# Power and the Church

Power in religious institutions is as inevitable and ubiquitous as anywhere else. It can be the power of good, a power for good – or morally ambiguous potency; it can come gorgeously vested or masked as unction or inspiration.

Martyn Percy examines its occasions both in the mainstream churches and in proliferating charismatic movements, expertly deploying the resources of sociological analysis. He is a fresh voice eminently worth serious attention.

*David Martin, Emeritus Professor of Sociology, LSE and Honorary Professor of Religious Studies, Lancaster University*

Few books contain quite as many subjects that make uncomfortable reading for church members, let alone office bearers: power, fundamentalism, sexuality, violence, and more. But put them all together and a sense of their connection emerges, and the discomfort starts to become creative, even empowering.

*Peter Selby, Bishop of Worcester*

# Power and the Church

Ecclesiology in an Age of Transition

Martyn Percy

**CASSELL**
London and Washington

Cassell

Wellington House, 125 Strand, London WC2R 0BB

PO Box 605, Herndon, VA 20172–0605

First published 1998

**British Library Cataloguing-in-Publication Data**
A catalogue record for this book is available from the British Library.

ISBN 0-304-70107-6 (Hardback)
ISBN 0-304-70105-X (Paperback)

Cover photo of author by Pippa Hague.

Typeset by Ensystems, Saffron Walden
Printed and bound in Great Britain by Biddles Ltd, Guildford and King's Lynn

# Contents

# Preface

A book about power may seem at first sight a curious project to attempt. After all, we all have experiences of power in one way or another. Language, concepts and encounters with power are a part of everyday life. Some may wield power, others may find themselves under it; some may think they know what the power of the Church is, or claim to know the power of God directly. Can it be possible then, that a book can look at something that is so often taken for granted, and illuminate the subject? Indeed, what would a set of studies about power tell us about ourselves, our theology, the religion to which we might subscribe, or the one from which we most readily flee? This book is a preliminary set of essays that sets out to discuss the diversity and digressions of power from a theoretical and applied perspective in terms of their relation to theology and religious studies. They are focused on the Church, or rather, churches. There is not just one 'church' to discuss in relation to power. Different ecclesial bodies handle power in different ways, and the powers themselves encountered therein are often quite different.

In choosing the theme of power as a way in to a variety of issues, I am suggesting that a sound focus on power has the potential to create a 'Master Key' for theology and religious studies. Initially, this key opens methodological doors in both theology and sociology. In turn, this gives access to a corridor of issues covering a diverse range of topics: violence, polity and authority to name but a few. True, a focus on power is no metanarrative in itself. Yet I do hold that attention to the theme of power creates the possibility of theology working with religious studies in a mutual and dialogical fashion: that in itself has methodological implications. Thus, the type of reflection on offer here is not Confessional theology. Nor is it an entirely dogmatic or systematic theology in which religious studies is simply tolerated as a lately-developed and faddish derivative. Neither is it a thorough-going form of religious studies in which theology has become entirely subsumed as a discipline. This is theology done, as Daniel Hardy would describe it, in 'a fourth way'. It is an open encounter and dialogue with issues of power in which insights from theology, religious studies, sociology and political science are permitted to inter-react with relative freedom. From that perspective, new modes of theological reflection may develop that have both applied and theoretical repercussions. Indeed, following Kieran Flanagan, John Milbank and others, it is possible to see this work, in combining sociology and theology, as a work of ecclesiology. This book is, after all, a study of power in the Church. Yet the bodies of Christ discussed here are not treated to an exclusive diet of reductive sociology or Confessional theology: the book intentionally treats churches and their faiths seriously, but not uncritically.

In outline then, the first chapter considers some key theoretical models of power and their relationship to theology and ecclesiology. The central thesis being advanced is that the project of Enlightenment has led to two responses to religious power. First, rational or established religion has tended to invest resources in socio-theological ideas like the incarnation, which steps back from absolute power. Second, enthusiastic or non-established religion has done the opposite, namely appealed to absolute power in a pre-Enlightenment form, and produced doctrines and ecclesiologies to match this. There is some analysis of sociological, ideological and theological writings on power. Dispositional and facilitative notions (philosophical), sociological concepts (exchange, dispersal), theological and anthropological ideas about power are also noted.

Chapters 2 and 3 are a pair. Chapter 2 looks at healing in the Gospels and offers a sociological treatment of biblical material. What kind of power is being witnessed to? This essay argues for miracles as being seen as 'interpretations' of events with social and political ramifications, and against copying miracles today as demonstrations of power. Chapter 3 (written with Anthony Bash) is also concerned with biblical material, and examines leadership and power in the New Testament, looking at the concept of weakness and suffering as central to authentic leadership. As with Chapter 2, there is an implicit argument against totalitarian, success-dominated forms of ecclesial governance. The New Testament principle of 'ambassadorship' is invoked and explicated.

Chapters 4, 5 and 6 are concerned with contemporary religion. Chapter 4 examines fundamentalism and power, and looks at the use of agencies, texts and organization in ecclesial and socio-political manipulation. As Kathleen Boone notes in her perceptive study of fundamentalist discourse, 'in fundamentalism, it is never the Bible that rules, but always the interpreter'. How do fundamentalist movements manage to control their adherents? Why is fundamentalism such a diverse and schismatic move- ment, and what does this tell us about the nature of power in tightly- controlled ecclesial communities? Following on from this, Chapter 5 attempts to explicate the anatomy of violence in established and new religious movements. It is suggested that force is a 'response' to the loss of power. Focusing on new religious movements, millennial movements and other religious groups, the work of scholars such as Rene Girard and Hannah Arendt is used to explore how violence is used by totalitarian groups. This raises questions over how minority religious groups are to be handled in liberal democracies, especially with the advent of the millen- nium. Chapter 6 examines the Toronto Blessing using sociological and anthropological theories of exchange that would more commonly be applied to materials. Yet the 'commodification' of the blessing leaves the Toronto Church unusually susceptible to sociological analysis. In this discussion, the body responsible for the globalization of the Toronto Blessing emerges more as a charismatic shrine than a church, in which believers are able to exchange perceived powerlessness for re-empower- ment, provided they exchange their rationality for a form of pseudo- mysticism.

Chapters 7 and 8 are also a pair of a kind. Both deal with the topic of ideology. When notions of divine power embodied in ecclesial structures have been so profoundly disturbed and eroded by modernity, how do churches respond to the loss of power? Chapter 7 suggests that established religion tends to resort to bureaucratic ideology. In assessing what is now known as *The Turnbull Report*, this essay explores the polity of oppression in organization and authority in the Church today. What happens to priests and laity when the Church attempts to adopt 'monarchical' forms of government in a post-monarchical State? The essay highlights how founders of ecclesial polity such as Richard Hooker can be abused in contemporary situations. Chapter 8 recognizes that ideology in charismatic religion is not carried in dogma or bureaucracy, but in charisma and agreed sense of feeling. Controversially, but not uniquely, the essay argues that a discourse of eroticism plays a major part in configuring notions of divine power in contemporary enthusiastic western religion. The search for healing, fulfilment and empowerment are underpinned by the language of worship (a 'grammar of assent') that establishes romantic genres in charismatic religion. Jesus emerges as the 'hero' who vanquishes compet- ing powers, with spiritual relationality assured through rational abrogation and passivity.

The final two chapters are also a pair, and they look at the fragility of ecclesial polity in late modernity. Both established and free churches seem to be producing an increasing number of schisms, suggesting that the

power of 'universal truth' and of central ecclesial government is failing –
not even the Roman Catholic Church is immune from this development.
Chapter 9 examines how issues of gender and sexuality have threatened
the order of established churches in Britain and the USA. The essay is
principally concerned with the struggle for space, equality and justice in
women's religious movements, and looks at the ordination of women in
Anglo-American Anglicanism. Chapter 10 returns to the phenomenon of
charismatic religion, and looks at why its power is constantly dissipated
through schisms caused by new 'waves' of revival. Can anything keep
charismatic religion from persistently falling apart? There is a brief
conclusion, which is naturally concerned with ecclesial power in a post-
traditional (or post-foundational) world. The essay tentatively suggests the
possibilities for divine power in the future, and how churches will attempt
to carry forward their agendas in a new millennium.

Inevitably in a book about divine and human power, some will feel that
issues or insights have been missed. For example, there is no one explicit
essay in this volume that deals with sexism or feminism. However, I
should say here that feminist insights and concerns imbue nearly every
essay in the book, and the decision not to treat 'women' as an issue was in
itself a deliberate choice. In terms of power, I have aimed to show that
feminist perspectives are quite plural and do not belong to a ghetto, but
can in fact infuse any discussion of power and ecclesial polity at any level.
Many of the essays (e.g. Chapter 2) have implications for studies in racism,
sexism, discrimination against those with 'handicaps' and the like. The
fact that these issues are not made explicit is, to an extent, a necessary
consequence of focusing on the actual dynamics of power, yet at the same
time not wanting to turn the theme into a metanarrative in its own right.
It is possible that two future projects may redress the balance. With the
grace of the publishers permitting, a second book could expand the field
of enquiry from the Anglo-American concerns discussed in this book, and
look more at Roman Catholicism, global and indigenous Christianity. A
third book might look at the theme of power in other religions. Both
these volumes – *Bodies of the Spirit* and *Bodies of God* – would require many
international contributions.

Finally, there are a number of publications and people to thank in the
making of this book. A number of the essays and insights in this work
appeared as shorter and earlier drafts in a variety of academic journals. I
particularly wish to thank and acknowledge the editors of *Studies in World
Christianity* (Edinburgh University Press), *Theology* (SPCK, London), *Anvil*
(Tyndale, Bristol), *Latimer Studies* (Latimer House, Oxford) and *The Journal
of Theology and Sexuality* (Sheffield Academic Press) for permission to print
previously published material. *The Journal of Contemporary Religion* (Carfax
Publishing, Oxford, OX14 3UE) has given permission for reproduction of

the following previously published material: 'Fundamentalism: A Problem for Phenomenology?', vol. 10: 1, 1995; 'Power and Fundamentalism', vol. 10: 3, 1995; 'The Post Evangelical', vol. 11, 1996; and 'Falling out of Love: The Ordination of Women and Recent Anglo-American Schisms Explored', vol. 12: 1, 1997. Thanks are also owed to Amnesty International, who have sought advice and socio-theological reflection on violence and New Religious Movements over the past few years. At their world conference in Edinburgh (1995) and their student conference in Birmingham I was able to present preliminary and shorter drafts of Chapter 5. Dr Andrew Walker of King's College, London, also invited me to address the 'Religion as Abuse' Conference in 1995, where further opportunity to refine my reflections was gained: my thanks also to him. Part of Chapter 10 is extracted from an essay I wrote for the recent volume on Neo-Pentecostalism led by a team from the University of Reading (*Charismatic Christianity: Sociological Perspectives*, ed. T. Walter, S. Hunt and B. Hamilton, Macmillan, London, 1997). I am also grateful to the same Faculty of Sociology for the opportunity to present and cultivate my work on exchange theories at a conference on charismatic renewal during 1996; that can be found in Chapter 6. Generous grants from Christ's College and the Divinity Faculty at the University of Cambridge also enabled me to visit Toronto and study 'the blessing' in some detail during 1996. Reflections on that visit have found their way into more than one chapter in this book, and I am grateful to the fund managers for their backing. I gratefully acknowledge the following authors and publishers for permission to quote from their material: 'The Kingdom', reprinted from *Later Poems*, by R. S. Thomas, London, Macmillan, 1983; 'The Second Coming', in *Collected Poems*, by W. B. Yeats, London, A. P. Watt Ltd, 1921; 'Canto CXV', in *Drafts and Fragments*, by Ezra Pound, London, Faber, 1969; 'Meditation on the Third Station of the Cross', in *Meditations*, by Sylvia Sands, Belfast, Oasis Community Project, 1996; 'Out of Fundament' (unpublished), by Cal McCrystal, 1995. By permission of Bloodaxe Books Ltd and the author, 'Motet' and 'Freedom' are reprinted from *Hail! Madam Jazz* by Micheal O'Siadhail, Newcastle upon Tyne, Bloodaxe Books Ltd, 1992. 'Jesus Take Me As I Am' by Dave Bryant, 1978, is reprinted by kind permission of Kingsway's Thankyou Music, Eastbourne, East Sussex. 'Your Prayers Are Very Precious', from *Songs of the Vineyard I* and 'I Will Be Yours, You Will Be Mine' ('Eternity'), from *Catch the Fire Again*, are reprinted by kind permission of Copycase UK.

Normally, I tend to dedicate all published work to my wife Emma, and our children. It is they who have to suffer a distracted and distant husband and father while the project is in gestation. I am no less grateful to them this time. Anthony Bash has also given of his time to this book, and has made detailed and helpful comments, for which I am grateful.

Yet for various reasons, this particular book is dedicated with affection and gratitude to Daniel Hardy, sometime Van Mildert Canon Professor of Theology at Durham University and Director of the Center of Theological Inquiry at Princeton. My work on the theme of power in contemporary religion began in a typically stretching graduate supervision class with Daniel Hardy, almost ten years ago. Through his encouragement and support, with his passion for knowledge, as well as his commitment to an expansive framework for conceiving theological work, many have benefited from his teaching. I count myself fortunate to be one of a number of graduate students to have worked under him. My wife was also an undergraduate of his when reading theology in preparation for ordination, so we feel to a large extent that our debt is doubled. What we have especially cherished is his pursuit of wisdom, his orthodox and gracious brand of liberalism, his willingness to try something new, his appreciation of innovation, his sense of awe and wonder, the commitment to dialogue, and his thorough and kind interest in all his students. And so it is with pleasure and admiration that this book is dedicated to Professor Daniel Hardy. How does the poet put it?

> Infinities of space and time. Melody fragments;
> a music of compassion, noise and enchantment.
> Among the inner parts of something open,
> something wild, a long rumour of wisdom
> keeps winding into each tune: *cantus firmus*,
> fierce vigil of contingency, love's congruence.

Micheal O'Siadhail, 'Motet', from
*Hail! Madam Jazz* (Newcastle upon Tyne: Bloodaxe Books, 1992)

Martyn Percy
Lincoln Theological Institute
University of Sheffield, 1997

A blown husk that is finished
but the light sings eternal
a pale flare over marshes
where the salt hay whispers to tide's change.

Ezra Pound
'Canto CXV' in *Drafts and Fragments, 1969*

*For Daniel Hardy*
*Friend and Teacher*

# 1
# Some models of power

Power is one of the central concepts in political theory. Distinctions between authority and force, between violence and resistance, between will and desire all lie at the heart of the subject. Power is the ability of its holders to carry out their will, exact compliance, exert force and compel obedience. To touch on authority, as part of power, is to study relations, rules and regulations. To focus on force, as another arm of power, is to consider compulsion, threats and violence. In any consideration of politics or society, the subject of power (and its legitimacy) is never far from the surface.

This is a book about power and religion. More specifically, it is a collection of essays that identify power as a subject for study in relation to Christianity and the Church. Ironically, this is often a neglected area in the fields of applied theology, sociology and ecclesiology. Imprecision over definitions and methods has often meant that its consideration only arises in broad disciplines such as feminist or liberation theology, or then again in social or psychological studies of religious groups. The aim of the book is to suggest a variety of different ways in which a focus on power may illuminate and impact the study of religion more widely. The subjects are mainly contemporary and Christian, but the insights offered certainly have a bearing on other faiths and alternative forms of social and moral coherence. No one uniform theory of power is being advanced, as will become obvious to the reader. Because this is a preliminary study of sorts, variety of method is a deliberate choice over uniformity of theorem. In common with Nicholas Lash, John Milbank and others, I am not proposing to 'speak of everywhere from nowhere in particular'.[1] A destructive metanarrative of power that imposes the universal over the particular is an abrogation of responsibility in handling and examining power.

Equally, I hope to avoid a postmodern power game in this work, in which every expression of truth is assumed to be nothing but a local ritual. So, dismissive reductionism is out, as much as I hope it is obvious that a blind act of faith affirming all claimed forms of divine power is also excluded. There is, in the nicest possible way, an orthodox liberal stance at the centre of this work. 'Liberalism' here should be taken to mean a viewpoint rather than one single coherent systematic position: it is a fluid tradition, but with respect for foundationalism. In my view, there is a genuine story about religious power to be told which does have a bearing on this book. The story is of the power of reality and the reality of power.[2] Whilst it is not the only story that could be told, it is an important one in the history of ideas: the relationship between religious or divine power, and modernity.

## A Short Story: Divine Power in Modernity

Modernism works with certain assumptions. It is a progressive, evolving and self-improving account of life. Reason can discover central 'truth'. Religion is a husk of 'myth' that might contain 'truth'. The endeavours of modernity have ushered in an age of industry, the welfare state, Fascism, socialism, Marxism – concepts that were all-embracing. Modernists are, characteristically, optimists and humanists, believing that humanity is capable of explaining and critiquing the present world and constructing a better one.[3] Established religion inevitably felt threatened by this post-Enlightenment agenda: but the response to the situation was to posit that God still ruled over all, from far and beyond. Apart from the occasional challenge, represented on the one hand by John Robinson's *Honest to God* (1963), and by Karl Barth's *Epistle to the Romans* (1918) on the other, Modernism has continued to see itself as a largely positive exercise. However, if you happen to be religious, it might look very destructive: modernity seems to threaten the magical thread in religion, substituting the sense of the divine for something altogether more human and accountable. Theories of evolution and the fundamentalist reactions to them provide a good narrative account of how non-established religion has sought to claw back what it feels has been lost by 'reductive' approaches to faith.

Modernism tended to make distinctions between 'religion' and 'revelation', divorce 'myth' from 'history', and then try and separate 'reality' and 'illusion'. As a social phenomenon, it had a profoundly imperialistic approach to religion. It believed itself to be 'neutral', that religion was something that could be explained: the social, moral and scientific critiques never saw themselves as constructions of reality – only their

2

subjects were these. Underlying the peak of Modernist thinking was a philosophy of suspicion that saw religious behaviour and language as ascriptive, whereas the student of religion was neutral and descriptive. The culmination of this reductionist approach was the 'projectionist' theory of Ludwig Feuerbach's *The Essence of Christianity* (1841) and *The Essence of Religion* (1845): 'theology is anthropology writ large' – 'God is the highest subjectivity of man abstracted from himself'. Feuerbach was to influence Marx and many other 'deconstructors' of religion, who primarily distinguish between its 'essence' and 'manifestation'.[4] In the light of this distinction, positive reductionists attempted to rescue the kernel of the Gospel from the obscuring husk of 'myth'; negative reductionists saw only self-delusion with moral and material pragmatism.

In Modernism, the problem of explaining religious power lies in the terms of reference applied to the subject. For Durkheim, a founding father of sociology, religion was just one means whereby society became self-conscious – a system of signs and symbols that were socially relative and relevant that enabled a form of moral ordering: 'A religion is a unified set of beliefs and practices relative to sacred things, that is to say, things set apart and forbidden, real and ideal . . . sacred and profane.'[5] For Freud, however, rituals were to do with primal needs, and religion appeared to be something we did with our repressed feelings and desires, or perhaps with symbols of our parents:

> In 1912 I tried in my book *Totem and Taboo* to reconstruct the ancient situation from which these (religious) effects issued . . . Once a year, however, the whole clan assembled for a feast at which the otherwise revered totem was torn apart and eaten . . . the correspondence of the totem feast (according to Robertson Smith's description) with the Christian Communion has struck many authors before me.[6]

Marx, who, unlike Freud, was no armchair-to-couch philosopher, theorized about the function of religion in relation to what he had seen in various European working-class situations:

> man makes religion, religion does not make man. In other words, religion is the self-conscious and self-feeling of man who has either not yet found himself or has already lost himself again . . . Religion is a general theory of [the] world . . . [it] is the sigh of the oppressed creature, the heart of a heartless world . . . it is the opium of the people.[7]

These Modernist thinkers all shared a belief, namely that religion was a form of social cement that bound people together, for good or ill, into a form of community. The fundamental task of each of their critiques was to expose what they saw as the underlying structure: social, psychological or moral.

Generally speaking, the responses to these metanarratives of religion fall into two camps. Theologically speaking, one could adopt the line taken by Grenz and Olsen in their sophisticated description of post-Enlightenment theology. On the one hand, there was an attempt to 'reconstruct' transcendence through immanence: Schleiermacher and liberation theology are cited as examples. On the other hand, there was a revolt against immanence in the work of Barth and other neo-orthodox theologies.[8] Ecclesiologically, with which we are more concerned here, the divisions are slightly different: Rational, established religion of the nineteenth and early twentieth centuries tended to retreat into a culture of high liberalism or conservatism. In terms of power, theology tended to stress the embodied but ambiguous power of the incarnation, yet assuming the immutable. Religious power became intrinsically social, and joined forces with the Modernist enterprise of welfare, justice and peace. William Temple's *Christianity and the Social Order* (1942) is but one good example of this synthesis. In contrast, non-established Christianity tended to re-appeal to the absolute power of God, either through quasi-rationality (fundamentalism) or through re-awakened religious experience (Pentecostalism and revivalism), or through theological imperialism, such as the Roman Catholic Church's development of the doctrine of Papal infallibility. The consequence of this has been at least two different versions of theological and ecclesiological power. One is committed to a form of democracy, the other to theocracy. One continues to see the power of God in loose, rather ambiguous but nonetheless real terms;[9] the other in absolute, unequivocal terms. Both these responses will constitute part of the focus for this study, by looking at how their ecclesial traditions within contemporary Christianity perceive the nature of divine and human power.

In telling the story in this way, I am of course describing the general anomie of Modernism which has seen the final breakdown of a culture of Christendom, but at the same time the failure of secular reason in its place. Of course, it is not as simple as that. But according to Durkheim, this anomie leads to individuals and groups becoming disillusioned, feeling a sense of powerlessness and alienation, experiencing a lack of community, and eventually moral relativity leading to social disintegration.[10] Steve Bruce, echoing a Weberian point, uses a musical analogy, suggesting that the 'grand symphony' of religion has gone, only to be replaced by 'small groups of enthusiastic music-makers'.[11] In short, perceptions of spiritual power have fragmented to the point where society can no longer presume that divine power can be really known, or that it even necessarily exists. Modernism questioned the interests and social function of divine power, with reductionist approaches suggesting that projection was the key. Postmodern affirmations of power take seriously its meaning, but (usually) deny its reality and truth. One of the simplest ways of tracking this history is to note the differences between Anglican Collects for Harvest Festival. *The Book of Common Prayer* is not shy of asking for rain and fair weather for good crops; the *Alternative Service Book* makes no such petition, but instead takes the crop yield for granted, and expresses the hope that God will 'give us grace to use them rightly'.

The issue of the power of God in relation to ecclesiology in modernity is clearly crucial.[12] Nancey Murphy notes how conservative theologians have retreated from the challenge of modernity into what she calls 'propositionalism'; liberal theologians have sought safety in 'expressivism'. In turn, conservatives have sought to hold on to an 'interventionist' view of the power of God, with liberals adopting a softer line with immanentism.[13] Yet as Murphy points out, *both* these responses to modernity are characterized by modernist presuppositions: a 'quest for universal knowledge ... and indubitable foundations'.[14] What separates them is their attitude to revelation, verification, data and disclosure. In terms of divine power, the immanentist-liberal view opposes the *laissez-faire* Deism that sees God outside the world, yet is also hostile to the conservative-interventionist line. Conservatives, on the other hand, feel that the privilege of the power of God is robbed of its meaning, and that liberals make divine power in their own image.

In summary then, Murphy sees the liberal tradition on the power of God as being conceived in terms of immanentism. Knowledge is mainly experiential, language mainly expressive, and a right relation with science essential. Conservatives see divine power as interventionist, knowledge as scriptural or 'revealed', language as propositionalist, and science as something that is judged by revelation.[15] In setting up her argument in this way, she is able to press for a synthesis between the two traditions, arguing that intervention and immanentism need not be mutually exclusive. In other words, God works in natural processes, but is not constrained by that method alone.[16]

In offering narratives of the power of God in the context of ecclesiology and the modern situation, I should make it clear that this book is not just a retrospect. It very much stands in the present, but also looks forward to the prospects for religious power and the groups who claim it, and their futures. I fully appreciate that many would criticize the bracketing off of 'power' to explain religion. The idea that one can suspend one's beliefs and approach a subject through a neutral lens has itself been deconstructed: there are now philosophies of suspicion *about* philosophies of suspicion.[17] In short, the modernist, reductionist veto is a metanarrative that is being exposed as something that can be turned in on itself. But at the same time the exercise of Modernist explication does provide a basis for development of social, theological and functionalist theories to be evolved that can be profoundly helpful to the student of religious studies. The aim of this book therefore, at least in part, is to deploy a variety of disciplines relevant to a study of religious power, but in such a way that any explanation is complementary rather than comprehensive.

## Models of Power in Relation to Religion

Definitions or explications of power are, practically speaking, a dime a dozen. The concept of power in social science and theology has no unity of discourse. Part of the problem lies in Peter Morriss' observation that 'power' is what we call 'something': it is primarily a noun, not a verb.[18] Although the verb does exist in the sense that we may speak of empowering, the fact that it is mainly a noun has implications for the way in which 'power' is described and studied. All too commonly, power is run together with verbs that are deemed to be its associates. For example, and from a sociological perspective, a theoretician like Dahl describes power by contrasting it with near-synonyms like 'influence', so that power becomes *like* influence.[19] Then again, the problem becomes more obvious in Rollo May's *Power and Innocence: A Search for the Sources of Violence*, in which the noun again assumes the characters of the nearest relevant verbs. For May, power is exploitative, manipulative, competitive, nutrient or integrative.[20] Each of these types of power represents a different level of threat, force or coercion, ranging from the mutually empowering (integrative) to the potentially violent (exploitative). Thus, 'power' loses its reality in some sense here, precisely because the verbs are allowed to project on to a passive noun. Perhaps this is why deconstructors of power such as Foucault have looked at power and seen nothing – only reciprocal relations.[21]

No

Yet as Morriss points out, careful attention to the etymology of power reveals its own diversity, prior to any linkage to verbs. Power is 'ability to do or effect something or anything . . . energy, force, effect . . . an active property, capacity of producing . . . possession of control or command over others . . . dominion, rule, legal ability, commission, faculty . . . political or national strength'.[22] That there is an overlap with verbs about power is clear, but that there is not complete synonymity is also clear. (As will become clear in this study, differentiating between the power of God as a source and subsequent ecclesial praxis is vital in any study of religious power. The verb that conveys the noun is not always a good indication of what might lie at the centre of divine intention, as in the case of the practice of authority.) Morriss' thesis is an attempt to argue for a dispositional understanding of power. That is to say, power is seen as a relatively enduring capacity within any given object. Dispositional views of power are held in contrast (but not necessarily in opposition) to episodic ideas, that see occurrences or events as specific exercises of power. However, Morriss does point out that this power is not something that can be observed.[23] Power is known only by its reification, which is ultimately an indirect but material way of inferring what power might be at work. This conclusion underlines his plea for power not to be studied in isolation: the subjects and objects of power require a methodological tolerance in the spheres of theory and evidence.

In many ways, this is precisely what has been attempted in Stewart Clegg's exemplary *Frameworks of Power*.[24] The genius of the work lies in its conciliatory tone and laudable syncretism of earlier theories. Clegg effectively constructs an open theory of power based on the concept of circuits, nodal points and agency: it has political, organizational and theological resonance.[25] As he says, 'a theory of power must examine how the field of force in which power is arranged has been fixed, coupled and constituted in such a way that, intentionally or not, certain "nodal points" of practice are privileged in this unstable and shifting terrain'.[26] In other words, this is a theory that is beyond dispositional and episodic ideas of power, and beyond the faulty attachment inclinations of Dahl and May. Yet it has space for their insights, recognizing that dispositions, episodes and influence or violence all play a part within an overall framework.

Clegg begins his book with an overview of earlier theoreticians such as Hobbes and Machiavelli. This is followed by discussions and critiques of Dahl, Russell, Bachrach, Baratz, Weber and Wrong, revolving around the two faces of power, namely the relationship between intention and structure, and which enjoys supremacy in society. These debates, naturally enough, were eclipsed by more substantial models. Steven Lukes proposed a three-dimensional model of power by identifying the centrality of interests; Habermas focused on ideal speech situations, ideology and hegemony; Giddens on the relationship between agency and structure in terms of power. But Clegg moves beyond each of these explications, working Parsons, Foucault and Mann (amongst others) into an overall integration that respects the dispositional and facilitative approaches to power, besides stressing the vital role of strategic agency. This is a rich theory, yet he concludes with the warning that forgetting power may be the fate of our times. The more difficult power becomes to locate, the harder it becomes to discern its veracity and to resist it when necessary.

A discussion about the true nature of power and where it lies is at the heart of religious belief.[27] Liberation theology, feminist theology and other new disciplines should be seen mainly in terms of re-constituting the balance of power in ecclesial and social structures. These theologies are effectively a form of revolution and resistance. The effect of the stress on power has led to more self-conscious questioning by some writers who are beginning to question the nature of the power that would generally be uncritically appealed to. For example, a recent book on concepts of truth in evangelical thinking recognizes that the appeal to divine power through agencies such as authoritative scriptures has a pharmacological quality about it. That is to say, the power is both medicine and poison: incorrect prescription and dosage leads to harm, not good.[28] The solution, they posit, is to *trust* in anti-totalizing metanarratives: real power that is freeing, not coercive.[29] In a similar way, and from an Anglican perspective, Richard Roberts has attacked Stephen Sykes' work on power for its uncritical conflation with concepts of authority, which is then invested, on behalf of the Church, in theologians and the Episcopacy. Although Sykes, in much of his work, periodically genuflects to the powerlessness of Jesus Christ, there is no escaping the apparent appeal to power and 'rightful hegemony' in his work.[30] This is achieved, in Roberts' view, by the 'assertion of essence' in constructing identity: this, of course, is to be done by theologians, who gain their authority by their self-representation as interpreters and arbiters of power.[31]

As we noted earlier with respect to Clegg and Morriss, one of the difficulties of studying power is that it is not one thing to be observed. The advantage of Clegg's conceptualizing of power in terms of circuits, flow and agency is that we can often identify the delimited field of power (such as an organization), the directionality of power within the structure (flow or hegemony) and the specific nodal points of power such as a guru, an infallible text or a law. In contemporary religious studies, purchase on the study of power depends, for example, on recognizing that power is linked to charisma, force and effect, although not synonymous with them, as Morriss noted. That would be to ignore its dispositional nature. Insights from other disciplines can be helpful in the pursuit of wisdom.

Gerardus van der Leeuw's work can be described as a phenomenology of power: he cannot prove there is such a thing, but he does seek to draw our attention to 'it' – the things of power. His thesis is that sensitivity to power has been largely forgotten in modern society, but in primitive society power developed into religious monism, which reached its climax in monotheism. In contemporary society, power is not encountered in nature or personality, but in the dispersed forms of social organization.[32] However, the essence of religion is power, driven towards monism, which has a tendency to conflate the psychological with the cosmological, the sociological with the theological: religion is a description of concepts of power and their use.

More recently, and from an anthropological viewpoint, I. M. Lewis has also argued that although religious power assumes many different forms (which may appear to be unrelated or mutually exclusive), it is an appropriate theme through which to approach religion holistically.[33] For Lewis, religious power is best understood as a negative force which opposes malign spiritual powers. Thus, the shaman assumes the charismatic role *par excellence* – being able to exorcize the evil and prepare the way for blessing. In effect, the shaman stands between negative and positive power as a broker, a fixed point of passage and determinacy that both creates and obviates power. Like van der Leeuw, Lewis cannot 'see' power, except in the way that it is related to, and in the social and ritual structures that are based on its assumption.

Sociologically, the conceptions of power can be divided into two very broad categories. On the one hand, there are those which are asymmetrical, stressing conflict, will, resistance and the like: social relations are assumed to be competitive, conflictual and dialectical. On the other hand, there are conceptions that imply that all may make some gain through power. Here, power is a collective capacity or achievement, born not out of conflict, but communal welfare.[34] Although it is helpful to be mindful of these two broad categories, it should be noted that they are somewhat inadequate in the analysis of religion. To an extent, all religious movements have elements of both categories within them. This must be because the religious-social system itself is one of exchange alongside being one of power, which therefore allows for conflictual and communal action together. Beyond this, however, there is no account of subliminal power, which is so important in understanding religious behaviour. Power is not just attached to structures and positional personality, but also to non-structural interaction and roles.[35] Yet we must agree with Talcott Parsons in eschewing 'canonically correct' definitions of power: it actually covers more than it can define.[36]

Then there is the question of luck. Keith Dowding, drawing on the work of exchange theorists such as John Elster, attempts to explain why some groups get what they want without trying, whilst others struggle and fail.[37] Dowding is concerned to get beyond questions of intention (such as 'Who benefits?'), and develops a structural theory that gives some kind of account for what he terms 'systematic luck'. This is a slightly different way of looking at episodic and dispositional power. The relevance of this to divine power lies in the field of attribution: how do you know the difference between God intervening in response to prayer, and a lucky break? Although Dowding is not concerned with any analysis of religious power, his methods are capable of limited translation into cause and effect relationships in miracles, prayer and apparent instances of intervention.

Given the myriad of studies on power and attendant methods, the most practical way forward in my view, especially given the multifarious nature of power that occurs within religious movements, is to return to the agents or nodal points of power identified by Stewart Clegg, and focus on their relationality. To recap, his theory of circuits of power does not attempt to marry the non-realist tendencies of Foucault with the identification trends of someone like C. Wright Mills.[38] Instead, he chooses to describe power in terms of circuits, which are organized through agencies. However, he is careful to note that the agencies cannot be seen as 'effortlessly rational or powerful', since their 'carrying capacity is itself opened up for scrutiny in power terms'.[39]

This view of power is altogether more contingent than monolithic. For example, it has space for dispositional, facilitative and episodic power within the same or overlapping frameworks. Dispositional power, as its description suggests, is the tendency or habit of an individual or group: in many religious movements, this is reflected in the 'grammar of power as a concept' that helps form the ecclesial community. Appeals to an almighty God, to a Lord, or to more specified concepts of omnipotence have direct social consequences. Facilitative power describes the points of access through which power can be reached, reified and exchanged. Episodic power can be used to describe the surges or events of power that may alter the shape, perceptions or behaviour of individuals and groups. Central to these three circuits is organization, and many a religious movement is able to demonstrate systematic configuration in each field. For example, the ideology present in postmodern charismatic worship could be said to be dispositional; the charismatic leaders are facilitative; the invocation of the Holy Spirit is a cue for episodic manifestations of power to be unleashed.

As I suggested earlier, the agents – which could be a guru or leader, a desired personal experience that is valued by the group, or an inerrant Bible – belong to a circuit: they usually control the distribution of power and direct its flow, but they can also be by-passed by power. Ecclesial communities, especially those that are revivalist and postmodern, frequently change their shape and direction in response to cultural trends. Their pragmatism can also lead them to question power sources that are inefficient, and to remove them from the equation if necessary. One consequence of this is the necessary conflation of divine and human agency as a means of survival within the framework. Leaders cannot just be good at what they do; they must be gifted to last, supernaturally endowed with qualities which make them indispensable. In terms of exchange, as Weber has noted, this fixes them as obligatory passages through which the best blessings flow. We can go further here, and say that there is an equation between the power a leader ascribes to a miracle or text, and then the power he has, which in turn relates to the perceived benefits of belonging to the group offering the blessing. This in turn has implications for the size of a group.

Yet to characterize an ecclesial community that appears to be subject to charisma, flux and change is to ignore the rationality of such bodies. Churches, generally, are organized – but how? Clegg suggests that there are modes of rationality that come into operation in a given power circuit, especially in a community in a postmodern context that has shuffled off the burden of comprehensive metanarratives. For example, in charismatic renewal, churches usually subscribe to a mode of rationality that is effectively an account of disorder, that stresses that there is no such thing as a total explanation for an occurrence of power. Thus, modes of rationality focus on efficiency – 'How do you *feel* after that prayer? – rather than on ultimate cause and effect relationships. Naturally, this posits power in the hands of the leaders, since modes of rationality are ultimately determined by them: apparent innovation is, ironically, the path to domination.[40] To gain one form of empowerment is to be relatively disempowered in another way.

What I am suggesting here is that the charismatic leader, as part of a system of flux, must avoid severe routinization or pure bureaucratic efficiency in the interests of keeping power. Such a position would mean power could revolve around the leader instead of *through* him or her; it might imply that the community was dynamic, and the leadership static. Thus, movement and change in modes of rationality are key; in my own observation of charismatically-led churches, it is not unusual to hear leaders state that we used to do this or think that, but 'now we have moved on'. Depending on your point of view, this is either an orthodox notion of developing doctrine, or sheer pragmatism in the face of theological rootlessness. Even so, it remains the case that the movement is still mostly driven by the charismatic personality. Here we have an irony. The modernist state has tended to routinize, even obviate charisma. The conditions of postmodernity however, have offered a new lease of life to the charismatic agent who can adapt to religious and cultural flux, mastering it and perhaps even 'surfing' the waves of renewal.

Perhaps the best way of understanding the place of agencies in circuits is to see them as *process* of power-exchange, a mechanism if you like, where power is given up or received, or raw material transformed into a type of power. A simple example of this would be to evaluate the nature and function of charisma at this point. According to Weber,

> 'Charisma' shall be understood to refer to an extraordinary quality of a person, regardless of whether this quality is actual, alleged, or pre-sumed. 'Charismatic authority', hence, shall refer to a rule over men, whether predominantly internal, to which the governed submit because of their belief in the extraordinary quality of the specific person.[41]

Although quality is at issue here, Weber's definition works just as well for efficiency or outcomes, or any other net result gained through exchange.

Indeed, Weber knew only too well that charismatic authority was quite capable of competing with rational or traditional patterns of power: charisma derives its authority through the devotion it inspires and the benefits it brings to believers.[42]

For Weber, the oldest of all vocations was the shaman or diviner, who is permanently endowed with charisma and is able to experience and pass on ecstatic states. Whilst Weber may have thought that this vocation was lost, or routinized in offices (such as priest or pastor) in the modernist-rational world, it is very much alive again in the postmodern world. An account of the resurrection of the charismatic religious leader in postmodernity lies, in part, in Weber's own writings. Weber differentiated between 'religion' and 'magic' in the way that he differentiated between ancient and modern. Religion was rational, organized and functional. Magic was primitive, a legitimate form of domination, and placed power outside ordinary temporal spheres.[43]

Within magic, there were prophets, magicians and shamans. Weber saw the prophets as the most significant bearers of charisma, since their claims were based on personal revelations that ultimately developed a personal following.[44] Yet he knew these distinctions to be fluid: priests and prophets practised magic, and there was routinization in the prophetic as much as in the religious.[45] The key to understanding the durability of charisma today lies in seeing Weber's vision of charisma as being too in debt to modernist notions of social and economic organization, which all too easily assume its routinization. The advent of postmodernity, ironically, creates a set of conditions under which the magicians, shamans and prophets can thrive. The absence of certainty, history devoid of teleology, progress questioned and a return to pre-critical classicism or romanticism, put competing powers and alternative world-views back into the centre of public space.[46]

What I am suggesting here is that some elements in an over-developed, postmodern culture are looking beyond religion and *back* to magic; Eliade says as much in his *Patterns of Comparative Religion* (1958). This is still no guarantee against domination, but it does at least ensure diversity. And to the believers, it at least appears to offer a place for ritual and symbolic power-exchanges that routinized religion may not be offering.

Some further remarks on the function of charisma as an agent or nodal point within a distributive power circuit are necessary here. First, it is clear from Weber that charismatic leadership is a form of domination *and* a method of power-exchange. Theologically, one could express the implications of this idea like this: God does not come to us neat, but only through things. To be in a charismatic situation, or under a charismatic leader is to 'know' something of the (alleged) power of God – the agent suggests a source. Yet conflation between agency and source is always a risk, and all agents have the capacity to dilute or distort their own source of power. Second, charismatic leaders have the potential to challenge existing order, are typically disruptive and innovative: something new is being offered in place of the old. Yet their weakness lies in having to constantly prove their powers, which are inevitably personal. This means that any delegated succession of leadership is open to the charismatic situation, not subject to it. The meek do not inherit the earth here, and neither, necessarily, does the chosen successor: the leader of the charismatic group will always need to be, definitively, the one with the most anointing – the most charismatic, even if that power is hidden.[47] Charismatic situations are notoriously susceptible to coups. Third, the form of domination in charismatic leadership is consensual. Disciples and believers enter into covenants with charismatic leaders because they wish to lose some things and gain others. Weber believed that charismatic domination emerges (or was demanded?) in times of crisis, or the cultural situation of anomie, to which I referred earlier. When established paths are seen not to be delivering, the charismatic leader emerges to renounce some aspects of the past, to embrace others, and to lead forward. The true prophet is not a seer, but 'reveals' and reads the present.[48] Fourth, charismatic domination stresses the ideal over the real, the spiritual over the material.[49] The consequence of this is that it is never easy to test the reality of power for the believer. In the dissonant community, the charismatic leader is able to dominate by naming the goals of belief and realizing them. If they are not achieved, the goal-posts can be moved, or results re-interpreted. The pyramidal structure of the power-exchange process, which mirrors the convergence of belief and the gradual restriction of critical horizons, is carefully controlled by the organizational agency of the charismatic leader. It is under these conditions that power flows: the circuits, although in a state of flux, are always carefully delimited by the ultimate power brokers. Only the death of a leader or the emergence of a competing power circuit can alter this. Thus, charisma is a dominating nodal point in a circuit of power, which is also a place of limited exchange for believers. They must be willing to shed material or ideological baggage and suspend belief above reality, but in return for this they receive power themselves, and feel blessed. The more you give, the more you get.[50]

How is it though, that a movement that claims to be and is experienced as powerful and liberating, should in fact be described as one that induces domination? To an extent, the answer lies, as we have already suggested, in the linking of power to verbs such as force, violence or influence. Violence may be deemed to be an agent of ultimately benevolent power, and seen as redemptive: freedom is removed in the interests of the believers' fulfilment and salvation. Gently administered, corrective force can be normative. In short, the end may justify the means. Jeanette

Winterson's *Oranges Are Not the Only Fruit* or Margaret Atwood's *The Handmaid's Tale* are two novels about religion that illustrate this aptly and with subtlety.[51] Yet the domination of a powerful, charismatic leader may arise through an accident, or out of ignorance, as Jane Rogers shows in her historical novel about early nineteenth millenarian sects:

> *Hannah:* But for a prophet: a man of God: a leader? I am at a loss. Nor can I determine to what degree he play-acts. I am sure he is a charlatan, but, I suspect, an unknowing one. That is to say, he is a simple soul who believes (deludedly) that he is chosen of God. There is too much awkwardness and nervousness about him to be an out-and-out rogue: although he is clearly clever, and used to twisting people to do his will. 'Be it menial or trivial, ye do it for the Lord' – sound advice for the household drudges, equal in cleverness to the economical suggestion that our reward for such labours shall be in heaven (at God's expense) rather than on earth at his own.[52]

Here, Mr Wroe, a charismatic prophet, has called seven virgins to work in his household, after being instructed in this matter 'by the Lord'. Seven women from his church are duly persuaded or volunteer for God's work, and Rogers describes the dynamics of religious submission through each of the female characters. The rhetoric of power, however, is much more obvious in contemporary ecclesial movements that are concerned with interventionism rather than sectarian control. From a revivalist perspective, the myths created by authors such as Frank Peretti portray power with undue clarity: demons and angels waging war, with both sides eroding human freedom in the process.[53] As Walter Wink notes, it is the coerciveness of Peretti's vision that is most striking:

> We have here a case of the total projection of evil out on others. The view of evil is scary but finally trivial; his demons are simply imaginary bad people with wings, and the really mammoth evils of our day – racism, sexism, political oppression, ecological degradation, militarism, patriarchy, homelessness, economic greed – are not even mentioned. It is simply Pentecostal political naiveté writ large on the universe.[54]

Equally, the history of hegemonic structures in revivalism such as 'shepherding' bear ample testimony to the domination that can take place inside the ecclesial community, once the believer is properly protected from malign powers and under the influence of godly power. Andrew Walker's perceptive sociological critique remains a seminal work.[55]

There are a number of theological critiques that are alive to these dynamics. For example, Walter Wink's trilogy on power plots a middle course between passivity and aggression towards power, and argues for a sensitive and discerning form of praxis that names, unmasks and engages with corruptions of power that abuse and dominate in social and ecclesial communities. He recognizes, however, that the present dominating systems are, to an extent, inevitable in the Church, although he reminds his readers of the eschatological dimension. In terms of power, this hopes to replace power-over with partnership, exclusiveness with inclusivity, and indoctrination with enabling.[56] The ultimate goal is God's domination-free order, a clear echo of the 'non-order' conceptualized more richly in David Ford and Daniel Hardy's *Jubilate*.[57]

Yet as Hollenweger notes, the problem with some postmodern religious groups and power, to some extent, might be traceable to the order or hierarchy of salvation or blessing that is present in much Pentecostal, 'New Age' and fundamentalist dogma. Although talk of 'doctrine' is problematic with these groups – they are mainly about religious experience, not formulas – there is a definite grading of blessing taught. Typically, in revivalist churches, there are notions of post-conversion second blessings: tongues, fillings and anointings. But beyond this, there is scope for having more or less power than other Christians: the more you know the power of God, the more you can rule and reign over others.[58] David Nicholls' study of recent images of God in terms of their socio-ecclesial capacities for power is aware of how complex social systems are funded through theological conceptions.[59] For example, Nicholls makes the point that monotheism, as a theological belief, has lent a significant hand in our developing understanding of monarchy. The links between Arianism and imperialism, and between Trinitarianism and pluralism or liberal democracy, are more than mere coincidence.[60]

In the light of these remarks, it is appropriate to suggest that the claimed power of God often leads to the establishment of a form of *Kyriearchy*. The appeal to God as Lord typically leads to a profound conflation between the leader of a given movement and the 'God' that is appealed to, that rules the rest of the ecclesial community. In feudal terminology, a Lord is in total charge, and requires obedience and subjugation. A Lord can also appoint an elite to carry out instructions and to rule in his place. A Lord may also be benevolent, bestowing favours on the faithful. The celebration of Lordship, at the heart of many contemporary and new religious movements, is the magnification of a certain kind of governance: freedom is necessarily restricted, force (or spiritual violence) justified, and conformity required. The power of the Lord is given first to the leaders, whose power and its interpretation become inextricably linked to and conflated with the power of God. In the present postmodern context, the implications of this are more serious than they might at first appear. The loss of metanarratives, metatheories and the collapse of the public forms of truth lead to competing forms of power and truth, spearheaded by tribal or feudal-like interests. It is almost impossible to keep up with 'policing' the emerging developments. One consequence of this is a significant rise in new churches, new religious movements and the like, all configured around concepts of alternative power sources, yet with a correlative rise in the manifest abuse of power within these movements. Typically, this will be domination in the name of the deity. Or, just another local *kyriearchy* conflating charisma, power and order with a selection of notions about God, for the sake of socio-ecclesial order.

## Summary

When one speaks about power in relation to the Church or to God, this awakens many thoughts and emotions. This book is not offering one way of conducting a conversation, but it is alive to many issues that concern the exercise of power. All too frequently, the power of the Church is remote for those who need it most: the poor, the persecuted and the politically disadvantaged. At the same time, there is no denying the capacity of power within the Church to effect change, bring order, transform and challenge. Frequently, the history of the Church in late modernity is caricatured by concepts of power and weakness: it often feels pressurized into making a choice between the false dichotomy of meekness and majesty. But the reader will not find a manifesto in this book. The genesis of the project lies in the simple observation that the power of God is deemed to be known by some religious groups, and is then handled in a particular way. This is therefore about the paths and pathologies of power that exist in ecclesial communities, their variety and vagaries. It is therefore about corpora Christi – 'bodies of Christ' – rather than one body, corpus Christi. In focusing on agency, structure, organization and polity, issues of orthopraxis are constantly being pressed. In choosing to use sociology and theology together, the book is essentially an offering of ecclesiology that is concerned with the knowledge of and use of divine and human power. For behind the reality of power lies a very different reality that is grounded in love and truth, and is willing to be made known in weakness – and even death.

## Notes

1 N. Lash, *The Beginning and End of Religion* (Cambridge: CUP, 1996), p. 197; J. Milbank, *Theology and Social Theory: Beyond Secular Reason* (Oxford: Blackwell, 1989).

2 See Peter Selby's essay 'The reality of power and the power of reality' in *God and Reality: Essays on Christian Non-Realism* (London: Mowbray, 1996).

3  For a useful introduction to the concept of modernity, see A. McGrath (ed.), *Encyclopaedia of Modern Christian Thought* (Oxford: Blackwell, 1993). Differentiation between modernity, late modernity and postmodernity is discussed later on.

4  For a critique, see Van A. Harvey, *Feuerbach and the Interpretation of Religion* (Cambridge: CUP, 1995).

5  E. Durkheim, *The Elementary Forms of Religious Life*, trans. J. Swain (London: Allen and Unwin, 1915; New York: Free Press, 1965), p. 62. First published in French in 1912.

6  S. Freud, *Moses and Monotheism*, trans. K. Jones (New York: Vintage, 1939), pp. 160–9. First published in German in 1937.

7  K. Marx, 'Contribution to Critique of Hegel's Philosophy of Right' [1844] in K. Marx and F. Engels, *On Religion* (Moscow: Foreign Languages Publishing House, n.d.), pp. 41–2.

8  S. Grenz and R. Olsen, *20th Century Theology: God and the World in a Transitional Age* (Carlisle: Paternoster, 1992).

9  I have especially in mind the work of Charles Hartshorne *Omnipotence, and Other Theological Mistakes* (New York: New York State UP, 1984). Naturally, the work of Don Cupitt as a post-liberal non-realist offers a different view on divine power.

10  See Steven Lukes, *Emile Durkheim: His Life and Work* (Harmondsworth: Penguin, 1973), pp. 210–18.

11  S. Bruce, *Religion in Modern Britain* (Oxford: OUP, 1996), p. 234.

12  Cf. Stephen Toulmin, *Cosmopolis: The Hidden Agenda of Modernity* (New York: Free Press, 1990), for a particularly enlightening account.

13  Nancey Murphy, *Beyond Liberalism and Fundamentalism: How Modern and Postmodern Philosophy Set the Theological Agenda* (Valley Forge: PA, Trinity Press International, 1996), pp. 2–3, 6–17. See also Claude Welch, *Protestant Thought in the Nineteenth Century*, 2 volumes (New Haven: Yale UP, 1972), vol. 2, p. 232.

14  Murphy, *op. cit.*, pp. 13–23.

15  Murphy, *op. cit.*, pp. 71, 80.

16  Murphy, *op. cit.*, p. 156.

17  See for example Gavin D'Costa's accessible and recent 'The End of Theology and Religious Studies', *Theology* (June 1996). For a more in-depth perspective, see John Milbank, *Theology and Social Theory: Beyond Secular Reason* (Oxford: Blackwell, 1989). Kieran Flanagan's work, *The Enchantment of Sociology: A Study of Theology and Culture* (London: Macmillan, 1996), is kinder to the social sciences.

18  P. Morriss, *Power: A Philosophical Analysis* (Manchester: Manchester UP, 1987), p. 9.

19  See R. Dahl, 'The Concept of Power', *Behavioural Science* (1957), no. 2, pp. 210–15.

20  R. May, *Power and Innocence* (Glasgow: Fontana/Collins, 1976), pp. 99–110.

21  See M. Foucault, 'Space, Knowledge and Power' in *The Foucault Reader* (ed. P. Rabinow) (New York: Pantheon-Random, 1984), p. 247.

22  Morriss, *op. cit.*, p. 10.

23  Morriss, *op. cit.*, p. 145.

24  S. Clegg, *Frameworks of Power* (London: Sage, 1989).

25  For further discussion of this, see my *Words, Wonders and Power: Understanding Contemporary Christian Fundamentalism and Revivalism* (London: SPCK, 1996).

26  S. Clegg, *op. cit.*, p. 17.

27  For some preliminary discussions, see Klaus Hemmerle, 'Power', in Karl Rahner (ed.), *Encyclopaedia of Theology: A Concise Sacramentum Mundi* (London: Burns and Oates, 1975) and K. Rahner, 'The Theology of Power' in *Theological Investigations*, Vol. 4 (London: DLT, 1966), pp. 391ff.

28 J. R. Middleton and B. J. Walsh, *Truth Is Stranger than It Used to Be: Biblical Faith in a Postmodern Age* (London: SPCK, 1995), p. 84.

29 *Ibid.*, p. 107.

30 See R. Roberts, 'Lord, Bondsman and Churchman' in D. Hardy and C. Gunton (eds) *On Being the Church: Essays on Christian Community* (Edinburgh: T. and T. Clark, 1989). Roberts is commenting on Sykes' *The Integrity of Anglicanism* (London: SPCK, 1978) and *The Identity of Christianity* (London: SPCK, 1984).

31 *Ibid.*, pp. 188–9.

32 See G. Van der Leeuw, *Religion in Essence and Manifestation*, trans. J. E. Turner (London: Allen and Unwin, 1938); see also J. Bettis (ed.), *The Phenomenology of Religion* (London: SCM, 1969), pp. 56ff.

33 I. M. Lewis, *Religion in Context: Cults and Charisma* (Cambridge: CUP, 1996) (2nd edition).

34 Steven Lukes, 'Power and Authority' in T. Bottomore and R. Nisbet (eds) *A History of Sociological Analysis* (New York: Basic Books, 1978), p. 636.

35 Kingsley Davis, 'A Conceptual Analysis of Stratification', *American Sociological Review*, vol. 7, no. 3 (1942), pp. 315–16.

36 See Talcott Parsons, *Structure and Process in Modern Society* (Glencoe Illinois: Free Press), pp. 220–1; this is a critique of C. Wright Mills, especially his *The Power Elite* (New York: Oxford University Press, 1956) and 'The Structure of Power in American Society', *British Journal of Sociology*, vol. 9, no. 1 (March 1958), pp. 29–41, and reprinted in *Power, Politics and People* (New York: Ballantine Books, 1963).

37 Keith Dowding, *Power: Concepts in the Social Sciences* (Buckingham: Open University Press, 1996). See also John Elster, *Nuts and Bolts for the Social Sciences* (Cambridge: CUP, 1989). (Elster's work has influenced Chapter 6.)

38 For a fuller discussion, see my *Words, Wonders and Power* (SPCK, 1996), and 'Power and Fundamentalism', *Journal of Contemporary Religion*, vol. 10, no. 3 (1995). See also J. Beckford, 'The Restoration of Power and the Sociology of Religion' in T. Robbins and R. Robertson (eds), *Church–State Relations* (New Brunswick, NJ: Transaction Books, 1987).

39 S. Clegg, *Frameworks of Power* (London: Sage, 1989), p. 239.

40 *Ibid.*, p. 238.

41 Max Weber, 'The Social Psychology of the World Religions' in H. H. Gerth and C. Wright Mills (eds), *From Max Weber* (New York: Oxford University Press, 1946), p. 295.

42 Max Weber, *Economy and Society*, (vol. 1) (New York: Bedminster Press, 1968), pp. 24–5.

43 Max Weber, *The Theory of Social and Economic Organisation* (New York: Free Press, 1947), pp. 358ff.

44 Max Weber, *The Sociology of Religion* (London: Methuen, 1965), p. 46.

45 For a good discussion of Weber's sociology of religion, see Brian Morris, *Anthropological Studies of Religion* (Cambridge: CUP, 1987).

46 See Anthony Giddens, *The Consequences of Modernity* (Cambridge: Polity Press, 1990), p. 46.

47 See J. Hughes, P. Martin and W. Shorrock, *Understanding Classical Sociology: Marx, Weber, Durkheim* (London: Sage, 1995), p. 115.

48 See Eric Hoffer, *The Passionate State of Mind* (London: Secker & Warburg, 1956), p. 105.

49 For an excellent discussion of domination and charismatic authority, see Ken

Morrison, *Marx, Durkheim, Weber: Formations of Modern Social Thought* (London: Sage, 1995), pp. 284ff.

50 See Percy, *op. cit.*, 1996, p. 121.

51 J. Winterson, *Oranges Are Not the Only Fruit* (London: Pandora, 1985); Margaret Atwood, *The Handmaid's Tale* (London: Jonathan Cape, 1986).

52 Jane Rogers, *Mr Wroe's Virgins* (London: Faber & Faber, 1991), p. 43.

53 See F. Peretti, *This Present Darkness* (1986) and *Piercing the Darkness* (1989) (Westchester, Ill: Crossway Books). Peretti's books have sold in their millions to revivalists all over the world.

54 W. Wink, *Engaging the Powers: Discernment and Resistance in a World of Domination* (Augsburg: Fortress Press, 1992), p. 9.

55 For a discussion of submission doctrines within the Shepherding Movement, see A. Walker, *Restoring the Kingdom* (London: Hodder & Stoughton, 1988) (2nd edition), pp. 88–93, 147–53.

56 W. Wink, *Engaging the Powers* (1992), p. 46. See also *Naming the Powers: The Language of Power in the New Testament* (1984) and *Unmasking the Powers: The Invisible Forces that Determine Human Existence* (1986) (both Philadelphia: Fortress Press).

57 (London: DLT, 1984).

58 W. Hollenweger, 'From Azusa Street to the Toronto Phenomenon' in J. Moltmann and K. J. Kuschel (eds), *Pentecostal Movements as an Ecumenical Challenge* (London: Concilium/SCM, 1996), no. 3, pp. 3–14.

59 D. Nicholls, *Deity and Domination: Images of God and the State in the Nineteenth and Twentieth Centuries* (London: Routledge, 1989).

60 Nicholls, *op. cit.*, 1989, pp. 234ff. I point out that the hegemonic structures in revivalist churches are partly derivative of the absence of a Trinitarian doctrine: Percy, *op. cit.*, 1996, p. 182, note 11.

# 2

# The healing benediction: a sociological and narrative theology of miracles in the Gospels

A most miraculous work in this Good king,
Which often since my here-remain in England
I have seen him do. How he solicits heaven
Himself best knows; but strangely-visited people,
All swollen and ulcerous, pitiful to the eye,
The mere despair of surgery, he cures,
Hanging a golden stamp around their necks,
Put on with holy prayers; and 'tis spoken,
To the succeeding royalty he leaves
The healing benediction.[1]

Malcolm's speech in Shakespeare's *Macbeth* reflects on the healing proper-
ties of Edward's tomb, and of touching. In healing ritual and praxis, touch
is usually vital. The laying on of hands, the grasping of a relic, the
location of a shrine, or an inner sense of being disturbed by the grace of
otherness constitute part of the grammar of healing and touch. To be
healed often begins by an awareness of being connected – of being touched
by something else. Naturally, this renders accounts of healing peculiarly
susceptible to social readings, and the purpose of this essay is to indicate
something of the power of Jesus in miracles by focusing on the *types* of
people he touched, rather than the method, although the two are linked.
All of us, believer and sceptic alike, use the word 'miracle' to refer to
events which seem unlikely, beyond our understanding, or even apparently
impossible. Yet it is only when we more specifically assert that God
intervenes in the ways of the world, such that the generally accepted laws
of nature are suspended, that major theological problems arise. However,
I want to suggest that the real problem with miracles, especially healing

miracles, is not so much their plausibility as their purpose. What was the point of miracles in the Gospels? To what end did Jesus perform them, and what did his disciples understand by them? Are they meant to be repeated today as demonstrations of the power and love of a living God? If so, what would they tell us about God, the nature of the world, and their relation to each other? And, in the light of this, what conclusions might we draw about the mission of today's Church?

These questions, amongst others, are particularly important when one considers the emphasis placed on miracles by some movements within contemporary Christianity. For over a decade the influential Signs and Wonders Movement has held that public demonstrations of the miraculous may be a pre-eminent form of evangelism. Those at the hub of the Movement urge churches to practice the miraculous in their congregations and beyond, in order to verify that the power and presence of God is within them.[2] Sometimes, the claims made by such groups in respect of being able to reproduce the miraculous lie beyond the borders of credibility: it is claimed that the dead are raised, the chronically and terminally ill healed, the handicapped made whole, and global disasters accurately predicted, with revivals following.[3]

Allied to this, the twentieth century has witnessed a revival in specifically religious healing methods in response to illness. A number of healers claim that they are operating within a 'revival tradition' that can be traced back to the New Testament, but point to specific periods of history when the Church has re-discovered its healing mandate. However, this account of history depends more than a little on literal and naive readings of the past.[4] Although relatively little has been done in terms of intellectual evaluation of the revival, the field is wide open for a range of assessments.[5] It should be noted that the interest of the Christian Church in healing coincides precisely with the staggering achievements of modern secular medicine, whereby people in Western societies have never enjoyed better physical health and lower mortality rates. There are no doubt many reasons for this ironic happenstance: the response of Christianity to secularization and the competitive conditions of postmodernity; a perception that the vision of modernity has failed; and, a desire originating from within certain strands of Pentecostalism and Fundamentalism to reclaim some of the original experiences that first empowered early Christianity.[6]

Of course, it would be misleading to suggest that healing movements in this century are solely confined to Pentecostal and fundamentalist groups: the Anglo-Catholic Guild of Health was founded in 1904, which emphasized the efficacy of healing though the main sacraments of the Church.[7] But the more usual tradition in this century is the belief in and practice of direct divine healing[8] which is commonly found in churches and groups influenced by charismatic renewal, Pentecostalism and certain types of neo-fundamentalism. Typically, this tradition sees the healer as being particularly gifted (continuing in the ways of Jesus and the Apostles), and the healing itself as being evidence of God's direct supernatural intervention in the world.

Most healers acknowledge the haphazard aspect of their ministry: some of the 'ill' are healed, some are not; some receive healing in different ways from those they expect; some healings are instant; some take place over a considerable period of time. The variations in types of healing claimed after ministry are even more diverse: from the trivial headache or cold, to the severity of cancers, deformed limbs and blindness. Beyond this lies the bizarre. Rex Gardner, in his *Healing Miracles: A Doctor Investigates*, cites the case of some South American Indians who received miraculous fillings for their tooth cavities, each with a little cross on![9]

To be sure, evaluating the effectiveness of methods of healing is an important medical, theological and phenomenological task. One of my main contentions is that the Signs and Wonders Movement is not a gospel for the poor; it primarily blesses those who already have health, wealth and more besides.[10] I am conscious that this is a serious charge, but it can be defended by attending to the following example. Suppose a middle-aged man attends a healing meeting at which healing ministry is being offered. At the close of the meeting he is approached by someone who claims to have a word from God for him about his chest pains. The man is astonished at the accuracy of the prophecy; he does indeed suffer acute chest pains. He is prayed for, feels touched by God, and returns home rejoicing. But his problems really begin here: he returns to his home which happens to be on one of the most depressed and crime-ridden housing estates; unemployment is very high, community amenities scarce, and debt and stress-related poor health common. He takes up smoking again, and his pains soon return: his smoking is related to his stress which is in turn, related to his social conditions. Globally, the biggest single cause of illness and disease is poverty. In the example above, the pain may well be psychosomatic, but no true healing can take root until the social conditions are materially transformed. (If this is true for the man in our example, how much more true is it for the millions who suffer illness because of malnutrition, or living in slum conditions, or who are the victims of war.) By contrast, a Signs and Wonders approach to healing generally deals with inner or unseen transformations in middle-class groupings. The kind of healings claimed are usually for things that can neither be seen or tested: headaches, backaches, heart problems and depression are typical. Mention of social transformation however, as a means of healing, especially for the poor, is very rare.

But my purpose here for the moment is not to examine whether or not modern Christian healing methods 'work'. Clearly, many people believe they do. What is perhaps of more importance is to enquire into the original purpose of miracles, particularly those in the Gospels. I wish to argue that the Gospel miracles should be read as primarily political and social actions, with consequent implications for their audiences and the disciples, and, therefore, for the Church today. In saying 'primarily', I would want to make it clear from the outset that I am not claiming to have constructed a complete scheme for interpreting miracles in the Gospels; there will be exceptions to the rule. Equally, miracles in the Old Testament and in Acts have not been considered, which some readers may also find problematic. However, I still wish to argue that the task of miracles in the Gospels may well have more to do with social, political and ethical considerations than with naked demonstrations of divine power simply intervening in often tragic human situations.

## Miracles as an Issue for Theology

One of the problems in the past that characterized the discussion of miracles in theology was the dialogical chasm that existed between those of conservative and liberal positions. With some exceptions, this is still true today. For example, Maurice Wiles in *God's Action in the World* argues for an understanding of creation which dispenses with specific divine interventions in history. In this view, creation is to be understood as a continuing activity in which God's concern to create self-determining, independent creatures who are themselves truly creative, cannot logically be overridden in any way. So, God works his purposes out in terms of 'bias implanted in matter' which is itself not a 'pre-packaged blueprint'.[11] Many would see this approach as being far too 'reductionist'; miracles emerge as feats that are attributed to Jesus and to God retrospectively by faith communities, in order to secure their sense of divine power and favour. Indeed, the work of Wiles seems to be giving fresh impetus to the Enlightenment theology of the likes of Troeltsch, Strauss and others.[12] Troeltsch, in particular, with his view of history and historical criticism, coupled with his use of analogy and correlation, effectively rules out the possibility of miraculous intervention; were he ever to be confronted with one, it is unclear what he would do, since his historical method ruled them out from the start.[13] Those of a more conservative theological outlook would argue that those writers just mentioned display a 'closed world-view' that is no better or worse than their own; why not begin a theological method by assuming that miracles do occur and that God does intervene, as the Bible seems to suggest? And so the chasm remains fixed.

Clearly any reflection about miracles belongs to a wider discussion about the nature of God.[14] David Jenkins argues that because God's self-revelation is love, not primarily power, miracles must be understood as 'gifts of love to be received by faith' that do not compel belief, but lead to freedom.[15] Miracles do not actually *prove* anything about God, therefore the focus of discussion ought always to shift from their actuality to the nature of God, in whom truth alone resides. This is a neat side-step, but the argument itself will not halt the process that Troeltsch sought to correct, namely the use of miracles in establishing doctrine and subsequent ecclesial power.

An alternative strategy in dealing with miracles is not to accept the sceptical traditions of the Enlightenment in the first place. ( I will qualify how this can be done in more detail later, avoiding liberalism and literalism.) The arguments of David Hume – that it was unreasonable to accept an account of an event that was an exception to the usual course of nature – have been widely accepted by natural scientists, philosophers and theologians. Hume's legacy is his definition of a miracle as a putative event which violates the laws of nature. This he finds unreasonable, and therefore processes of deconstruction or demythologizing automatically arise out of reading accounts of the miraculous.[16] But his definition and the consequences need not be accepted. Sarah Coakley has recently challenged Hume's treatment of the resurrection by critiquing his concept of history, which she finds inadequate. Her discussion broadens to include Swinburne and Pannenberg,[17] concluding that a focus on 'metaphor' in miracle accounts may provide further developments in 'a debate that has otherwise settled into rather predictable contours'.[18]

Equally, the divorce between natural and supernatural has been challenged in J. Houston's *Reported Miracles*. Houston argues that Hume was wrong about the conceptual aspects of miracles in Christian tradition; for both Augustine and Aquinas, miracles did not violate nature so much as transcend it. God's apparent intervention in the world is part of the creative and redemptive processes, and does not run counter to their normal functioning. Houston resources his argument with writings from the Fathers to the Middle Ages, and concludes that theism makes more sense of our experience than the closed world of Enlightenment philosophy.[19] It is this kind of theology that does much to bridge the gap between the false polarization of history and faith that has characterized so much discussion on miracles. Yet awkward questions remain: how precisely are the Gospel accounts of Jesus' miracles to be read? In spite of much theological water passing under the bridge, a 'literal' reading feels naive (and perhaps dishonest?) against a weighty background of theological and philosophical inquiry. Equally, a reading funded by a rigorous Enlightenment standpoint can been shown to be problematic in its foreclosure of mystery and miracle. Perhaps the first step must be to establish what purpose the miracle accounts might serve in the Gospels, especially in relation to Jesus and the nature of God. Is there any discernible political and social agenda within the miracles themselves, and their retelling by the Evangelists?

## Reading Miracles

To some extent, the territory of this article has been sighted by New Testament scholars for some years, yet few have chosen to tread its paths. Liberation theologians, to date, have shown some reluctance in systematically interpreting miracles in the terms I've so far outlined, for reasons one can only guess at.[20] Jon Sobrino's *Jesus the Liberator* deals, as one would expect, with the importance of the poor for Jesus, making much of his solidarity with the innocent and victimized at the hands of the rich and powerful. Yet the miracles of Jesus, prominent in all four Gospels, are only treated by Sobrino as a means to critique those who (in his view) 'spiritualize' the Kingdom of God out of existence, such as Charismatics, Evangelicals, and even Mother Teresa: unlike Jesus' miracles, the work of these movements and people do not forward the kingdom.[21] Sobrino's work is typical of many liberation theologians. The Gospel miracles it seems, remain 'unread' in any meaningful political sense, except for a few isolated comments and commentaries on specific texts.

Outside the realm of liberation theology, Alan Richardson's *The Miracle Stories of the Gospels*, published in 1941, attempted a symbolic reading which might be construed as the beginning of a systematic political 'reading'. Richardson maintained that all the Gospel miracles should be understood as a dramatized form of essential Christological teaching. In other words, they were enacted parables, not mere 'wonder stories' or historical reminiscence.[22] The work of Howard Clark Kee develops Richardson's thesis in line with modern historical methods. Kee concludes that miracles have a fourfold function, based on his reading of comparable literary genres such as Tacitus and Josephus. First, miracles have an apocalyptic dimension, serving to instil fear in readers and remind them of the coming parousia. Second, and allied to this, they have a romantic function in the post-resurrection age. Third, they work as universal symbols for the power of God, which, fourth, allows them to be used as propaganda against pagan beliefs and the forces of scepticism.[23] All this may be so, but it is unfortunate that such a highly developed symbolic reading should lead to reductive rather than productive conclusions.

Of course, Richardson and Kee are vehemently opposed by scholars such as James Kallas, who insist that the miracles are not 'employed for expressing a truth which is quite independent of them – they are, instead, themselves the message!'[24] Kallas is a rich resource for fundamentalists and Charismatics who wish to licence their current healing practice, since his readings of the Gospel miracles accept (uncritically) the heaven/hell and Satan/God dualism inherent in some miracle stories; but he writes with more passion than depth. A more sophisticated and moderate voice is that of Reginald Fuller, who believes in the authenticity of miracles, but regards them as possessing a symbolic power as well, which points to the redemptive work of Christ in a social as well as a spiritual context.[25] Fuller's carefully nuanced thesis culminates in a discussion of the point of miracles for the Church today: they cannot be proofs or persuaders, but are rather part of the 'works of Christ' on a par with words and sacraments – a pointer to the new order and creation, but not a compelling sign, except to those who already believe.[26] Fuller completes his thesis by suggesting how miracles can be preached on (including an illuminating discussion of the 'nature' miracle in Luke 5:1–11: the 'miraculous draft of fishes'), before offering an appendix that is critical of the approaches of both Kallas and Richardson. However, these examples only serve to illustrate that the chasm between liberal and conservative positions remains, in spite of the synthesis attempted by Fuller, which has its origins in differing views on the nature of God, scripture and consequent praxis.

One of the most developed theories of miracles as a form of political activity can be found in the work of Gerd Theissen. In agreement with Clark and Richardson, Theissen opts for a symbolic interpretation of miracles over a literal one. Further still, he contends that the genres of the accounts contain many dualities, such as those between rich and poor, included and excluded, and so forth. For Theissen, the miracles have socio-economic connotations and implications, which, although not explaining their presence in the Gospels, nor indeed why they might have been performed, are nonetheless one aspect of the dynamic to be noted by the reader.[27] As examples, he cites the marriage at Cana as having (likely) implications for providing for the poor at feasts, and the saving of the disciples in the storm on Lake Galilee as signifying God's concern for the protection of the poor at work in dangerous situations: the contemporary correlations are obvious, and do not need spelling out. Thus, for Theissen, the miracle stories have a power to change the world, and, whether read 'literally' or not, are parables of action for the Church. Yet Theissen is tentative in extending the range and scope of this reading to the rest of the gospel miracles. This is unfortunate, since it leaves the Church without a clear agenda that both liberal and conservative expositors might be able to agree upon and act upon. What follows may go some way towards bridging that gap, whilst at the same time eschewing unnecessarily spiritualized or demythologized modes of interpretation.

## Re-reading Healing in the Gospels: Comparing and Contrasting

Jesus' healing ministry as recorded in the Gospels appears to be extremely discriminating. On only four occasions is a healing recorded in a building used for religious purposes (see Mark 1:23–27, Mark 3:1–5, Matthew 21:14 and Luke 13:10–13, and their Synoptic parallels). In two of these four cases, it is a woman who is healed, whose actual right to be there must be in some question. In every other case, healings by Jesus take place outside any community of faith, except where crowds or the poor are deemed by an Evangelist to constitute a group of faithful people. Jesus' friends or relatives are not usually the beneficiaries of his healing power either.[28] In fact, of those who are healed, we know little, not even a name, and certainly nothing of the long-term response of those who are healed. This may be partly due to the fact that those who are healed are either poor, voiceless, marginalized or despised within society. The form of healing engendered by Jesus is also ambiguous, extending well beyond physical changes in a person. For example, Zacchaeus has his place and relationship with his community restored through a symbolic gesture initiated by Christ, which called into question the demonizing tendencies of a hostile public in response to an unfair tax (Luke 19:1–10). Others are forgiven before they can even confess their sin (e.g. Luke 7:36ff. and John 8:1–11), resulting in a form of healing. Where some would indict the individual sinner, Jesus seems to recognize the corporate and societal pressures that produce the wrong. The equation between sin and suffering is one that Jesus seems to query rather than endorse.[29]

In virtually every healing story (and there are over forty in the Gospels) the person healed is politically, socially or religiously disadvantaged – unloved or unnoticed by the majority of onlookers or witnesses. The Gospel miracles, then, are a record of Christ reaching out to those marginalized, dispossessed, cursed in society and cast out from faith communities: Christ seems to embrace those who few would consider touching. There is even a sense of urgency about this within the context of the Messianic mission. The woman healed of a crippling infirmity in Luke 13:10–17 is healed on the sabbath: first century Rabbinism allowed for such healing, but only when there was danger of death, which the narrative strongly suggests was not the case. Fitzmyer describes this healing as 'the welfare of a human being [taking] precedence over . . . religious obligations'.[30] The thrust of the narrative is to contrast the jealousy or scepticism of the 'leader of the synagogue' (v. 14) with the plight of the 'daughter of Abraham': Jesus emerges as Lord of the synagogue and sabbath in the space of seven verses, a healer whose responsiveness and urgency of ministry reflects his overall mission.

Other commentators have suggested that the link between healing and the forgiveness of sins must be connected to the perceptions of onlookers. In effect, it is only for this reason that the Gospels reflect the linkage: they are not trying to make a theological point, but rather to subvert a commonly held premise.[31] Not only that, but authors such as Fridrichsen, Geisler, and Ernst and Marie-Luise Keller suggest that the act of repeating a miracle may diminish its value, relegating it to the ranks of thaumaturgy.[32] The more thoughtful approach of the Kellers is, in my view, of greater value than the positivism of Geisler. The Kellers' exegetical readings allow them to see miracles as signs that had a unique function which in turn have been imbued with a unique status: in this respect, they are close to Fuller.[33] But their shrewd analysis of the treatment of miracles in philosophical theology and Biblical literature places them in a good position to discuss the reality of miracles. They see them as 'something localized [from] beyond this world . . . concentrated in mysterious centres of action'. They are primarily revelations that point to the ultimate dissolution between the natural and supernatural order, but this dissolution is held in the crucified, raised and ascended Christ, which is not always consonant with the activity of the Church.[34] In short, they are part of the created order, but not supra-creation in terms of eschatology; as such, critiques of their function and place are to be welcomed.

By way of comparison, much of what passes for the 'healing movement' in today's church is very different. Evangelists and healers who offer ministry usually do so in the context of a church or faith-gathering. The ministry on offer is inward-looking, intended for those who join or become members; it largely leaves the dispossessed and marginalized of society alone. Where they are included, the terms are often strictly defined, whereas those who were encompassed by Jesus' healing ministry had no obstacles placed in their way, at least by him. The modern healing movement only appears to work for 'believers', or in order to make people believe who would not otherwise. Frequently, those who claim to be healed already possess significant social, moral or religious status, whereas the healings of Jesus seem to be directed at people who are exactly the opposite.[35] In fact, Jesus, both in parable (e.g. Luke 15 – the Prodigal Son) and activity (Luke 7 – the Woman at Simon's house) demonstrates the importance of the assurance of forgiveness being offered before the respondent can speak or confess their sin; the Gospels seem to be saying that you can only truly confess once you have heard the words of absolution.

In contrast, many exponents within the healing movement would insist on confession of sin as a precondition to being offered healing ministry. In saying this, I am not dismissing accounts where sin and sickness are bound up together. For example, Matthew 9:2–7 records the paralytic, where Jesus originally says to the man: 'Your sins are forgiven.' The teachers of the law, scandalized by this, question Jesus' authority to forgive, upon which Jesus simply instructs the man to walk, which he does. The social construction of reality concerning the relationship between sin and sickness in Jesus' day was complex, involving processes of hereditary curse, personal responsibility, third-party blaming and psychosomatic causes. Jesus' attitude to the perceived cause and effect relationship between sin and sickness is, to say the least, ambiguous; he simultaneously rejects and accepts it, treating it almost playfully at times. It is not unfair to suggest that when he does appear to acknowledge it, agreement with the link is not necessarily implied.[36]

The disparities between the way in which Jesus conducted his healing ministry and the way in which modern healers usually proceed are numerous. However, what is perhaps more striking, as the table below shows, when compared to the subsequent list of healing miracles, are the *types* of people healed by Jesus, and the consequent implications for the church in liberal and conservative spheres.

---

## TYPOLOGIES OF GOSPEL HEALINGS

1. The demonized (by society?), mentally ill, and therefore ostracized from society and faith community (1, 9, 17, 21, 22).
2. The handicapped – marginalized in society – due to inability to function or fit in normally (6, 7, 15, 16, 18, 40).
3. Lepers and other Untouchables – banned from society (5, 11, 34).
4. Children and widows – little social status (10, 14, 17, 30, 38). [Also single mothers: 14?, 30].
5. Women adjudged unclean through sin/sickness (11, 31, 32; see also Luke 7, John 4 and John 8).
6. Others judged to be ill through sin (40; but possibly the case with most sickness – see John 9).
7. People of other faiths (14, 19, 34, 38).
8. 'Multitudes' – seemingly indiscriminate, except insofar as the gospel writers use the term multitude to refer to those excluded from normal religious activity and the poor in society. They are to be distinguished from the religious of the day such as the Pharisee and Saducee denominations, as well as Elders, Scribes and Priests (3, 13, 23, 24, 25, 26, 27, 28, 36, 37).

### AN OVERVIEW OF THE HEALING MINISTRY OF JESUS

| Description | Matthew | Mark | Luke | John |
|---|---|---|---|---|
| 1 Man with unclean spirit | | 1:21–28 | 4:31–37 | |
| 2 Peter's mother-in-law | 8:14–15 | 1:30–31 | 4:38–39 | |
| 3 Multitudes | 8:16–17 | 1:32–34 | 4:40–41 | |

## AN OVERVIEW OF THE HEALING MINISTRY OF JESUS (*Cont.*)

| Description | Matthew | Mark | Luke | John |
|---|---|---|---|---|
| 4 Many demons | | 1:39 | | |
| 5 Leper | 8:2–4 | 1:40–42 | 5:12–13 | |
| 6 Man with palsy | 9:2–8 | 2:3–12 | 5:17–26 | |
| 7 Man with withered hand | 12:9–14 | 3:1–6 | 6:6–11 | |
| 8 Multitudes | 12:15–16 | 3:10–11 | | |
| 9 Gaderene demoniac | 8:28–34 | 5:1–17 | 8:26–39 | |
| 10 Jairus' daughter | 9:18–19, 23–26 | 5:22–24, 35–43 | 8:40–42, 49–56 | |
| 11 Woman with bleeding | 9:20–22 | 5:24b-34 | 8:42b-48 | |
| 12 A few sick people | 13:58 | 6:5–6 | | |
| 13 Multitudes | 14:34–36 | 6:54–56 | | |
| 14 Syrophoenician's daughter | 15:21–28 | 7:24–30 | | |
| 15 Deaf and dumb man | | 7:31–37 | | |
| 16 Blind man | | 8:22–26 | | |
| 17 Child with evil spirit | 17:14–18 | 9:14–27 | 9:38–43 | |
| 18 Blind Bartemaeus | 20:29–34 | 10:46–52 | 8:35–43 | |
| 19 Centurion's servant | 8:5–13 | | 7:1–10 | |
| 20 Two blind men | 9:27–31 | | | |
| 21 Dumb demoniac | 9:32–34 | | | |
| 22 Blind and dumb demoniac | 12:22 | | 11:14 | |
| 23 Multitudes | 4:23 | | 6:17–19 | |
| 24 Multitudes | 9:35 | | | |
| 25 Multitudes | 11:4–5 | | 7:21–22 | |
| 26 Multitudes | 14:14 | | 9:11 | 6:2 |
| 27 Great multitudes | 15:30 | | | |
| 28 Great multitudes | 19:2 | | | |
| 29 Blind and lame in temple | 21:14 | | | |
| 30 Widow's son | | | 7:11–17 | |
| 31 Mary Magdelene + others | | | 8:2 | |
| 32 Woman bound by Satan | | | 13:10–13 | |
| 33 Man with dropsy | | | 14:1–4 | |
| 34 Ten lepers | | | 17:11–19 | |
| 35 Malchus' ear | | | 22:49–51 | |
| 36 Multitudes | | | 5:15 | |
| 37 Various persons | | | 13:52 | |
| 38 Nobleman's son | | | | 4:46–53 |
| 39 Invalid man | | | | 5:1–9 |
| 40 Man born blind | | | | 9:1–7 |

The typologies in these tables have their modern equivalents, and it is clear that the overwhelming focus of Jesus' ministry lay with the poor, unknown and excluded of his day. So, the healings themselves can be seen as an activity which characterizes the love of God for the forsaken and damned, especially those who are victims of religious, moral and societal exclusion. This love even extends to including those of other faiths, with no conditions attached; nobody becomes a Christian in the Gospels, or is compelled to believe anything, because of a miracle. The activity therefore stands as a literal as well as symbolic sign of God's love for the oppressed, and questions the role of religion and society in colluding with or instigating that oppression. As Mary Grey says, the healings of Jesus are 'characterised by a redemptive mutuality in which people come into their own'.[37] This is endorsed in some of Jesus' encounters with others even where a physical healing does not take place. Mention has already been made of Zacchaeus, and, as Jean-Jacques Suurmond points out, the Gospels are full of playful political subversion and social healings: 'tax collectors become Robin Hoods who returned their money to the poor; common sluts become princesses of the resurrection preaching'.[38] Therefore to focus on repeating miracles as demonstrative acts of power for today misses the original context and target of Jesus' healings, which had radical political, social and religious dynamics that were usually missed in their day, but should not be ignored now.[39]

## Healing as Taking on Affliction

There is a further dimension to the healings of Jesus that should be mentioned, which places his ministry in sharp contrast to many of today's healing movements. It is the notion that there is some sense in which Jesus takes on the suffering and affliction of the individuals he cures, such that it becomes part of him. This view would not have been strange to the Early Church fathers, whose progressive move towards a richly incarnational theology required them to conclude that what was not assumed could not be redeemed. So, Jesus risks social ostracization when he dines with Zacchaeus, consorts with sinners, and receives women of dubious repute into his company, precisely in order to take on their brokenness, as well as take on the taboos of society that maintain structures that divorce the secular and sacred.

As Janet Soskice has pointed out, it is no different in the healing miracles themselves. Noting the story of the haemorrhaging woman in Luke 8:40–56 (cf. Mark 5:21–43 and Matthew 9:18–34), she points out that what is striking about it is Jesus' willingness to touch or be touched by an impure woman. Although modern readers of the text may find this aspect of the narrative difficult, the significance of Jesus' action should not be underestimated; '[she] defiled the teacher which, according to Levitical law, she would have done for she was in a state of permanent uncleaness, polluting everyone and everything with whom she came into contact'.[40] Her poverty – 'she had spent all she had' – is a direct result of her affliction. Yet Jesus, apart from healing her, also seems to challenge the social and religious forces that have rendered this woman contagious; he calls her daughter in all three accounts, and all three Evangelists stress the woman's faith. Interestingly, the Synoptic accounts of the haemorrhaging woman are all paired with the raising of Jairus' daughter. Again, the issues of impurity (touching a corpse) and of menstruation occur: the girl is twelve, and her untimely death clearly prevents her from entering womanhood. Jesus declares her 'not dead, but sleeping', and his touch, resulting in his defilement, raises the girl.[41]

Frank Kermode's work has important resonances with the observations made by Soskice.[42] Kermode's discussion of the purity issues in Mark 5 picks up on the fact that the stories of the haemorrhaging woman and Jairus' daughter have been paired and conflated. Kermode cites as evidence for this the undue prominence Mark gives to the narrative by the sharing of the number twelve (the girl is twelve, the woman has been ill for twelve years): 'this coincidence signifies a narrative relation of some kind between the woman and the girl ... an older woman is cured of a menstrual disorder of twelve years' standing, and is sent back into society. A girl who has not yet reached puberty is reborn ...'.[43] Kermode presses his claim that the narrative is centred on sexuality with some force: 'they take their complementary ways out of sickness into society, out of the unclean into the clean'.[44] Jesus does not negate the sexuality of either woman, nor does he demonize their afflictions, or imply that they are unclean – the healing comes from their being accepted by him as they are: defilement is done away with.

Whilst these elements in the Gospel accounts may be implicit in the text, or buried by traditional forms of exegesis, their uncovering raises serious issues for the contemporary Church in its healing ministry. The taking on of another's affliction is not something many would contemplate, particularly if that requires the healer to then be regarded as also being handicapped, defiled or a sinner. Nowhere is this issue more acute than in the field of care for victims of HIV/AIDS related cases, where defilement through touch stalks the mind of society like a ghost. My reading of the healing miracles in the Gospels suggests three things in this case. First, that touching and embracing the afflicted, in the widest possible sense, is critical to Jesus' ministry. Second, that judging the cause of sickness, or naming it as sin, has no place in Jesus' ministry. Third, that (somehow) inculcating the sickness itself into the body of Jesus was important. I am aware that this is effectively a call for the Church to live as though the 'body of Christ has AIDS',[45] fully assuming the personal, social, moral, medical and political problems that arise for sufferers. But to do less than this would be to fall into the familiar dualist trap of seeing the body of Christ as pure and unassuming rather than being engaged in complex, rich suffering and mutual intercourse with the world.[46] Sylvia Sands spells out the implications of this suffering solidarity in her poem *Meditation on the Third Station of the Cross – Jesus Falls for the First Time*:[47]

Eat dirt.

We all like to see the mighty fallen
Don't we?
So here's God in the dust.

Except,
Crumpled and tumbled beneath his cross,
He resembles nothing so much
As a Child.

Grown-ups don't fall down, do they?
Well, not often.
Not unless they are
Drunk;
Crippled;
Down and out;
Mugged;
Starved;
Queer-bashed;
Frail;
Raped;
Stoned;
Or
Plain suicidal.

He's there in all of them, of course.

Dear Jesus of the gutter I cannot forget
It was Roman feet you saw,
Ready to kick you onwards,
Just as later, your sisters and brothers
Would see jack boots
In Auschwitz.

So,
It's hard to watch you squirm,
Debased,
Degraded,
Filthy,
Beneath your cross.

But where and how else could we understand
Your solidarity
With
The Disposessed?

There is a fundamental sense, then, in which the suffering God needs to be brought alongside the Jesus of healing miracles. Moltmann's picture of the crucified Christ needs to be placed firmly in the centre of any theology of healing, not because Jesus' death somehow negates sickness, but because the death itself is the ultimate fulfilment of those miracles. In death, Jesus becomes the man who is going nowhere, an emblem of hopelessness, betrayed, vilified and cursed; he earns the scorn of society, for 'he saved others, but he cannot save himself'. So at the heart of the Gospels there is a profoundly broken person, who was prepared to be broken for others, and ended up by paying the ultimate price. This vision of Jesus flies in the face of the usual portrayals one encounters in the majority of modern healing movements. The emphasis is usually on Christ's strength and his ability to accomplish all things. Those who are afflicted must lose what afflicts them before they can join the company of the redeemed: that same company will certainly not be joining them, descending to their level. So as far as the Church is concerned, Paul's 'kenotic' hymn of Philippians 2 is reversed: individuals and society must empty themselves and rise to meet God on another plateau. Yet at the heart of the Eucharist, it is the action of breaking bread that signifies Christ's solidarity with his people, and points to the salvation beyond. When the Church lives like this, as the broken body of Christ for the broken themselves, there is healing and redemption in abundance: the work of many communities and individuals testifies to this.[48]

Before looking finally at the task of miracles, it perhaps apposite to ask 'did Jesus actually heal, or are the miracles just "signs"?' Part of the answer has to lie in locating the healing ministry of Jesus within the activity of incarnation, which, in some sense, is an ongoing process. In the incarnation, that which is symbolized in Christ is also actualized, and the hidden revealed: the Church is called to live out this life too, relating the inner to the outer in all spheres. So the miracles of Jesus are real in the sense that all symbolic action became focused in activity that was observable, reifiable and demonstrable. This apparently involves disturbing the laws of nature, but the laws are only subverted where they oppress or threaten, and Jesus' healing activity points to the importance of breaking through all oppressive barriers, be they legal, societal or natural. Again, this suggests that miracles can never be proofs or simple demonstrations of power: they always have a social-transcendent function which is primary.[49]

## The Task of Miracles

The social, moral, religious and political impacts of Jesus' healing miracles are inescapable. Part of the value of these miracles in Jesus' ministry, besides healing individuals, seems to be in questioning society over its attitude to sickness itself. The sin of the individual as a cause is uniformly rejected by Jesus. Instead, he tends to challenge crowds and onlookers, questioning their implicit or explicit role in the person's misfortune. For Jesus, healing is never just an action for an individual: there are always wider, corporate implications.

This observation is particularly pertinent in the context of the changes taking place in health-care at present. Besides the radical shake-ups in the financing of the National Health Service in the UK, there is also a political and moral shift taking place. People are increasingly encouraged to relate to a system as individuals in their own right, competing for funds, care and treatment. Increasingly, the causes of disease are portrayed as matters of individual choice: those who might have poor diets or smoke too much in, say, urban priority areas or inner city areas, are blamed for their own bad health. The rhetoric of choice somehow implies that those who are ill, disabled or marginalized have partly become so through their own free will. Even at its best, such rhetoric reduces the patient to the status of a unit of consumption, a figure whose only significance is their place on the balance sheet. This was brought home to me only recently, as I waited at my local Parent and Baby Clinic with my young son. A young mother came in, distraught because her village practice would not accept her because 'they had enough babies on their list'; she could not drive, and was now faced with an expensive taxi journey every two weeks. The days of a 'cradle to grave' health service are over for most people, unless one is fortunate enough to be able to afford private health care. Yet as we have noted, the healing miracles of Jesus are directed to those with little or no choice, some of whom have exhausted their resources or been worn down by persistent blaming.

So, the modern healing movement needs to bear in mind that the Gospels and the accounts of healing within them do not provide the reader with a kind of manual on how to heal, or what to think about sickness. Leaving aside the world-view of first century Palestinians, the healing stories of the Gospels are too symbolic to be read as aids to diagnosis and prognosis. (Presumably, one should be as cautious about adopting the demonology of the first century as about adopting the pre-Copernican cosmology and 'flat Earth' geography of Psalm 19, even if Jesus did believe it in his incarnate form.) Accounts of healing can't be read as a type of instruction book, any more than an artist's portrait should function as an anatomical guide for a surgeon about to perform an operation. 'Healing stories' are still-life pictures, pregnant with meaning, including the social and political, yet faithful to the original subject. What counts is our reaction to what we see, not whether or not we can copy the picture.

The modern healing movement, for the most part, is correctly diagnosed by Sobrino as being too spiritualized in its relation to the world. There are, no doubt, many benefits in being part of the phenomenological escapism that many believe constitutes a revival.[50] Healing rallies and conventions will continue to come and go; healers who emphasize methods, texts and types of faith will always abound; some people will always be helped by such things, whilst others will be hindered. But the healing task of the Church surely lies well beyond this horizon. What I am arguing for is a reading of the healing stories that involves eschewing literal or demythologized paths, conservative or liberal slants, seeking instead a shared agenda for social, moral and political praxis. There are implicit imperatives in the healing ministry of Jesus that the Church needs to heed.[51]

Healing benediction, I would suggest, will only come when there is a serious theology of touch in relation to pain. Touching is one of the most basic forms of human communication, and one of the most personally experienced of all sensations. Our tactile sense is the genesis of our individual and social awareness. Closeness and physical intimacy play a major part in addressing pain: a hand extended in friendship or consolation, a hug or embrace, can be more profound than a thousand words.[52] The remarkable story of Jesus' healings is his awareness of this dynamic: he was willing to touch and be touched – he expressed grace in his physicality.[53] Individually and socially, the Church needs to contemplate real touching in response to real alienation and pain. This engagement requires a deep reaching inside itself, as well as a reaching out, drawing on the the resources of the One whose incarnation is just that. Revival will only come when the poor are accounted for and liberated. Renewal will only come when the culture that has produced the blaming of individuals for their sickness, along with the purchasing of services and choices in levels of treatment in health care, is subverted by a corporate sense of responsibility and a spirit of true service. Healing benediction will always be about touching society at this point.

## Notes

1 William Shakespeare, *Macbeth*, IV, iii: Malcolm's speech.
2 In this respect, the expectations of such groups are similar to what Bryan Wilson identifies as 'thaumaturgical': 'magical dispensation by supernatural agencies from

the normal laws of causality'. See B. Wilson, *Religious Sects* (London: Weidenfeld & Nicolson, 1970), pp. 39ff.

3 The Signs and Wonders Movement sees itself as part of the Third Wave of the Holy Spirit in the twentieth century, the Second Wave being the charismatic renewal of the '60s and '70s. The Signs and Wonders Movement regards healing miracles as normative for a growing, successful church, and promotes revival and renewal across denominational boundaries. Leading exponents include John Wimber, Peter Wagner, Bill Surbritzky and Morris Cerullo.

4 For example, the Third Wave Movement sees itself as an heir of the revivals of Wesley and Edwards. But as the table below shows, this is suspect, especially when dealing with a phenomenon like 'being slain in the spirit', which is held to be 'scriptural' (cf. Matthew 7:16, Luke 5:8, Acts 9:4, I Corinthians 14:25).

**Comparative Chart of Revival Phenomena**

| *Focus* | *18th century* | *20th century* |
|---|---|---|
| Attributes of God and Response | Holiness/repentance | Power/healing |
| Needs of respondents | Sins forgiven | Made whole or empowered |
| Falling down at gatherings | Fell down on faces | Fall on backs |
| When falling takes place | During preaching | During special 'clinic' |
| Response to falling | Ignored or removed | Become focus of attention |
| Preachers | Discouraged phenomenon | Encourage phenomenon |
| Congregational proxemics | Fell individually | Fall within groups |
| Social teaching | Integral to message | Added as important |

5 See S. Pattison, *Alive and Kicking* (London: SCM, 1989), p. 50.

6 i.e., an 'inductive theological strategy'. A closer examination of this is available in my 'Signs, Wonders and Church Growth', Unpublished PhD thesis, King's College, London, 1992.

7 Pattison, *op. cit.*, p. 52.

8 *Ibid.*, p. 51.

9 Published by DLT (London, 1986). See Chapter 9.

10 Some would point to revival in the Third World at this point, to defeat my argument. However, there is a sober recognition of mortality and disease in the Third World, and the social and spiritual dynamics of revival in places touched by renewal do not remove the causes of disease such as poverty, privation or poor sanitation. Equally, the demonology present in some Third World cultures does not validate its occurrence in other societies: if the social construction of reality requires a belief in malign spiritual forces, that may not bear any relation to the truth of a situation which might have a better medical explanation.
Pentecostalism and charismatic renewal have, in any case, been divided on racial lines for most of this century. Ostensibly this has been about Trinitarian issues, but the wealth and race gap is equally significant.

11 See M. Wiles, *God's Action in the World* (London: SCM, 1986) and H. Montefiore, *The Probability of God* (London: SCM, 1985), p. 161.

12 See Troeltsch, *Über Historische und dogmatische Methode* (Eng. trans. by Olive Wyon, New York: Harper, 1960), p. 734, and G. W. H. Lampe, *God as Spirit* (Oxford: OUP, 1977).

13 Troeltsch, *op. cit.*, p. 740.

14 D. Jenkins, *God, Miracle and the Church of England* (London: SCM, 1987), p. 19.

15 *Ibid.*, p. 32.

16  D. Hume, 'Of Miracles' from *An Enquiry Concerning Human Understanding*, sec.x., reprinted in R. Wollheim (ed.), *Hume on Religion* (London: Collins, 1963), p. 224.

17  See R. Swinburne, *The Concept of Miracle* (London: Macmillan, 1970), and *The Existence of God* (Oxford: OUP, 1979).

18  Sarah Coakley, 'Is the Resurrection a Historical Event?' in Paul Avis (ed.), *The Resurrection of Jesus Christ* (London: DLT, 1993).

19  J. Houston, *Reported Miracles* (Cambridge: CUP, 1993).

20  My guess is that many still read miracles as acts of interventionist power and therefore as imposition. In attempting to reconstruct theology and society along more egalitarian lines, this reading of miracles and its underlying theory of power has little place.

21  J. Sobrino, *Jesus the Liberator* (London: Burns and Oates, 1993). For interest, readers are also referred to John Pilch's 'Understanding Healing in the Social World of Early Christianity', *Biblical Theological Bulletin*, 22 (1992), pp. 26–33.

22  A. Richardson, *The Miracle Stories of the Gospels* (London: SCM, 1941), p. 22.

23  H. C. Kee, *Miracles in the Early Christian World* (New Haven: Yale University Press, 1983).

24  J. Kallas, *The Significance of the Synoptic Miracles* (London: SPCK, 1961), p. 83.

25  R.H. Fuller, *Interpreting the Miracles* (London: SCM, 1963).

26  *Ibid.*, p. 116.

27  G. Theissen, *Miracle Stories of the Early Christian Tradition* (Philadelphia: Fortress Press, 1983).

28  Exceptions to what I have stated above are few. Peter's mother-in-law is possibly a friend of Jesus, and is healed (Matthew 8:14–15; Mark 1:30–31; Luke 4:38–39). However, she may have been a widow, and therefore her status as that may be more significant. Mary Magdelene is healed (Luke 8:2), but the precise nature of her affliction is unclear. Lazarus is raised to life (John 11:1–44) and is, according to John, 'beloved' of Jesus. However, caution should be exercised when reading parts of the Gospel of John: its allegorical and apologetic directionality suggest that it is not always to be treated as 'literal history' (see 1:1–18, 20:30–31, 21:24–25, etc.). This is not to say that the Gospel is untrue; just the contrary. The Fourth Evangelist is clearly aiming at revealing the Truth (i.e. the Christ) in his work, whilst being faithful to the historical Jesus, yet the Gospel is more than mere history. The 'I AM' sayings are, I think, more allegorical than historical, and the raising of Lazarus may be a myth (i.e. a story that is true on the inside, but not necessarily on the outside, like a parable) that is a vehicle for affirming Jesus as the Resurrection and the Life – a confessional story, in other words. We should note that John the Baptist is not healed by Jesus, in spite of their closeness (Matthew 14:1, Mark 6:14, Luke 9:7ff.). Nor should we forget that Jesus seems to be unable to heal the victims of natural disasters (Luke 13:1–5) or massacres (Matthew 3:16ff.). These instances raise important theological questions about the limits of Jesus' healing ministry: what sort of things could he not do?

29  For further reflection, see the discussion of Luke 13:1–5, especially verse 2: 'Do you suppose that these Galileans were greater sinners than all the others in Galilee, because they suffered this fate?' in Joseph Fitzmyer's commentary, The Gospel According to Luke X–XXIV, *Anchor Bible Commentary 28a* (New York: Doubleday, 1985), pp. 1003ff. Fitzmyer points out that when the 'sin-suffering equation' is pressed by Jesus' audience, Jesus turns the question on its head to speak about the need for all to repent. Cf. Luke 13:36ff.

30  *Ibid.*, p. 1011.

31 See *The Problem of Miracle in Early Christianity*, Anton Fridrichsen (Minneapolis: Augsburg Publishing House, 1972).

32 See N. L. Geisler, *Miracles and Modern Thought* (Grand Rapids: Zondervan, 1982), and E. and M. L. Keller, *Miracles in Dispute* (Philadelphia: Fortress, 1968).

33 *Ibid.*, pp. 226–40.

34 *Ibid.*, pp. 241ff.

35 The question over the social status of people who are healed is a contentious one. Wimber's healing meetings seem to primarily cater for 'white American, European and Commonwealth middle-class people'. But other healers do operate in different racial and social contexts with equally dramatic effects. For a fuller discussion of this see my *Words, Wonders and Power: Understanding Contemporary Christian Fundamentalism and Revivalism* (London: SPCK, 1996).

36 Fitzmyer, *op. cit.*, pp. 1003ff.

37 Mary Grey, *Redeeming the Dream* (London: SPCK, 1989), p. 51.

38 Although I dislike the word 'slut' in this quote, it nonetheless serves its purpose. See Jean-Jacques Suurmond, *Word and Spirit at Play* (London: SCM, 1993), p. 51.

39 The revivals of the 18th century may have been closer to this goal, insofar as they were often worked amongst the new poor of urban society. A discussion of the contrasts between elements of the Wesleyan 18th-century revival with that of the 20th-century revivalist, John Wimber, can be found in my *Words, Wonders and Power*.

40 I am indebted to Dr Janet Soskice for some of these insights, in her paper 'Blood and Defilement', given at the Annual SST Conference (1994).

41 *Ibid.*, pp. 8ff.

42 See F. Kermode, *The Genesis of Secrecy: On the Interpretation of Narrative* (Harvard: Harvard University Press, 1979).

43 *Ibid.*, p. 132.

44 *Ibid.*, p. 134.

45 I have borrowed this phrase from Prof. Anthony Dyson's paper delivered at the Annual SST Conference in 1992.

46 For interest, readers are referred to the work of Walter Wangerin's tale 'Ragman', in which a Christ-like figure takes on the infirmities of all those he touches in exchange for their healing. See W. Wangerin, *Ragman and Other Cries of Faith* (London: Spire, 1993).

47 Sylvia Sands (1996). Sands has written fourteen *Meditations* on the Stations of the Cross, and has broadcast her poems on BBC Ulster and RTE, Dublin. Her work is available from The Oasis Community Project, Richardson Street, Belfast, BT6 8DY.

48 See J. Hadley, *Bread for the World* (London: DLT, 1989), p. 87.

49 I am grateful to the insights of Werner Kelber here, who set me thinking along this path. See *The Passion in Mark* (Philadelphia: Fortress Press, 1976), especially chapters 2, 3 and 7.

50 See *Words, Wonders and Power*, chapter 8.

51 See Pattison, pp. 55ff. The theory that healing movements are a reflex response to secularization and postmodernism remains unchallenged. I have been especially impressed with the work of Charles Davis in relation to some of these problems. See his *Religion and the Making of Society: Essays in Social Religion* (Cambridge University Press, 1994), pp. 199–201, on religious hope and praxis.

52 Two very helpful books in this regard are Norman Autton's *Touch: An Exploration* (1989) and *Pain: An Exploration* (1986), both London: DLT.

53 See Autton, *Touch*, pp. 138–41.

# 3

# Wisdom and weakness in ministerial formation: 'ambassadors' as a paradigm for the Early Church

## with Anthony Bash

This chapter begins with two case studies about powerlessness. A chaplain of an Oxbridge college found himself unable to do his job. It was not that he was incapable or unwilling; on the contrary. The problem was with the way in which the institution was structured. The chaplain was deemed by his employers to be neutral by virtue of the clerical nature of his vocation. This meant that he was routinely and systematically excluded from all councils, committees and bodies, in order that the neutrality was never compromised by the public expression of his opinion. The hierarchy saw clerics as ornaments – there for the right occasions with the comfortable words, but otherwise out of sight and mind. Religion was seen as a private, subjective matter, and an unsuitable force to participate in the shaping of public policy. The situation had existed for almost fifty years. The chaplain was expected to perform pastoral and liturgical duties, teach and take part in college life, but never interfere with the machinations of college politics. Arguably, in a well-run, just and fair institution, this could work as an arrangement. But the chaplain regularly dealt with a litany of pastoral problems that arose directly out of the structural hegemony of the college.

What was to be done? True, meekness is sometimes desirable, even godly. But when meekness is not chosen but imposed (and absolutely) in order to maintain existing power structures, it is simply legislation for submission. Feminist and liberation theologies owe their existence to this very fact. In the face of powerlessness, the chaplain worked for a voice on the college's governing body. Many life fellows and tutors who were avowedly anti-clerical opposed the move. The head of the college, who owed his election to these two groups, spearheaded the drive to maintain the *status quo*. In the end, a compromise was reached, with the chaplain

40

allowed to sit on the governing body and speak; he was denied a vote, supposedly to maintain the principle of neutrality. But it had been a hard battle, waged against the disparate forces of an uncritically established tradition that were decidedly parsimonious when it came to sharing power. Joan Chittister knows this dynamic well: 'Scripture is one long ledger of small people in contrast with great groups who overpower them, then overwhelm them, outnumber them and often seem to destroy them entirely ... one after the other they confront forces too mighty for them and survive to begin again.'[1]

Or take another example. A student in a theological college was training for ordination. The sponsoring body for the student required the college Principal to report regularly on the student's progress. The purpose was to ensure that the student remained and developed as a suitable candidate for ordination. Reports were usually written after a series of interviews and discussions with the student, and the findings shared with the student before the report was sent out. However, in the case of this student, the normal procedures were overlooked. The college Principal wrote a report after only one interview, and despatched it before the student had any chance to comment. The report cast considerable doubt on the student's aptitude and integrity, questioning the appropriateness of ordination. In this situation, the student was powerless: there was nothing she could do for herself. There were few criteria or procedures for appeal: a good character and candidate had been blemished unfairly.

What was to be done? Once again, a compromise was struck, with the student making representations to her sponsoring body about the in-built injustice of the system of assessment. An agreement over a supplementary report was reached, which subsequently overturned the original findings. As with our first example, the battle was hard fought, with the student needing to overcome a position of powerlessness which had not been anticipated.

These are but small examples of powerlessness. Christian history is littered with far grander and large-scale struggles. Women who have had to fight against all manner of prejudice and tradition to be ordained as priests. Black Christians in America who have had to march for liberty. The poor and dispossessed who have had to campaign, struggle and fight for justice. Martyrs for faith, who have stood against government and paid with their lives. Others who have chosen non-violent resistance, and triumphed – or been crushed. In all these cases, the resources of the Old and New Testaments have endorsed the path from the valley of powerlessness to the plain of equality. Yet paradoxically, powerlessness as a virtue remains close to the heart of the Christian kerygma: but how is it possible to embody and preach a gospel of power in a form of powerlessness?

Whatever the biblical witness to weakness is, powerlessness is not a cherished icon in contemporary Christianity. Size, success and power are frequently its dominant motifs.[2] The irony is, as Bonhoeffer knew, that for the Church, success in the world is a form of failure. Ecclesiologically speaking, the Church stands in the gap between power and the powerless, between strength and weakness, between absolutism and outright vacuity. As the social transcendent community, a particular kind of body, it has knowledge but not certainty, boundaries but not limits, is discerning but open, is for the other and others but not for itself. It is allowed boundaries and borders, but not barriers. In this essay, we shall be exploring the value of weakness and suffering in ministerial formation, paying particular attention to the wisdom it brings. In the experience of powerlessness there lies something that is close to the revelation of God in Jesus Christ, and we wish to suggest that the special form of simultaneously embodying power and weakness in a person is an incarnational testimony. There is, of course, nothing new in that observation. So our concern is to go beyond this, and look at a model of authority and leadership, namely the concept of ambassadorship in Paul's writing, that communicates the quintessential double bind at the centre of ministerial orthopraxis.

## Exploring Apostolic Power

One crucial question to ask is why did Paul the Apostle bother to appeal to his hearers to respond to the gospel which he unfolded and explicated in his letters? As an apostle, why did he not simply demand obedience, and punish disobedience if compliance was not forthcoming? Why did he not exercise his apostolic power, punish his recalcitrant hearers and readers, and leave them to suffer the folly and consequences of their disobedience and resistance?[3]

There is one strand in Paul's writing in which he appears to intend to act like that. In 2 Corinthians 10:6, he warns the Corinthians that he is ready 'to punish every disobedience when your obedience is complete'. He claims to have authority from God and warns that he may be severe in his use of it, even possibly destroying the Corinthians if they fail to mend their ways (2 Corinthians 10:8, 13:10). The unmistakable implication of 2 Corinthians 1:23ff. is that by not visiting the church at Corinth, he had spared the church severe discipline and that he would 'lord it over' their faith, if they did not fall into line. In an earlier letter to them, he asked whether they would have him come with a rod, presumably to lash them for their disobedience and to beat them into submission (1 Corinthians 4:20).[4]

And yet, despite the threats and bluster, Paul apparently did little more than write letters[5] in order to bring the wayward churches into line. Certainly some claimed his presence apparently had little effect (2 Corinthians 10:10). His apostolic office, doubted by some who suspected him of being a zealous bigot who had usurped the title apostle, seemed to count for little among those in his churches who simply did not want to accept what he said and what he did. He could only mouth threats against the visitors to Corinth who, he claimed, had hoodwinked and seduced the Corinthians, and then pathetically and – by his own admission – foolishly[6] try to defend himself against them.

Central to this issue are three simple groups of questions. First, was Paul an apostle? If he was not, was Paul, then, no more than a bully, browbeating his churches to conform to his gospel while not in fact having any more right to do so – if right there ever could be – than any first century Quintus, Sextus or Septimus? Second, if Paul was an apostle, what authority did Paul have as an apostle to promote 'the obedience of faith' (Romans 1:5) to the gospel? What was that authority and what were its parameters? Third, what power did Paul have as an apostle? What was the nature of that power? What did it mean for Paul – and what did it mean for his churches – for Paul to have that power?

Sadly, simple questions rarely have simple answers. Though it is undeniable that Paul thought he was an apostle who had authority and power to promote the obedience of faith, it is exceedingly hard to verify his claim to apostleship, to define and describe what it was that constituted or demonstrated his supposed authority and power, to set out what were the boundaries of his authority and power.

New Testament scholarship is in a mess on the first question we have set out. Despite two thousand years of trying, scholars have been unable to establish what constitute adequate criteria for establishing a valid claim to apostleship.[7] It seems that the problem goes back to the first century, because even the New Testament bears evidence that Paul's claim to apostleship was denied by some and that Paul himself denied the claim of others to apostleship. For example, E. Käsemann has properly identified that the real object of the debate in 2 Corinthians 10–13 was the legitimacy of Paul's apostolate – and the legitimacy of the supposed apostolate of those whom Paul so bitterly denounces.[8]

In addition, on the second and third questions, New Testament scholars have also consistently confused the discrete ideas of 'power' and 'authority'[9] and are unable to agree on the nature and effects of apostolic power or how to identify its legitimate exercise. To locate the origin of apostolic power in the supposed office of apostle, as some have tried to do, renders a claim to apostleship dependent on appeal to tradition or to principles of legitimization of which none irrefutably occurs in the New Testament.[10] The nearest supposed solution was put forward in the 1930s by the

German theologian K. H. Rengstorf, who identified apostles with Jewish *shalichim*, that is, authorized and accredited representatives. The problem with Rengstorf's solution is that in the period of the New Testament *shalichim* as he describes them simply did not exist: he interpreted a later, second-century Jewish practice – made necessary by the destruction of the Jewish cult in Jerusalem – as being in existence in the first century. It was not; and his supposed solution has befuddled much scholarly thinking on the subject until recently.[11] His solution also introduces into the discussion the very confusing idea that there was an office of apostle in the first century – something which many New Testament scholars doubt. Others, following Max Weber's discussion of charismatic power,[12] have sought to locate the origin of apostolic power and position in the apostles' charisma. This is, however, no help because self-evidently the apostles were so frequently ignored – and sometimes supplanted by others, such as the Corinthian intruders in 2 Corinthians 10–13 who apparently had better charismatic endowments of power – that this solution is circular and only restates the problem in another form.

In this essay, we must set to one side the vexed question of how it is we can establish a valid claim to apostleship. More specifically, we will assume that Paul's claim to apostleship was a valid one and so we confine our discussion to an exploration of the nature of apostolic power and authority. Even this is difficult because the two notions are frequently conflated in Paul's mind – and in fact not even modern sociologists[13] can agree on a normative basis for understanding the nature of power and authority, for it is always easier to observe the effects of power than to identify its nature or basis.[14]

What is generally agreed by sociologists is that authority is power expressed or interpreted in a particular situation and that the ultimate source of authority is power. It is also possible to describe specific aspects of the nature of authority: for example, according to D. H. Wrong, authority is legitimate, competent and personal. We must also distinguish between a description of what authority is and a description of what authority does with power.

In the case of Paul, he does not describe what his authority is; he simply assumes its existence and seeks to exercise it. He did so on occasions by issuing commands as a person with 'perceived status, resources and personal attributes',[15] in order to induce compliance. Even so, although Paul did believe that he had authority and that his apostolic teaching was authoritative, his preferred way of influencing people, as we shall show later, was usually other than by issuing commands. From the point of view of those who were the recipients of Paul's intended exercise of authority, we can say, following Dennis Wrong's classification set out above, that compliance was by those who believed that Paul legitimately exercised authority because he had power as an apostle; by those who believed Paul had special skill, knowledge and competence by virtue of his being an apostle; and by those who had confidence in Paul's personal qualities.

One consequence of this approach to the nature of authority is that where a person's authority is rejected because that person is perceived as not having 'status, resources or personal attributes', then that person cannot be said to have authority in that situation. In other words, the existence of authority is dependent upon the response of the person over whom it is intended to be exercised; it exists if it is recognized as existing by its receiver but not otherwise. To say that a person has authority among people who reject or do not recognize that supposed authority is to propound a piece of sophistry which is as absurd as it is fanciful. One can go further: if such a person's authority is rejected, it also follows that that person's power (if it can be said to exist at all) is nullified because the receiver's response precludes the expression or interpretation of his or her power.

This precisely illustrates Paul's problems with his churches. For example, it certainly appears to be the case that the Corinthians had doubts about Paul's apostolic legitimacy. Hence, they doubted his apostolic authority and so they impugned his apostolic power – but they welcomed others whom they supposed to be apostles (referred to in 2 Corinthians 10–13)[16] and so apparently also welcomed their authority and power. On the other hand, in other letters Paul wrote, such as those to the Philippians and to the Romans, there is evidence that Paul was favoured and his claim to apostolic power was recognized.

As for power, one of the most widely accepted ways to describe power is by reference to the effects of its exercise – it can be identified as existing where its effects can be seen.[17] For Dennis Wrong, power is 'the capacity of some persons to produce intended results and foreseen consequences on others'.[18] In this connection, it is also necessary to distinguish latent power (having power)[19] from actual power (the successful exercise of latent power).

In Paul's case, there is a dichotomy between his latent power – the power that he thought he had – and his actual power, measurable in terms of his success in exercising that power and achieving the results and consequences that he hoped for and intended. It is certainly clear that he regarded his latent power as deriving from his call to apostleship, from the gospel he preached and, when he was engaging with a church which he had himself founded, from the fact of having founded that church. But in fact his latent power was sometimes denied, often because his legitimacy was doubted or repudiated; in this situation, he had apparently no actual power (despite what he may have thought) and there occurred what D. H. Wrong has called a 'breakdown of the power relation'. For example, the visitors who opposed Paul in 2 Corinthians 10–13 and who (according to Paul) called themselves apostles, based their claim to legitimacy upon external criteria of validation, such as their performing the 'signs of an apostle'. They apparently rejected Paul's legitimacy, persuaded the Corinthians to do the same, and so negated Paul's actual power among the Corinthians.

Can we see the exercise of actual power by Paul? Paul certainly thought that he had actual power.[20] However, only one of the four criteria for identifying the existence of actual power set out by Wrong applies in the case of Paul – and that one criterion can only infrequently be identified as evident. For Paul exercised neither force (the infliction of bodily pain), nor injury (the withholding of true intentions) nor persuasion (arguments, appeals and exhortations intended to be critically evaluated as to suitability for the basis for behaviour). Neither, strictly speaking, did he always or even often exercise authority, that is, utter commands to induce compliance; though occasionally he did command obedience and thought he had the power to do so, his typical practice was to persuade, appeal and exhort. In fact, Paul's supposed apostolic power was inherently weak, for without the consent and submission of those whom he commanded, there was in fact little he could do – and little he did successfully do. To this extent, he made a virtue out of a necessity.

Nevertheless, the literature on the nature of power and the exercise of actual power does not take account of the fact that to appeal, reason, exhort and persuade (that is, actions which New Testament scholars call *paraenesis*[21]) are valid ways to exercise actual power – and it may even be that a person with actual power (characterized by force, injury, persuasion or authority) may choose to limit the exercise of that actual power to *paraenesis*. Paraenetic appeal is a valid way to exercise actual power, for its model is the God who gave himself voluntarily for humanity and who invited from humanity both the response of faith and an *imitatio* of that voluntary self-giving. It is a way of exercising power which is the most Christ-like as it involves a voluntary self-limitation of capacity and even effect.

## The Model of Ambassador

A recent book by one of the joint authors of this chapter[22] explores precisely this point. Is it not odd to the modern reader that though calling himself an 'ambassador for Christ' in 2 Corinthians 5:20, Paul should choose to limit himself to an appeal to his hearers? Why was it that God's own ambassador apparently gladly boasted of his weaknesses and powerlessness and seemed unwilling to exercise the powers and privileges which one would typically associate with an ambassador?

This thinking is based on a fundamental misunderstanding of the nature and form of ambassadorship in the first century. To be an ambassador did not mean then, as it does today, to be a diplomatic representative of one country permanently stationed in another country and representing the interests of the sending country. This is to import into a Graeco-Roman practice a concept which did not arise until the Middle Ages. In the first century, an ambassador was an *ad hoc* representative, usually of a community, though occasionally of an association or individual, commissioned to carry out a particular task and who returned to the community, association or individual on completion of the task. Almost invariably, at the heart of an ambassador's task was an appeal to the person or community who received him.[23] Typically, a community or person sent an ambassador in circumstances of weakness, dependence or vulnerability. Ambassadors were often dispensable people, who in many cases had to extol a brief that simultaneously made them expendable and integral.

Essentially, ambassadors were suppliants – even though often they were also people of high standing in the communities from which they came. To be a suppliant was to stand in the tradition of an ancient religious and social institution to which certain ritual acts pertained.[24] For example, suppliants stretched out olive branches covered in wreaths of wool to signify their condition and intentions. In addition, it was regarded as impious and an affront to the gods to mistreat a suppliant. To be a suppliant involved certain ritual acts of self-abasement and to supplicate in accordance with the traditions and practices of the ancient institution was to undertake an honourable task. Even though the religious and social institution pertaining to suppliants had died out by the first century, many of the social customs and privileges still obtained.

Paul's choice of the metaphor of ambassador precisely illustrates his understanding of his power – and weakness – as an apostle of Christ.[25] It illustrates that he was a leading representative of the community from which he came – that is, that he was an apostle of the church of Christ. It illustrates that at its heart, his task was to appeal, to supplicate, to beg and to entreat. And it illustrates that though Paul believed he could have exercised power in other ways, he was voluntarily limiting himself to the exercise of his power by appeal – and was not commanding obedience. His affront at his treatment – and mistreatment – by those who spurned him and his paraenetic appeals can in part be explained as outrage at the way the ancient institution of supplication was being disregarded.

The choice of the metaphor also illustrates something of Paul's own christological understanding too. First, Paul interchangeably speaks of being an ambassador for Christ and of making an appeal on behalf of God. In the ancient records, without exception, an ambassador's appeal was made on behalf of the person who sent him. The apparent exception in Paul's writings – that is, as an ambassador for Christ he was making an appeal on behalf of God – in fact only serves to show that in Paul's mind God and Christ were one and the same. Second, ambassadors were usually sent by communities or individuals who were in need, usually because of weakness or vulnerability. In presenting himself as an ambassador for Christ, Paul was making a statement about the God whom he represented. That God was not a God who was coming to humanity compelling or requiring submission; rather, that God was coming to humanity through an ambassador whose task presupposed vulnerability, dependence and need. Since Paul was a suppliant as an ambassador for Christ, so too was the one he represented. And the one Paul represented was, like Paul, entreating humanity to yield in obedience.

What, then, is true Christian weakness?[26] It is the powerlessness which arises from choosing to appeal for consent rather than to demand – and to compel – submission. It is the powerlessness which arises from choosing to exercise power other than by force. It is the powerlessness which arises from preferring to be rejected and so to suffer than to impose and get one's own way. It is also the powerlessness which Paul himself modelled – the powerlessness of weakness and vulnerability, the powerlessness of being self-questioning, self-critical, self-disclosing and deeply aware of personal weakness and need.[27] For at the heart of the Christian gospel is a God who chooses voluntarily to limit himself to making appeals to humanity – and to appeal with humility and self-abasement. Divine power lays aside its rights and privileges – its authority and imperatives – to beg humanity to respond. To be an ambassador for Christ is to model and illustrate the self-emptying of Christ referred to in Philippians 2:6–8. For just as Christ humbled himself to become a human being and further humbled himself to die on the cross, so too he comes in that same humility through his supplicating ambassadors who model his *kenosis*.

## Drawbacks to the Model of Ambassador

The metaphor of ambassador would have sounded quite shocking to Paul's hearers and readers. For if Paul came as an ambassador, it meant that the God on whose behalf he was supplicating was somehow in a situation of weakness, need, dependence and vulnerability. An ambassador's task almost always necessarily presupposed such a condition on the part of the person who sent him. The Corinthians, to whom the letter using this language was addressed, would have been affronted at such an idea. For they favoured the strong and powerful and, according to Paul, they had been duped by the 'superlative apostles' (2 Corinthians 11:5, 12:11) to whom Paul allusively refers in 2 Corinthians 10–13. Their favourites were the self-confident emissaries who were eloquent, plausible, educated and awash with manifestations of the Spirit and power.[28] Yet for Paul, a supplicating God who came to humanity to confront and affront human pride was the God who also came to shame and bring down the strong, the powerful and the apparently important so that no human being could boast in God's presence (1 Corinthians 1:27–30).

There are also other reasons why Paul's choice of the metaphor of ambassador was highly unsuitable. Ambassadors were expected to be good rhetoricians – Paul clearly was not, certainly face-to-face. His manner and bearing were apparently unimpressive and he was not a good speaker (2 Corinthians 11:6). Ambassadors were also supposed to be leading citizens in their local communities: Paul at best was an apostle, a title and claim which seemed to count for little, so far as concerned Paul, among the status-conscious Corinthians, and one which seemed to be doubted by some. In addition, ambassadors were typically distinguished citizens, exemplifying statesmanship and excellence of character. Paul, however, could not point to civic honours and his integrity was heavily impugned.[29] By choosing to use the metaphor of ambassador, Paul was creating legitimate expectations about himself, his standing and his abilities which he was clearly unable properly or completely to fulfil. In fact, his gospel of a God who chose the weak, the foolish, the disparaged and the despised in order to humble the wise, powerful and rich (1 Corinthians 1:27ff.) confronted his very choice of metaphor: for ambassadors were precisely the people whom Paul would have said God intended to humble by the gospel of grace. It was as if Paul was, to some extent, claiming back the advantages, attributes and qualifications which he said he had, for the sake of Christ, renounced (Philippians 3:7–8). The metaphor was in fact inappropriate and unsuitable and it led to confusion and disappointment.

Although he did not argue the point, it is worth considering what answer Paul might have given to the objections we have raised. He might well have said that since the cross of Christ remodelled all human actions and values, the cross also remodelled the practice of ambassadorial communication. Ambassadorial communication as he practised it could have been – and in Paul's hands was in fact – transformed by the gospel and so become an *imitatio* of it. In other words, if the metaphor failed to work, it was because of the unsanctified expectations of the Corinthians, not the foolish choice of the metaphor by Paul. Nevertheless, in choosing to use the metaphor, Paul failed explicitly to divest the metaphor of some contiguous contemporary social norms and expectations to which the gospel was opposed but which the Corinthians, from a social point of view, might legitimately have expected to see present. It is true that Paul did use language creatively and his choice of the metaphor of ambassador is one example of that creative use of language; nevertheless, he failed adequately or clearly enough to rewrite the metaphor he chose and so brought suspicion upon himself and his ministry.

Another question about Paul's use of the metaphor has to be faced. Did Paul really believe, as a suppliant for Christ, that his pleas could be rejected? Did he believe that, notwithstanding his apostolic status, the Corinthians really were free to say 'no' to his entreaties? The answer is 'clearly not' – and after the failure of his ambassadorial appeal, he abandoned such language in a later letter to the Corinthians[30] and resorted to the language of compulsion, obedience and injunction. When he wished, he could express his task militantly (10:3–6), reserving the right to exercise discipline when he thought it was appropriate (10:8, 13:2, 10). It is hard to avoid the conclusion that the metaphor of ambassador was used by Paul when it suited him – and the metaphor was dropped when it did not. The apostle–ambassador metaphor is not only paradoxical but also, in the hands of Paul, it is self-contradictory.

The lesson we can also draw from the life of Paul is that it is almost impossible to exercise power by limiting oneself to *paraenesis*. It is indisputable that, when confronted with outright rejection and refusal, Paul resorted to threats to impose his apostolic power and authority. Those threats compromise, distort and pervert the gospel Paul preached and contradict the idea that Paul was presenting a God who appeals to – not compels – humanity voluntarily to give itself to him out of a response of love. Paul would have called down 'more than twelve legions of angels' (Matthew 26:53) whereas Jesus did not.

## Wisdom, Weakness and Human Pathology: Concluding Reflections

It is interesting, in this connection, to ask how and why New Testament scholars have consistently failed to understand the language of ambassadors which Paul employed. Almost without exception, for hundreds of years writers on the New Testament have assumed that language about ambassadors had to do with power and strength.[31] The opposite is true. For although ambassadors were very often men of considerable importance and influence in their local communities, they were almost invariably those sent to supplicate on behalf of the one sending them. To supplicate presupposes weakness, need and dependence.

New Testament scholars have been led into this confusion in part because one Latin word *legatus* (pl. *legati*) and its cognate, *legatio* (an abstract noun referring to the task or function of a *legatus*), refer to two quite different ideas. On the one hand, the word *legati* refers to imperial or senatorial delegates in the period of the Roman Republic (and, later, of the Roman Empire) who had been entrusted with specific governmental tasks. The word also refers to governors of imperial provinces and to commanders of legions in the period of the Empire. In other words, *legati* refers to governmental agents who had been entrusted with military, political or administrative tasks on behalf of the Roman rulers.

Interpreters of the New Testament have latched onto this aspect of the meaning of the words *legatus* and *legatio* and have interpreted the New Testament accordingly. They have confused a political practice of the Latin-speaking west of the Roman Empire (the dispatch of governmental agents) with a quite distinct, indigenous practice of the Greek-speaking east (the dispatch of supplicating ambassadors). For example, A. G. Deissman has been widely quoted as interpreting Paul to be referring to himself as akin to the 'the Emperor's legate'.[32] He has been cited with approval as recently as 1994 by M. E. Thrall in the first volume of her magisterial commentary on 2 Corinthians.[33] C. Spicq, a scholarly French lexicologist of the New Testament, interpreted the equivalent Greek words in the New Testament as referring to imperial legates and chose this interpretation of Paul's language, notwithstanding that he identified the usual meaning of the Greek word he was considering as referring to ambassadors in the senses we have set out above. He therefore concluded that Paul had conferred on himself a dignified title of someone at the top of the military hierarchy.[34]

But this view of Paul's language is mistaken and ignores another highly significant stratum to its possible meaning. For the same Latin words – as do their equivalents in Greek – typically refer to ambassadors in the senses we have been describing, that is, those sent to supplicate for another. This is the meaning which most readers or hearers of Paul's letters would have been familiar with – not least because it is typical of the language they would have read in inscriptions and heard heralds proclaim.[35] The word referring to Paul as ambassador in 2 Corinthians 5:20 (the Greek verb *presbeuein*) is, moreover, never used of republican, senatorial or imperial representatives but is typically used of supplicating ambassadors in Greek literary and epigraphic records. In addition, the language is set in the context of Paul's appeal to the Corinthians to be reconciled to God: he does not command, require or insist, but he begs and supplicates, exactly as an ambassador would do.[36] It is an extraordinary confusion of thought to fail to observe a contradiction between Paul's supposed status as akin to that of an imperial representative and his choice of language to that of humble petition and supplication.

Given the scholarly consensus, it is not surprising, therefore, that so many commentators on the New Testament should assume that when

Paul calls himself an ambassador he is using language to do with power and strength. The opposite is the case. It is language to draw attention to the one who was weak on whose behalf he supplicated. But is the error on the part of scholars so surprising? Is there not something almost repellent about the Gospel's insistence that we should repudiate the authoritarian exercise of power and limit ourselves to paraenetic appeal? Is not the paradox of a God of strength who chooses to be weak so perverse that to expect us to follow his model is almost unthinkable? The human condition predisposes us all naturally to tend towards the exercise of power and authority with force and compulsion and human scholarship is often the projection of human pathology.

Yet a body of 'knowledge' should not constitute a form of force that is 'power over' in this way. For Christians, it is the case that the infinite expansiveness of God is his wisdom. More generally for humanity, wisdom is simply knowing your place before God. The beginning of wisdom, writes the Psalmist, is appropriate awe – a 'fear' of the Lord.[37] The specific tradition of Wisdom literature is therefore a matter of orientation rather than answers: it is sustenance for the journey and direction, but it is not the destination. But wisdom is not a commodity of power, although it can be used in that way. More properly, it is a form of discourse that enables individuals and groups to acquire insight for the contexts and situations in which they find themselves. In these moments, powerlessness can be understood, as in the case of the Book of Job. Or, in the Book of Jonah, the right and merciful use of power (restrained) is articulated. Omnipotence, omnipresence and omniscience belong to the god and ideology of absolute forms in Platonic traditions. The God of the Christian scriptures is more subtle, one whose being lies in love, whose desire lies in relationality, and whose disclosure of power is invariably shaped eschatologically.[38]

Although wisdom is typically couched in words, it is also an activity that balances power interests. The wisdom of Solomon cannot undo the tragedy of a cot death, but it is able to stop the course of justice being perverted.[39] Wisdom is, in part, a process of coming to terms with reality and then transcending its limits. For the those who acquire it, there is a new liberty – a truth that sets free. The poet Micheal O'Siadhail expresses it like this:

> Enough was enough. We flew
> nets of old certainties,
> all that crabbed grammar
> of the predictable. Unentangled,
> we'd soar to a language
> of our own.

> Freedom. We sang of freedom
> (travel lightly, anything goes)
> and somehow became strangers
> to each other, like gabblers
> at cross purposes, builders
> of Babel.
>
> Slowly, I relearn a *lingua*,
> shared overlays of rule,
> lattice of memory and meaning,
> our latent images, a tongue
> at large in an endlessness
> of sentences unsaid.[40]

In the poem, the first two stanzas pitch 'fixed beliefs and norms' against knowledge and a language that is anti-foundationalist.[41] Totalitarian certainty opposes a discourse that has no correspondence with reality. Only in the third stanza do we meet wisdom, a *lingua* through which an infinity of meaning is matured to speech. Yet many would say that O'Siadhail's vision of wisdom is pathologically weak: a lattice is hardly an image of strength, and latent images look vulnerable to misconstruction.

Yet paradoxically, weakness and wisdom are allies in Christian tradition. The wisdom of God is present in Christ who suffered, though it is folly to the world. In the thought of Paul, for example, the 'wisdom of the world' is set in opposition to 'the wisdom of God' (1 Corinthians 1:20ff). Human wisdom for Paul demands signs and wonders or relies on sophisticated philosophical deliberation (1 Corinthians 1:22). The human longing for power and knowledge remains ultimately unfulfilled if it denies or repudiates the weakness which God demonstrated in the cross. Why is this so? The reason is that human self-sufficiency exploits and perverts power so as to control, oppress and crush the weak. But power and knowledge gained God's way not only demand an understanding of the weakness of the cross but also require a participation in that weakness. This is the place where true wisdom and strength lie and where power can be exercised in such a way as to bring life and health (1 Corinthians 1:23ff.). It is only when the weakness of Jesus is shared that 'participation in the wisdom of God through Jesus Christ' can lead to reconstitution, restoration, re-proportion, healing and the end of alienation.[42] Out of this dynamic flows praise. For this reason, Paul can write, daringly, 'We rejoice in our sufferings . . .'.[43] Weakness, when wisely directed to God in praise, becomes something that can be filled with constancy of God, adding to the deficiencies of our human integrity.

But who would want to be weak? At the heart of many church

strategies, discipleship schemes, courses in spirituality or apologetics, the emphasis is placed firmly on strength and knowledge. Weakness is a sign of faithlessness, and it invites scorn, abuse, pity or patronage. But as Sue Rose points out, it is the poor and weak (or meek) who are blessed in the Beatitudes.[44] Rose goes on to distinguish between two types of weakness: one to be emulated, the other to be overcome. The first of these is the weakness of Christ that is to be shared. An appropriate weakness is a sign of humility, and therefore the beginnings of wisdom. The second kind of weakness is to be overcome: it could be personal, social, or moral weakness, but it is the kind of condition that leads to despair, not hope. Yet the pursuit of wisdom lies at these cross-roads. Sheila Cassidy writes of her work in a hospice:

> Slowly, as the years go by, I learn about the importance of powerlessness. I experience it in my own life and live with it in my work. The secret is not to be afraid of it – not to run away. The dying know we are not God. They accept that we cannot halt the process of cancer . . . all they ask is that we do not desert them: that we stand our ground at the foot of the cross. . . .[45]

Rose is arguing that there is a paradoxical relationship between weakness and strength, and that the realization and reconciliation of that paradox is a path to wisdom.[46] In the writings of Paul, as we have seen, a similar pattern can be traced. Paul's vocabulary of suffering is vital to his self-understanding as disciple, apostle and Christian. The harsh reality of his afflictions actually has a role in his ministry, and leads to its maturing. For this to happen, there must be grace in abundance, and above all a trust in God. Resurrection only comes when we let go and allow death to be.[47] Letting power slip from our grasp is alien to our human nature, but it is not alien to God's. Jesus himself brings about salvation, in part by not clinging to power, but through disowning it.[48] This situation arises through the particular act of the incarnation – Christ the Word, coming as a baby, initially unable to speak any words – as much as it does in the significance of Jesus' choices in the temptation narratives.[49] It is through this profoundly *kenotic* activity that a new power is gained, yet it is one that does not and cannot dominate. Rather, resurrection power transforms, by inviting participation into the being and communion of God.[50] As we noted earlier, ambassadors in the ancient world, though highly gifted, eloquent and bringers of peace and reconciliation, were sometimes deemed to be expendable. They were integral yet peripheral, vital yet incidental. They were just the messenger, not the message. It is in sharing this dynamic that ministers as ambassadors can enable that most fundamental of ministerial tasks, first given to John the Baptist: 'He must increase, I must decrease.'[51]

What wisdom does this model of weakness and suffering bring us as we think of ministerial formation? We would like to suggest four concluding but preliminary insights. First, paraenetic appeal on the part of Christian ministers is an *imitatio* of the gospel and of the ministry of Christ. For if God himself in his incarnational form expressed himself to human beings in voluntary self-limitation and appealed to but did not compel men and women to follow him, then Christian ministers must surely do the same. There is no place to compel or require this or that course of action or form of behaviour. Second, any appeal must be expressed in the form of a genuine appeal and not in fact constitute a weighted or emotionally loaded *diktat*. Failure to do so undermines the right and responsibility of men and women freely to choose and subverts their God-given capacity to choose. Third, history teaches us that Christian ministers have experienced enormous difficulty in exercising power in a Christian way. Paraenetic appeal all too often gives way to authoritarian abuse. Not only are frequent personal reflection and self-examination essential but also rigorous supervision by those unconnected with the minister's own situation. Fourth, it is enormously difficult to grasp that true strength and power may be seen in voluntary self-limitation and that where many would see only human weakness, others would see an entry-point for divine power. Ministerial formation must teach that models of ministry based on the exercise of power which compels, punishes and bullies, actually distort and pervert the gospel and eclipse the life and presence of God.

## Notes

1 Joan Chittister, *The Fire in These Ashes* (Leominster: Gracewing, 1995), p. 68.
2 See M. Percy, 'How to Win Congregations and Influence Them: The Anatomy of the Church Growth Movement' in *The Contours of Christian Education*, ed. J. Astley and D. Day (Great Wakering, Essex: McCrimmons Publishing, 1992), pp. 177ff.
3 Cf. Acts 5:1–11 in the case of Peter the Apostle. See also 1 Corinthians 5:3–5 on Paul's juridical presence 'in spirit' at the trial and punishment of an offender.
4 For a critical account of Paul's views on and use of power, see G. Shaw, *The Cost of Authority* (London: SCM, 1982).
5 B. Holmberg in *Paul and Power: The Structure of Authority in the Primitive Church* (Lund: CWK Gleerup, 1978) identified Paul's power as being limited to his influence as founder of churches, his personal presence, his representatives and his letters (pp. 72–88).
6 2 Corinthians 11:21, 12:11.
7 See, for example, K. H. Rengstorf, *Theological Dictionary of the New Testament*, Vol. I (Stuttgart: Kohlhammer, 1964), pp. 398–447; W. Schmithals, *The Office of Apostle* (Nashville: Abingdon Press, 1971); J. A. Kirk, 'Apostleship since Rengstorf', *Journal of New Testament Studies* 21 (1975), pp. 249–64; F. Agnew, 'On the Origin of the Term *Apostolos*', *Christian Biblical Quarterly* (1976), no. 38,

pp. 49–53; C. K. Barrett, 'Shaliah and Apostle' in Donum Gentilicium, ed. E. Bammell et al. (Oxford: Clarendon, 1978), pp. 88–102.

8 'Die Legitimität des Apostels', Zeitschrift für die NT Wissenschaft (ZNW) 41 (1942), pp. 33–71, G. Strecker, 'Die Legitimität des paulinischen Apostolates', Journal of New Testament Studies 38 (1992), pp. 566–86.

9 On the separation, see R. H. Roberts, 'Lord, Bondsman and Churchman' in On Being the Church, ed. C. E. Gunton and D. W. Hardy (Edinburgh: T. & T. Clark, 1989), pp. 197ff. and B. Holmberg, Paul and Power (1978), pp. 124–35.

10 See S. J. Hafemann, 'Self-Commendation and Apostolic Legitimacy', Journal of New Testament Studies, 36 (1990), pp. 66–88 on some of the contradictions involved.

11 See K. H. Rengstorf, Theological Dictionary of the New Testament, Vol. I, pp. 398–447 and the criticisms of W. Schmithals in The Office of Apostle in the Early Church (1971) and C. K. Barrett, 'Shaliah and Apostle' in Donum Gentilicium, ed. E. Bammell et al. (1978), pp. 88–102. J. T. Greene's work on messengers in the Old Testament provides no support for Rengstorf's solution; see The Role of the Messenger and Message in the Ancient Near East (Atlanta, Georgia: Scholars Press, Brown Judaic Series, no. 169, 1989).

12 Weber distinguished between traditional, rational-legal and charismatic authority in Economy and Society (New York: Bedminster Press, 1968). On charismatic power, see M. Weber, op. cit., pp. 215–16, 241ff., 1111ff. and B. Holmberg, Paul and Power (1978), pp. 136ff., especially pp. 149–50.

13 Modern sociologists have built on the work of M. Weber, op. cit., who distinguished power (Macht), domination (Herrschaft) and authority (Autorität). Weber's categories are regarded as overlapping.

14 See B. Barnes, The Nature of Power (Oxford: Polity Press, 1988), pp. 1ff., who understood power in terms of 'capacity for action' (p. 57). For the principal modern views, see S. Lukes, 'Power and Authority' in A History of Sociological Analysis, ed. T. Bottomore and R. Nisbet (Oxford: OUP, 1979), pp. 633–76 and S. R. Clegg, Frameworks of Power (London: Sage, 1989).

15 D. H. Wrong, Power: Its Forms, Bases and Uses (Oxford: Blackwell, 1979), p. 35.

16 Their identity is disputed and no certain conclusions have been reached. Current scholarship offers three possibilities: Palestinian Jewish Christians who were either Judaisers (C. K. Barrett, Essays on Paul [London: SPCK, 1982]) or a delegation from the Jerusalem apostolate (E. Käsemann, 'Die Legitimität des Apostels', ZNW 41 [1942] pp. 33–71); Gnostic Jewish Christians (R. Bultmann, Exegetische Probleme des zweiten Korintherbriefes [Darmstadt: Wissenschaftliche Buchgesellschaft, 1963] and W. Schmithals, Gnosticism in Corinth [Nashville: Abingdon, 1971]); or Hellenistic Jewish missionaries who were either theioi andres (D. Georgi, The Opponents of Paul in Second Corinthians [Edinburgh: T. & T. Clark, 1987]) or adherents of Stephen (G. Friedrich, 'Die Gegner des Paulus im 2. Korintherbrief' in Abraham unser Vater, ed. O. Betz et al. [Leiden: E. J. Brill, 1963], pp. 181–215).

17 Some others, e.g. B. Barnes in The Nature of Power (1988), p. 57, understand power in terms of a 'capacity for action'.

18 D. H. Wrong, op. cit. The idea of intention and foreseeability in the description of power has been heavily criticized.

19 It does not necessarily follow that no power exists where its effects cannot be seen if the power is latent power. Even so, there has to be a belief in the probability of the holders of the power exercising it (D. H. Wrong, op. cit., p. 8).

20 e.g. Philemon 8.

21 First made widely known by M. Dibelius in *From Tradition to Gospel* (London: SCM, 1935), pp. 233ff.

22 A. Bash, *Ambassadors for Christ: An Exploration of Ambassadorial Language in the New Testament* (Tübingen: J. C. B. Mohr (Paul Siebeck) (WUNT, II, 92), 1997).

23 The male pronoun is used deliberately. Ambassadors were invariably men in the epigraphic record; the few women who were supposedly ambassadors are referred to in literary accounts which are almost certainly legendary.

24 See J. Gould, *'Hiketeia' Journal of Hellenic Studies* 93 (1973) pp. 74–103.

25 On Paul's weakness and his ministry, see D. A. Black, *Paul, Apostle of Weakness* (New York: Peter Lang, 1984); J. T. Fitzgerald, *Cracks in an Earthen Vessel* (Atlanta: SBL, 1984); S. J. Hafemann, *Suffering and the Spirit* (Tübingen: J. C. B. Mohr, 1986); J. L. Sumney, 'Paul's Weakness', *Journal for the Study of New Testament* 52 (1993), pp. 71–91; and T. B. Savage, *Power Through Weakness* (Cambridge: CUP, 1996). Cf. S. B. Andrews, 'Too Weak not to Lead', *New Testament Studies* 41 (1995), pp. 263–76.

26 For an excellent recent exploration of Paul's paradoxical teaching in 2 Corinthians on power, weakness and Christian ministry, see T. B. Savage, *Power Through Weakness* (1996).

27 Despite the observations we made earlier about Paul's authoritarianism in 2 Corinthians 10–13, a balancing impression from 2 Corinthians and his other letters that he was inwardly reflective and aware, humble, loving and broken. These are not the characteristics of a bully but of a frail and sinful person, seeking to practise the message of the gospel.

28 e.g., 2 Corinthians 10:7ff., 12, 18; 11: 4–5, 20, 22–23. Yet Paul does defend himself before the Corinthians and argued that he was not inferior (11:5), had knowledge (11:6) as well as social and religious status (11:22–23). His ministry had power and authority (10:3ff. and 10:7ff.); he performed the signs of a true apostle (12:12) and he had visions and revelations (12:1).

29 e.g., 2 Corinthians 1:12ff., 10:2, 8, 11:16, 12:16–18.

30 Many believe that 2 Corinthians 10–13 are from a later, separate letter written by Paul: see M. E. Thrall, *2 Corinthians* (Edinburgh: T. & T. Clark, 1994), pp. 3–49 for a careful assessment of the evidence.

31 C. Breytenbach in *Versöhnung: Eine Studie zur paulinischen Soteriologie* (Neukirchen-Vluyn: Neukirchener Verlag, 1989) is a notable exception, although he mistakenly interprets Paul's appeal for reconciliation as characteristic of ambassadors' pleas: see A. Bash, *Ambassadors for Christ* (1997), pp. 24, 29–32, 97–103.

32 A. G. Deissman, *Light from the Ancient East* (London: Hodder & Stoughton, 1927), p. 374.

33 M. Thrall, *The Second Epistle to the Corinthians* (Edinburgh: T. & T. Clark, Vol. I, p. 436). A. T. Lincoln in his leading commentary on Ephesians also interpreted the language of Ephesians 6:20 in the same way: *Ephesians* (Texas: Word Books, 1990), p. 454.

34 C. Spicq, *Notes de Lexicographie Néo-Testamentaire*, 2 (Göttingen: Vandenhoeck & Ruprecht, 1978), p. 738.

35 For example, see M. Buonocore, 'Sulmo', *Supplementa Italica* no. 4, 1988, no. 58, ll. 42–3. and *Tituli Asiae Minoris* V.1 687, ll. 42–4. Until recently, Roman political historians have exaggerated the extent to which the ordinary people of the Greek east of the Roman Empire would have known, come into contact with and used language referring to Roman officials. This arose in part by a change in the way in which political scientists have understood the workings of the government of the Roman Empire. The seminal work of F. Millar in *The Emperor*

*and the Roman World (31 BC–AD 337)* (London: Duckworth, 1977), has led to the recognition that much communication and day-to-day business of government was in response to local initiatives. In particular, Millar has highlighted the enormous number of ambassadors from the disparate communities of the Roman empire who went to imperial officials to supplicate for their communities. It is with these people that the subjects of the Roman Empire would have had far more contact and familiarity than with imperial officials.

36 There are other reasons for rejecting the 'received' interpretation of Paul's language in 2 Corinthians 5:20 and these are set out in detail in A. Bash, *Ambassadors for Christ* (1997).

37 Psalm 111: 10.

38 Cf. D. Griffin, *God, Power and Evil: A Process Theodicy* (Philadelphia: The Westminster Press, 1976) and C. Hartshorne, *The Divine Relativity* (New Haven: Yale UP, 1948).

39 See I Kings 3: 16–28.

40 'Freedom' from Micheal O'Siadhail, *Hail! Madam Jazz*, (Newcastle upon Tyne: Bloodaxe Books Ltd, 1992).

41 For further discussion see Daniel Hardy, *God's Ways with the World* (Edinburgh: T. & T. Clark, 1996), p. 9.

42 *Ibid.*, p. 254. See also Rowan Williams, *The Wound of Knowledge* (London: DLT, 1979).

43 Romans 5: 1–3.

44 S. Rose, 'Who Wants to be Weak? Reflections on a Personal Pilgrimage', *Anvil*, vol. 6, no. 3 (1989).

45 Sheila Cassidy, *Sharing the Darkness* (London: DLT, 1988), p. 12.

46 For an autobiographical account of this dynamic, see Gillian Rose's *Love's Work* (London: Chatto & Windus, 1995).

47 See D. Hardy and D. Ford, *Jubilate* (London: DLT, 1984), pp. 166–7.

48 The necessity of this should be obvious. As George Daacon quips, somewhat ironically: 'If absolute power corrupts absolutely, where does that leave God?'.

49 Cf. Matthew 4 and Luke 4.

50 See Philippians 2: 1–11. The resurrection narratives in the gospels seem to suggest that not all who witnessed the risen Jesus were persuaded. Even here, the revelation of God is non-coercive.

51 John 3:30.

# 4

# Fundamentalism and power

What does it mean to be a fundamentalist? Does the term actually mean anything any more, or is it just a more sophisticated (but less accurate?) name for any individual or group that is fanatical? This essay is an exploration of the *phenomenon* of fundamentalism: is it now so broad as to need redefining? Second, what possible ways forward for reading fundamentalism exist which deploy both theological and sociological methods? Third, how might fundamentalism be seen as a religion of power, or as a mindset within religion that especially lends itself to concentrating on power for a particular end?

One of the effects of the proliferation of critiques of fundamentalism from a variety of disciplines has been the unconscious broadening of the category fundamentalism into which many groups may now be said to belong. When James Barr deployed the category in 1978,[1] he only had in mind certain American Protestants, and, in his view, their British counterparts. However, fundamentalism is not just a transatlantic phenomenon; it is now recognized in many studies that it is also transdenominational and transreligious, and ultimately common to individual and institutional experience. It is also not necessarily textually based. Inerrancy in scripture or articles of faith may be crucial, but experience can also function similarly as a fundament.

It is with this in mind that phenomenological studies have assumed a particular importance. Phenomenological studies lay special stress on experience, in the belief that the very structures of individual and communal consciousness will ultimately point to the experience and expression of belief. It is a different approach from many others, insofar as it often aims at returning to the originality or origin of the immediate experience. Phenomenology can be reduced to creating a typology of religious phenomena, or, it can sometimes be used as a tool for letting the religion speak for itself (i.e. claiming to be neutral). More properly though, phenomenology is a more developed discipline than this, often resting on a theory of religion and human nature. For example, Mircea Eliade's work on shamanism[2] is self-consciously influenced by Jung's theory of archetypes, which leads Eliade to suggest that there is a type of mythic ontology which some religious traditions and societies share. Indeed, some would see phenomenology as an ontology, the search for the fundamental categories we use in consciousness to interpret our existence, God and the world.[3]

Phenomenological studies have become especially prominent in the study of charismatic-fundamentalist religion, which includes Pentecostalism and the emergent charismatic movement within mainstream Christianity. Walter Hollenweger's *The Pentecostals: The Charismatic Movement in the Churches*[4] was the first work to draw attention to the sheer numbers of people caught up in the phenomenon known as charismatic Christianity. Hollenweger points out that although some fundamentalists deny the right of Charismatics to own the title fundamentalist, both groups do adhere to the inerrancy of the Bible and claim to uphold traditional or fundamentalist positions of Jesus' deity, virgin birth, resurrection and second coming. Charismatics and fundamentalists are also united in their opposition to theological liberalism. In fact, Charismatics and fundamentalists often cannot be distinguished in essence, but only in form. Therefore, both recognize that fundamental articles of faith serve to constitute the community that guards them, and the operation of those fundamentals is a guarantee, or deed of covenant, through which God mediates his past, present and future presence. The identity of the essentials of course, differs; yet Charismatics and fundamentalists often behave similarly.

Fundamentalists look to the givenness of the Bible; Charismatics look to the givenness of the Holy Spirit; Catholic Charismatics look to church dogma and the empowering possibilities of charismatic renewal. Yet all treat these quite different essences similarly: they are held to be absolutely authoritative, the word of God for given situations, indispensable and essential for the constitution of the individual and community in response to God. They are also regarded as weapons – somewhat mechanistically – as tools or objects that will advance the cause of Christendom in an age of unbelief.[5]

In the actual forms, the symptomatic expression of God's power appears to be different.[6] Charismatics lay stress on the value of personal and interpersonal experiences of God's power, such as healing, speaking in tongues or prophecy. Traditional fundamentalists stress the importance of correct belief, and tend to be anxious about doctrine. But even here, the forms are not as different as we might suppose: Charismatics are just as dependent on tight-knit doctrinal boundaries as they are on experience, and traditional fundamentalists depend heavily on the 'born again' experience and experiencing the Bible as they encounter it, often through an interpreter, who in turn re-interprets the texts in the light of particular contexts.[7]

There is a wide range of material engaged in the analysis of charismatic–fundamentalist groups. Hollenweger's work has already been mentioned, and his scholarly, historical overview of Pentecostalism on a world-wide canvas remains unsurpassed. His theological critique at the close of the book, however, is disappointing, and really only serves to underline the sectarian nature of charismatic–fundamentalist groups, whilst calling into question their ability to engage in dialogue, and hence, ultimately, the possibility of an ecumenical revival movement. Hollenweger recognizes that charismatic–fundamentalism is transdenominational, but this will not have a unifying effect on the denominations themselves, since this particular form of belief is non-dialogical in essence.

Other phenomenological treatments of charismatic–fundamentalism that are also worthy of note include Michael P. Hamilton's *The Charismatic Movement* (1975): he offers an analysis of the strengths and weaknesses of charismatic religion from the perspective of sympathetic and non-sympathetic participants. John Kildahl's *The Psychology of Speaking in Tongues* (1972) focuses on the personal experiences of individuals and suggests that speaking in tongues (glossolalia) should be understood as a variety of aberrant behaviour, like neurosis and other psychogenic disorders. Kildahl used psychiatric interviews and batteries of psychological tests to document his conclusion: that fundamentalists of this type are more submissive, suggestible, and dependent on leaders than normal.[8] Dale Bruner's *A Theology of the Holy Spirit* (1970) attempts to trace the present Pentecostal experience to the New Testament. His work is in two sections, the first dealing with the experience and understanding of the Pentecostals, and the second addressing Bruner's own New Testament understanding. James D. G. Dunn's *Baptism in the Holy Spirit* (1977) adopts a similar strategy, though his work is less comprehensive, and engages in a more exegetical study of the relevant portions of scripture. Though neither of these writers is Pentecostal, they nevertheless deal effectively with some of the essentials of the charismatic–fundamentalist tradition in their presentations.

It is clear even from our brief survey that fundamentalism as a movement (or individual fundamentalist exponents) could lay claim to being the 'Cinderella of theology'. There has been little in the way of serious theological engagement with fundamentalism in all its fullness. The undialectical forms of criticism are particularly problematic. The clear methodologies employed in analysis might lead one to believe that the critiques are just a developed list of complaints and personal dislikes. Although they contain much intuitive insight, which has some value, they tend to treat fundamentalism as cognitive reality, or simply as experiential and expressive. That is to say, authors like Barr appear to read fundamentalism primarily in terms of its propositions, which allows them to conclude that fundamentalists are at best simplistic and at worst anti-intellectual. But this fails to take account of the fact that a fundamentalist orientation is a complex, systematic world-view in its own right. Fundamentalism is a way of *relating*, not just thinking. The work of Kathleen Boone[9] goes some way to correcting the emphasis of Barr, but still reads fundamentalist discourse with an experiential-expressive template in mind. In other words, attention to the expression of discourse alone is sufficient for pursuing an understanding of the way in which authority is mediated and understood in fundamentalist communities, which her own work aims at.

All the critiques discussed, in general, fail to perceive that fundamentalism is a distinctive theological tradition and culture in its own right, with an accompanying appropriate discourse and method (or rhetoric). Such a complex system requires a systematic response if it is to be respectfully engaged with and understood. The critiques also fail to deliver a working definition of fundamentalism. Those that are available are either too narrow, too broad, or too pejorative. A good definition is needed that is accurate, conceptually sound and properly descriptive. There is also a failure to hunt out the deeper impulses that drive the fundamentalist tradition. Too many works address the surface aspects of the tradition, criticizing the symptoms, but not attempting to locate the cause. So, the scale of the problem before us is considerable. Any solution must therefore begin by working towards a more technical definition of what fundamentalism actually is.

## Fundamentalism: Clarifying Definitions of the Term

A number of scholars have argued that 'the term "fundamentalist" is now so broad as to be useless'.[10] So many groups are now labelled fundamentalist, that the concept has indeed become somewhat 'spongy', and is in need of redefinition. Conventionally, the word has usually been employed with reference to individuals or organizations that operate by 'strict adherence to traditional orthodox tenets (e.g., the literal inerrancy of scripture) held to be fundamental to the Christian faith', as well as 'being opposed to liberalism and modernism'.[11] Whilst this definition tells us something about part of the nature of fundamentalism, it does not go far enough. Fundamentalism is not just a set of constructive propositions designed to oppose modernist thinking and to advance what is held to be original orthodoxy. It is a relational phenomenon too, a way of being in the world, offering a social and mythic construction of reality for participants which offers a secure identity, along with personal and corporate value.

Following this, church historian Martin Marty has characterized fundamentalism as 'a world-wide reaction against many of the mixed offerings of modernity' appealing to those who look for 'authoritarian solutions' in relational problems.[12] He notes that differing fundamentalist groups are often deeply hostile to each other, even if there is a measure of broad agreement on the nature and location of fundamental articles of faith. Marty's explanation for this is that fundamentalism appeals to a particular class and personality type. Indeed, he sees the actual fundamentals themselves as a smoke screen, and goes so far as to state that fundamentalists are not so much motivated by religious belief as by psychological disposition, social forces and historical circumstance. Noting that Catholic, Jewish, Christian and Islamic fundamentalists all share the same mindset, he states:

> It is not productive to dwell on fundamentalist theology and point out its contradiction and errors. The (fundamentals) . . . are merely tools, excuses or alibis for the fundamentalist mindset. Without the mindset, the doctrines wither.[13]

Marty's observations are useful, yet he himself still tends to treat fundamentalism as though it were a unified phenomenon, its many adherents believing roughly the same thing, behaving essentially in the same way – but just getting on badly with one another. This is extremely problematic, since if we analyse how fundamentalists define and describe themselves, a wide polarity of views quickly begins to surface.[14] These defensive clarifications of fundamentalism in fact only serve to underline the scale of our systematic problem.

For example, many self-defined fundamentalists believe the charismatic (or Pentecostal) movement is, at best, contrary to the will of God: 'On the basis of Scriptural evidence we have concluded that . . . the modern tongues movement is not of God.' Meanwhile, Jerry Falwell, another self-confessed fundamentalist, points out in his *The Fundamentalist Phenomenon* that the 'Pentecostal-Charismatic movement . . . is based upon the fundamental doctrinal foundation'.[15] Other fundamentalists deny the right of people like Billy Graham to own the title fundamentalist – he is too liberal, they claim, and co-operates with Roman Catholics.[16] J. I. Packer, author of *Fundamentalism and the Word of God* (1958) would disagree, however. Although uneasy about the term fundamentalist, he nevertheless, as an evangelical, concludes that 'Evangelical doctrine is fundamentalist', with the term fundamental pervading most apologetic work done by self-confessed Evangelicals, anxious to distinguish themselves from some fundamentalist doctrine. Carl F. H. Henry conducts a sustained attack on James Barr in Volume 4 of his *God, Revelation and Authority* (1979). He questions Barr's broad and tireless use of the term 'fundamentalism', but then warns his readers not to reject evangelicalism which affirms 'the literal truth of an inerrant Bible'.[17] It is difficult to see here what upsets Evangelicals like Packer and Henry most about Barr's *Fundamentalism* (1978): his critique, or his terminology?

I have pursued this question of terminology here because it is an acute difficulty for those both inside and outside fundamentalist communities, and with good reason. Fundamentalist attitudes can be found in a wide variety of individuals and communities, and yet few wish to own a title with such pejorative connotations. However, from our brief survey so far, the term fundamentalism can at least be used to describe a set of common social, theological and ecclesiological outlooks, shared between traditional fundamentalists (i.e. Anti-Pentecostal), some Evangelicals, and those from the Charismatic movement or Pentecostalism. A good analogy might be to describe the movement as a dysfunctional family tree – all are connected and related, even if some members sometimes wish this were not so. Given this, I shall now advance a more specific definition.

First, contemporary fundamentalism is a 'backward-looking legitimation' for present forms of ministry and belief.[18] Present patterns of operation are justified in legalistic and historicist fashion via a claim on an exclusive validity for one line (or a very small core) of developments from Scripture, that refuses to recognize the diversity and development of others. In other words, an absolute authority must be established. This in turn affords participants a viable perception of reality in the modern world, a template through which experience can be processed. Some of these experiences themselves – as in the case of Charismatics or Pentecostals – can then become actual fundaments, although the validating line of interpretation – usually an interpretation of a text or texts, or possibly a written creed or articles of faith – often remains the supreme authority. This backward looking legitimation is subsequently represented by a myth or constellation of myths that are at home in the modern age. The metaphor *home* is not meant to connote an impression of happiness or comfort. Instead, it suggests that these mythic constructs provide a perception of reality that is more usually opposed to many aspects of Western culture. It is at home however, because it eclectically 'maps' traditional Christian mythologies and symbols onto the modern situation, thus forming a basic comprehensive cognitive picture of how the world is, how it should be, and how it will be. This cognitive picture is comprehensive enough to influence, amongst other things, family life, the role of women, attitudes to politics, other faiths, ethics, and questions about life after death.

Second, fundamentalism is dialectical: it exists in relation and opposition to trends in society that it perceives as modernist (i.e. where the authority of the existing tradition is challenged), pluralist (i.e. the dissipation of 'common beliefs' and moral values related to religion, giving rise to competition in society between competing convictions; what was once implicit must now become explicit in order to survive), or compromised. Thus, it is programmatic; it aims at reversing certain traits and establishing a new type of order or perceptions of reality. This is most commonly expressed in the controlling symbol of 'Holy War' that is variously employed. It is a primary perceptual and conceptual lens through which the past, present and future is processed. Fundamentalists see their enterprise as a struggle, in which the order they seek to advance must overcome the present (ungodly) order. The trends of modernity that fundamentalists oppose are to be resisted precisely because they represent a threat to the authority that they place themselves under. Therefore, we can speak of fundamentalism being non-dialogical. Fundamentalists have nothing to receive from the world, since the world must receive them first, wholesale. Some sociologists of religion (such as Bryan Wilson) identify this phenomenon as sectarianism, which is usually quite correct. However, caution needs to be exercised in using that word, since it might indicate that fundamentalists are somehow retreating from the world. In fact the opposite is true; they are engaging with it most forcefully, yet with a faith that is committed to addressing a monologue to the world that arises out of their authoritarian dogma.

Third, although fundamentalism now enjoys considerable breadth of expression, including its own competing sectarian factions that deny each other the right to the title, I nevertheless hold that there is a traceable phenomenon that we can call fundamentalism. By viewing it as a *tendency*, a habit of mind, rather than a single movement or body, it is possible to discern a phenomenon that is widespread, yet has common features. It is an attitude sometimes selective on subjects (e.g. sexuality) and found within traditions that are otherwise quite catholic or plural. These features generally include a hostile reaction to the mixed offerings of modernity, and to combat them, a set of fundamentals, such as a 'core doctrine', an absolute source of authority, a specific programme that is to be imposed rather than shared, clear patterns for mediating authority and power, and authenticating procedures (e.g. 'Have you been born again?') that validate and recognize existing members and potential recruits.

Fourth, fundamentalism, like liberalism, is not just a theological perspective localized to a particular denomination (or even religion, although here I am only concerned with Christian fundamentalism for the moment). It is a transdenominational phenomenon that denotes standpoints, attitudes, patterns of behaviour and theological methods. Although it has its origins in the emerging evangelicalism of the eighteenth century and in the historic fundamentalism of the early twentieth century, contemporary fundamentalism's chief nemesis is theological and ethical liberalism, which it opposes in varying degrees. In fact, what distinguishes fundamentalism from other similar faith perspectives is its opposition to liberalism: where opposition to liberalism is lacking, I hold that one cannot speak of true fundamentalism, but only of an analogue or close relative. At first sight, this might appear to rule out many charismatic or Pentecostal groups, but not so. These groups are just as anti-liberal; they simply construct their remedial programme differently. A good example of this is the British Evangelical Alliance, an umbrella organization incorporating many different fundamentalist groups from different denominations, in order to bring a greater degree of pressure to bear on certain issues.[19]

Fifth and last, fundamentalism is a cultural-linguistic phenomenon.[20] All of the studies discussed regard fundamentalism as a primarily noetic phenomenon, concerned with certain beliefs and doctrines, and propagating informational propositions. We have already noted this problematic aspect in Barr's treatment of fundamentalism, namely his habit of treating fundamentalism as a (primarily) credal phenomenon. For example, the doctrine of inerrancy does not just exist to counter the excesses of form-criticism and Darwinist ideas about the origin of man. It is more subtle than that. The cognitive approach does not do justice to the rich intricacy of the fundamentalist universe; it fails to attend to how a doctrine like inerrancy helps constitute a habit of mind, viable perceptions of reality, in short, a whole world. Stories also help constitute communities, not just propositions; it is often the group's own narrative that shapes its theology, as for example in the case of fundamentalist Afrikaaners. Equally, fundamentalism cannot be regarded as just a matter of expressing experience. There is more to fundamentalism than a primordial religious feeling, which when articulated becomes thematized into a type of determinate mystical language. For example, Methodists do not all seek to have their hearts 'strangely warmed' as Wesley did. It is the telling of the story, with its message of intervention and immanent change, the hope of transformation, and the renewal of inner beings, that helps place that story centrally in the Methodist tradition. The point of expressing experience belongs in a wider context.

Thus, I hold that fundamentalism must be read as a comprehensive interpretative schema, employing myths or narratives that structure human experience and understanding of the self and the world.[21] This view recognizes the power of language to shape, mould and delimit human experience, to the extent that it may be said that the way language itself is used can give rise to certain experiences. If fundamentalism can be seen as a cultural-linguistic system, the operating scaffold of symbolism within can be shown to be part of the idiom that describes realities, and formulates beliefs and the experiencing of inner attitudes, feelings and sentiments: in short, a complete interpretative framework. Like a culture or language, fundamentalism as a tendency is a communal phenomenon that shapes the subjectives of individuals and the objectives of communities, rather than being a manifestation of them. It comprises a vocabulary of discursive and non-discursive symbols, together with a distinctive logic or grammar in terms of which this vocabulary can be deployed. It is a way of life with cognitive and behavioural dimensions; its doctrines, cosmic understandings, myths and ethics relating to the ritual practices, the sentiments and experiences evoked, the actions recommended, and the subsequent institutional form that develops. All this is suggested in comparing fundamentalism to a 'cultural-linguistic system'.

With these five qualifying hallmarks in mind, I am conscious that the definition of fundamentalism proposed here is quite broad. Indeed, much of what could be described as Christianity fits the description I advance, but this does not invalidate the definition. Much of Christianity *is* organized around fundamental articles or excluding creeds, and many scholars have affirmed that Christianity has been a form of fundamentalism for much of its history. So, is there anything that separates fundamentalism from ordinary Christianity that simply organizes itself around a set of fundamentals? I would suggest there is, with the difference locating itself in a variety of arenas, of which I single out just three.

First, the fundamentals are held differently: doctrines tend to be 'tight', rigorously defined, and used as a controlling mechanism for the establishment of ecclesial order. The doctrine of an inerrant Bible is a clear example, being a symbolic reminder of the closed and complete revelation that orchestrates relationships and doctrine.[22] In contrast, non-fundamentalists generally recognize that their faith and 'knowledge is incomplete' (1 Corinthians 13:9), resulting in a commitment to dialogue and openness rather than monologue. Second, and linked to this is the question over the nature of truth. Fundamentalists deny the ambiguity or contradiction of truth, seeking to press for a uniformity of truth that will effectively govern life. Truth, and the homogeneous groups resulting from interaction with it, emerge as an exclusive concept, with no space for error, non-aligned interpretation or appropriate ambiguity. Non-fundamentalist Christians acknowledge the necessity of contradiction in truth, which generally gives rise to a higher degree of tolerance for plurality of truth-expression.[23] Third, non-fundamentalists also have a bigger *volume* of truth or tradition on which to draw: history, creeds, liturgy and the like. The actual size of Anglican tradition, for example, prevents its members from being fundamentalist: there are 39 Articles, a Prayer Book, priests, deacons and bishops, besides a well-developed 'quadrilateral' framework for processing theological and ethical questions. Anglicans only start to *become* like fundamentalists when they insist on the sole primacy of one aspect of tradition, such as the *Book of Common Prayer*.

## Fundamentalism as a Religion of Power

There is a general consensus that fundamentalism is one of the major forces at work in the postmodern world, especially as a new millennium approaches. However, what kind of a power or force are fundamentalists concerned with? To answer this question, it is important to understand how God, the Church and the world appear to individuals inside the movement. I therefore want to analyse the role (both perceived and actual), that the power of God, the Church and the world play in constituting the fundamentalist universe, with particular reference to Christian Protestant fundamentalism, although I hold that my comments are generic for other fundamentalisms. However, I remain mindful of Michel Foucault's suggestion, noted in Chapter 1, that,

> Nothing is fundamental. That is what is interesting in the analysis of society. That is why nothing irritates me so much as these inquiries – which are by definition metaphysical – on the foundations of power in a society or the self-institution of society, etc. These are not fundamental phenomena. There are only reciprocal relations, and the perpetual gaps between intentions in relations to one another.[24]

Of course, it is ironic that Foucault says that 'nothing is fundamental', and then says 'there are *only* reciprocal relations'. Relationships involve conflict, coercion, persuasion, adjustment and space. Foucault may be right in hinting that pure power as such does not exist; but that does not disallow discussion of power being fundamental any more than Foucault would be denied his attempt to place 'relations' as fundamental. Relationships are indeed fundamental, and where there are relationships, it is appropriate to speak of power.

So, in connection with fundamentalism, what definition of power might we work with? Basically, I hold that power is a multi-faceted reality, like fundamentalism itself. It is the force that can apply itself through and reify itself via agents (tools). It is dispositional, in the form of ideas, manners, bonding and unity. It is also episodic, in the form of specific instances, interventions and moments. It is a phenomenon present within all epistemological and social frameworks, usually encountered via its agents rather than the source itself. Power is a function of systems of social interaction.

Accordingly, this analysis of fundamentalism, using the theme of power as framework, is not an attempt to reduce the ultimate origins of all fundamentalism to concepts of power and powerful individuals. Rather, it is an attempt to investigate fundamentalist discourse and behaviour by analysing the inter-relationship of its various aspects. Moreover, this form of analysis has some urgency, especially in the field of ecclesiology. Ecclesiology once operated with a pattern that distinguished between order and organization: the essential structure of the visible church was a matter of revelation; the rest of it was held not to be theologically significant. The order–organization distinction provided Christian communities with a theological base for institutional structure, since organization followed logically from (revealed) order. In fundamentalist communities, where the revealed order is 'narrow' and non-negotiable, corresponding structural implications naturally arise, so that church administration has a clear theological base, from which subsequent theological constructions may be prosecuted or defended.

Understanding fundamentalist belief and organization requires the careful use of sociological tools that can bridge the gap between the language and models of fundamentalist theology, and the language and models of its modern organization. One way forward is to examine key concepts that inform a given community not only about its theology, but also about its ecclesiology. Clearly, one such concept is power, which functions analogously on both sides of the gap: the omnipotence of God, the Lordship of Jesus and the power are essential to understanding any Christian institution. In using the concept of power to interpret fundamentalism, we will gain an understanding of how individual fundamentalists regard God, as well as the communities in which they seek to serve him. We will proceed by discussing the central importance of a concept of power for a proper empathetic and systematic understanding of fundamentalism. In particular, the relational conflation between divine and human power in such communities will be explored, with its consequent implications for theology and ecclesiology. This agenda is set quite neatly in Jane Rogers' *Mr Wroe's Virgins*:

> *Hannah*: He has told me, half-jokingly, that he can do no right at the present. 'Elders Moses and Caleb fear my laxity, Sister Hannah. They urge the expulsion of all backsliders from our church. Did you know that only 144,000 may sit with Christ during his blessed reign? All who have shown the slightest deviation from right principle must be cast out: we tarnish our own purity by clutching sinners to our own bosoms. Should I cast you out, Sister Hannah? If Elder Moses knew of your beliefs, I am sure he would despatch you straight to hell.' He pokes vigorously at the fire with his iron rod, but his voice is weary. 'He would despatch us all to hell, if he could, and reign alone himself with God.'[25]

In Rogers' account, the concept of the 'body of Christ' has been entirely conflated with that of a local millenarian sect in the nineteenth century. The Elders, especially Elder Moses, take on the prophetic task of purifying their ecclesial body as though it were Christ's own body, removing every spot and blemish from it. The power wielded by the elders is therefore total: they propose to present Christ's body to himself, through the exercise of their power.[26]

Of course, every religion has a set of beliefs, either dogmatically set forth, or instinctively recognized and accepted by those who hold them. This set of beliefs includes an element of faith or trust, and perhaps a primitive view of cause and effect. The following of certain religious conventions ensures for the believer a better, more interesting and ultimately rewarding future; these promises are implicit in almost all religions. Power is clearly a fundamental issue in any such religion, and especially so in fundamentalistic expressions. Even writers sympathetic to American Protestant fundamentalism recognize that 'there is a striking difference in the desire of (contemporary) fundamentalism for power', that holds the system together, and magnifies it.[27] Naturally, that desire in fundamentalism is manifest in many different forms, and becomes concretized in various social and sacred activities. Political power, if achieved, can promote spiritual value on a wider social scale. Liturgical power can also organize and routinize a community.

Access to transcendent or charismatic power can enhance the position of a leader as the most viable mediator between God and humanity. Cheryl Forbes, in her influential critique of power in the contemporary American evangelical scene, notes that 'the point of power is to be visible, and it promises visibility to the worshipper'.[28] She cites modern evangelical leaders for their pursuit of success (Forbes equates this with power) – in all its spheres – and suggests that most churches fail to own up to their preoccupation with power and choose instead to mask it under a new vocabulary, with words such as leadership, authority or simplicity. Although the labour of her thesis is to exorcize the influence of 'possibility thinkers' from evangelicalism,[29] she makes a number of interesting personal observations that are useful. First, she notes the tendency of Evangelicals and fundamentalists to use stimulating and well-known personalities who have become Christians, in their evangelism. The appeal to a powerful personality who is a convert, she suggests, is a power-game. On one level, it assures more average believers (or interested non-believers) that they are correct in subscribing to this particular form of Christianity. Yet at a deeper level, she suggests that the use of a powerful personality from a profession (acting, politics, sport, etc.) is a way of not talking about powerless people who might also believe. She maintains that this is because the powerless, those who are sick, poor or handicapped, are not used in the service of the Church (in evangelism) because their lives do not apparently or immediately speak of God's power. Thus, she concludes, fundamentalists use power in the service of greater power. She carries this argument over into the realm of miracles, signs and wonders, and questions Evangelicals and fundamentalists as to whether or not they have moulded God in their own image, and then turned themselves into power-brokers, with potentially damaging results.[30] This reaches a peak for Forbes in her engagement with the Charismatic Movement (my emphasis):

> I attended the 'First International Conference on the Holy Spirit' as a reporter. Most of the attendees spoke in tongues and were convinced someone wasn't completely a Christian if they didn't. Since I was not a charismatic, I became the subject of much witnessing. People badgered me about speaking in tongues (there is no other way to describe it). One otherwise charming elderly woman told me that *God had sent me to the conference just so I would begin to speak in tongues.* And there were others, not quite as charming, who *upbraided me for not submitting to the Holy Spirit,* for being proud and defensive. *These people wanted power over my relationship with God.* They used every spiritual tactic they could think of to shame, harass, embarrass, and propel me into an experience that was for them the mark of a Christian.[31]

The experience of Forbes demonstrates the multi-layered way in which power is functioning in a charismatic community such as the one she describes. She is perceived by the conference participants to be lacking in some fundamental aspect of God's power. Consequently, power in the form of pressure is applied to her, with those applying such pressure presumably (and sincerely) seeing themselves as agents of God's power, through whom Forbes might ultimately be blessed.

## Key Issues in the Study of Power

There are two socio-theological reasons why it is important to understand what is meant by power. First, power is one of the primary religious ideas: humanity's awareness of God is an awareness of him as powerful. It is seen as a fundamental attribute of God. The possibility and existence of God reside in his omnipotence; the election and guidance of Israel are viewed as being marked by specific manifestations of power; Jesus' good news concerns the reign and kingdom of God, that is, the perfect expression of his power; as Christ the Lord, Jesus shares in that power, revealing new knowledge of the love of God which is now disclosed as being the central feature of God's power. Second, a right attitude to power is fundamental in human social relations. The source, practice and goals of power are important here. To Christ, all power in heaven and on earth is given, and the Christian's citizenship of heaven implies that a personal appeal may be made to a transcendent form of power. Yet the earthly authorities are also to exercise power and are to be obeyed by citizens as they carry out their work of administering justice as God's agents.

Both observations are crucial to this enquiry. In any type of fundamentalism under investigation, the distinction between *opus Dei* and *opus hominum* is usually blurred to the extent that it is difficult to perceive their precise nature and (subsequent) proper relationship. The use of the word distinction is not meant to imply a separation: it is recognized that all human action is dependent on God as its creative ground, and equally, that God's power must be made known through some form of created – often human – agency. In this sense, I do not agree with Foucault's non-realist position on power. I hold that there is a source: the issue to evaluate in ecclesiology (through sociology and theology) is how the power occurs in specific forms, and what is the intention particular to the agent.

Correspondingly, power is most often chiefly in question in the sphere of social relationships, since social power can be the will of individuals or groups exercising a determining influence on the communal life of a number of people within an organized structure. Such a will cannot be powerful by the mere act of willing, but by imposing what it wills externally. This external domain is the world in which the groups share their existence, and at the same time it also represents their will, by which they fulfil themselves in their world. If the powerful will works by the freely consenting wills of others from the same world, power assumes the form of force. But power and authority are at their strongest when being consented to, since power can then be drawn from within, and not merely from extrinsic means.

These observations have further implications for the study of fundamentalism. The powerful will must be at one with the consenting will of others, and yet it must also be at one with itself. This demands that what it wills ought to exist and its act ought to be posited (in this case, the nature and activity of God understood through a working power theology that will shape ecclesial behaviour and destiny); that is, this form of power must be good and rightful. The real purpose of power can be partly expressed here as (visible?) goal-attainment, namely increasing the power and influence of what is said to be good and right, in the interests of a common good. Power has both a horizontal and a vertical dimension: horizontally, it harmonizes community will, and vertically it attempts to be in harmony with the higher goals of what it believes to be normally right and good. In short, as far as the study of fundamentalism is concerned, power is the effective ordering of communities in relation to God and in relation to the world. For such purposes, both authority and force are legitimized in social relationships and theological dynamics.[32]

The exercise of power in fundamentalist theory and practice is intrinsically linked to the blur that results from the confusion over what is *opus Dei* and what is *opus hominum*. The fact that this confusion has arisen at all is traceable to the very foundations of fundamentalism. Fundamentalists have never been clear in distinguishing their own powers from that of God's power working within: rather than trying to clarify this tension, they have in fact built upon it. The results – traceable in all forms of fundamentalism – have consequently been three-fold. First, clear patterns for mediating (godly) social and theological authority or force have emerged: one primary leader, supported by a group of anointed underlings. Second, the authority of force of God has become merged – for the whole community – in the office of the leaders, making the distinction between human and divine power difficult to actualize. Third, the leaders have become the chief mediators of God's power, via the agency of, say, healing, prophecy or renewal. Therefore, the nature of power for the community concerned becomes identified with how that power is actually exercised.

We have argued earlier that power is a multi-faceted reality, like fundamentalism itself. It is the force that applies itself through and reifies itself via agents (tools). It can be dispositional, in the form of ideas, manners, bonding and unity. It can also be episodic, in the form of specific instances, interventions and moments. It is a phenomenon present within all epistemological and social frameworks, usually encountered via its agents rather than the source itself. Apart from the power of God, power is a function of systems of social interaction; power is one of the important means of social organization. Agents are things capable of motivity, that is to say moving or impelling power. Agents can be people, instances, doctrines, situations, and so on. Within a given world-view, agents are the nodal or fixed points that reify power or allow access to power, provide markers or boundaries for a circuit (group, identity, etc.), and ensure the connectedness of the power relationships. Charisma can be an agent as much as an individual doctrine, and each agent will have its own structure made up of other nodal points. What, though, are the likely effects of a power theology and power community on itself and on others? Here are some suggestions:

1. Finite power is always tempted to establish itself in self-assertion, to shut itself off in ostensible independence in the face of competition from other finite wills. This leads to the community and its main sponsors becoming non-dialogical and ultimately sectarian. Many fundamentalists have a policy of not answering criticism, not engaging

with critics, on the basis that it drains energy and diverts the attention of the community.

2. If divine power is conflated with human power in the face of this non-dialogical stance, the leaders themselves will become fundamental instruments of God. This is partly authenticated by the agency of charisma, which bears witness to the leader as God's elect, and often makes the community unmanageable after its demise, even if the ideology remains intact.

3. Failure to distinguish between *opus Dei* and *opus hominum* leads to a potentially damaging form of ecclesiology that can oppress individuals: this is particularly common in cults and sects. The preservation of the community's identity becomes too vital a task, since it identifies itself and its goals too closely with God and his purposes. Thus, what the community and its leaders want is what God wants. The task of the community moves from being a responsive, open engagement in social inter-relationships quickened by the Spirit (mission), to being a closed type of agenda, in which God and the community only confront the world in a defensive fashion, yet with clear targets in mind.

4. The power theology of fundamentalism is usually too stipulative and programmatic. Although individuals may find it initially progressive, it can be said to fail ultimately in its obligation as a form of truth in setting people free. The ecclesial structure – funded by charisma and ideology – is partly to blame. However, at the root of this, lies a theology that has not dared articulate the limits of God's power (albeit for apparently worthy causes) rather than be owned by it.

5. The theological and ecclesial work of fundamentalists is usually too mechanistic. Against the threat of randomness that modern plurality seems to suggest, fundamentalists offer a God who is in tight control of the world, even when the discovered nature of his creation seems to rule out such totalitarianism. Logically, it is almost impossible for fundamentalists to avoid determinism and its theological offshoots such as predestination. The evidence of such notions can be traced in most fundamentalist churches.

I am more than conscious that these are serious charges. However it is my expectation that the use of power as a framework in interpreting fundamentalism bears out these points. The methodology employed recognizes that disclosing the 'identity' of a given Christian community will depend partly on discovering that,

> the language of sociology and the language of theology may be separate, but the reality of divine and human power is not. It is not parallel or merely co-ordinated, it is inevitably, and dangerously, mixed.[33]

Ultimately, the 'Religion of Power', like all forms of fundamentalism, can be shown to be an insecure response to the modern and postmodern situation. Instead of grounding ecclesial, individual and theological identity in an open movement towards God and others, the search for the power of God tends to be laid to rest prematurely. The desire to channel the energy of God leads communities to refer what is finite and fallible only to itself and idolize it as infinite or infallible. We agree with Edward Farley when he states: 'Nurtured in insecurity, sin's motivation is to secure, to anchor human beings in a cosmos projected by itself, a creation of its own act of meaning or intentionality.'[34] In other words, fundamentalism is a *concentration* of power for particular ends.

## Conclusion

In ecclesiology, and perhaps to a lesser extent theology, power has been a neglected, even despised, concept. The common error of over-simply equating power with coercion has meant that theology has been reluctant to find a legitimate place for it in its doctrine. Embarrassment over the reality of power often leads to the concept being cloaked or misrepresented by associational rhetoric: 'authority', 'Lordship' or 'headship' are some examples. Evidently, before we can work with concepts like power and power structure in fundamentalist communities, we need a broader understanding of power, and for this we must turn to social theorists and philosophers. Once we have a grasp of how the concept functions in organizational theory, we can bring it back into theology and fundamentalist thinking, in order to see if we can make use of it.[35]

However, in our discussion of power we ought to clarify our terms of reference with regards to the concept of agency. A preliminary definition was advanced earlier, but it is now necessary to be more precise about the usage of the term. Working on the assumption that it is not possible ever to encounter the pure power of God, which would, presumably constitute meeting God (himself) face to face, theologians have to accept that God is encountered through agents of that power. These agents can either be of divine origin, as in, say, the case of creation, or they can be of human origin, as in, say, the case of a work of art. I am not denying here that the artist is inspired (the artist is the human agent through which God's grace flows, creating another agent, namely the work of art, which allows others to encounter God). Of course, it is sometimes difficult to decide what is a human agent and what is a divine one, particularly in fundamentalist communities where the power of God is often conflated with other powers at work in the community.

We should not be surprised at this distinction. Actually, fundamentalists tend to treat their primary agents for delivering divine power as (virtually) divine agents. An inerrant Bible is seen as a God-given agent – faxed from heaven – in the same way that 'signs and wonders' might be. However, the methods for using these agents or interpreting them are widely regarded as examples of human agency. In all cases, the primary function of an agent is two-fold: (1) to *reify* power, and (2) in so doing, to *control* people, doctrines, standards, etc. by the exercise of that power. That is to say, produce a result, product or benefit as a result of its exercise. When the term agent or agency is used in connection with power, the following assumptions can therefore be made: when the term is linked to fundaments, divine agency is implied; to methods or programmes, human agency is implied; to concepts such as charisma, there is conflation between the divine and human. How, though, does this discussion connect with ideas about power?

There is a debate among theorists of power as to whether the concept does necessarily involve the idea of coercion, or whether coercion is only one form of power or one way of using power. Some thinkers make power and coercion almost synonymous. For example, Sidney Hook says, 'What differentiates "power" as I use the term, from mere influence, authority and persuasion is the element of constraint or the threat of constraint that is integral to its meaning.'[36] However, Hook represents an extreme; most writers, even if they find that the concept of power has, at a foundational level, something to do with coercion, would include authority, persuasion and influence as types of power. Dennis Wrong includes all these, and defines power as 'the capacity of some persons to produce intended and foreseen effects on others'.[37] Others opt for an even broader definition. John Silber reaches back to Plato's equation of power and being (in *The Sophist*) and concludes, 'When we recognise that power is the ability to affect or to be affected we shall be able to recognise the family resemblances of power in its many forms, including the concept of force and the concept of authority.'[38]

It is this positivist definition of power which is most useful in organizational analysis, particularly when reading fundamentalist theology and ecclesiology. The limitation of the concept of power to coercion might attract some critics of fundamentalist thinking, but I hold that such a strategy is simplistic and narrow. Indeed, even the limitation to the productive intended and foreseen effect – the 'productive theory' of Dennis Wrong – has unfortunate consequences, since it inevitably focuses on reification (i.e. the result of power, or product of its exercise), but will tend to eschew ontological considerations. As Stewart Clegg has pointed out, understanding power structure in organizations requires a positivist definition rather than definitions which depend on intention: 'The individualistic and subjectivist concept of power cannot aid us in this kind of analysis. It merely disposes us to treat illusion as reality.'[39] The illusion of which Clegg speaks is that of individual power,[40] the idea that individuals make social change by their intention. While Clegg's early work was perhaps extreme in its insistence on the power of structure (including the ideological template), his point has won widespread acceptance. Increasingly, many scholars understand that changing the actors, even those in positions which seem very powerful, may do little or nothing to change the system.[41] A new Pope, a new President, a new chief executive or a new fundamentalist pastor, will still have to work within the same old structure. The structure, the system itself, is powerful; beyond, even despite, the intentions of individuals, it affects what happens.

Power is thus a multi-faceted phenomenon. It is a form of 'circuit' in which aspects of power are held, changed and disposed of within a given framework, in which the power source operates inductively. It is structure, resource, creativity and perversion. As Silber remarks,

> Power in its ontological meaning is good. That is, to the extent that power is being and being is good, there can be no power that is not in that sense good, and the more power the more being. It grows with fulfilment. Put theologically, in creation God shared his own power by extending it, or created more power by creating new being . . . The evil of power consists not in its being, but in the way that it is used.[42]

Silber's transition to a theological mode is most helpful, allowing us to foresee how power connects the theological and sociological realms of discourse. This is especially true in any careful analysis of fundamentalism. In this light, the omnipotence of God, the Lordship of Jesus, the power of the Spirit, the inerrancy of Scripture, and so on, become images, not of coercion (at least not exclusively or primarily), but of generation. Power and being, as we have already suggested, are not to be divided artificially: in this respect, we are not far from Aquinas' notion of God as *actus purus* (i.e. perfect actuality or actualization). At the same time, we must not lose sight of the Scriptural witness to power: it is not something inert, like a stone, that can be examined at our ease. In keeping with our positivist understanding of power, we can only see and read power as it is used and understood by a community. As Silber points out, it is not the being of power which is in question. What is subject to theological evaluation is the use and abuse of power as a process, at theoretical and practical levels, within fundamentalist communities.

# Notes

1 J. Barr, *Fundamentalism* (London: SCM Press, 1978).

2 M. Eliade, *Shamanism: Archaic Techniques of Ecstacy* (Princeton: Princeton University Press, 1964).

3 Cf. D. Stewart and A. Mickunas, *Exploring Phenomenology: A Guide to the Field and its Literature* (Chicago: American Library Association, 1974).

4 W. Hollenweger, *The Pentecostals: The Charismatic Movement in the Churches* (London: SCM, 1966), Eng. trans., 1972.

5 As I note later in this book, the term 'fundamentalistic' may be preferred to describe these disparate groups.

6 For a fuller discussion of differences in attitudes to divine power between fundamentalists and liberals, see Nancey Murphy's *Beyond Liberalism and Fundamentalism: How Modern and Postmodern Philosophy Set the Theological Agenda* (Valley Forge, Pennsylvania: Trinity Press International/Rockwell Lecture Series, 1996), pp. 62ff.

7 In terms of contexts, one ought to add that the primary one for fundamentalism is that of modernity. However, the periodization of the history of thought (pre, modern and post-modern, etc.) is fraught with difficultuies in relation to the study of religion. Two useful books that would offer introductions to this avenue of enquiry are Stephen Toulmin, *Cosmopolis: The Hidden Agenda of Modernity* (New York: Free Press, 1990), and Michael Buckley, *At the Origins of Modern Atheism* (New Haven: Yale UP, 1987).

8 Tongues should really be described, medically speaking, as a 'sound salad', not unrelated to the 'word salad' that describes the discourse of some schizophrenics. In preferring 'sound' to 'word', I am suggesting that 'tongues' is never a language, but is rather a form of ecstatic utterance, the mind and mouth speaking harmonious babble when words have ceased to express praise or anxiety adequately.

9 K. Boone, *The Bible Tells Them So* (London: SCM, 1990).

10 *Ibid.*, p. 10.

11 This is a standard definition. See for example the *Oxford English Dictionary*.

12 M. Marty, 'Fundamentalism Reborn', in *Religion and Republic.* (Boston: Beacon Press, 1987), pp. 299–300.

13 *Ibid.*, p. 3.

14 On Islamic fundamentalism for example, see Richard Buckley, *The World of Islam* (Cheltenham: Global Issues Limited, 1996), no. 2.

15 See N. C. Sellers, *Biblical Conclusions Concerning Tongues* (Miami: n.p., 1972), p. 76. See also J. Falwell (ed.) *The Fundamentalist Phenomenon: The Resurgency of Conservative Christianity* (Garden City: Galilee-Doubleday, 1981), p. 71.

16 See J. Falwell, *The Fundamentalist Phenomenon* (Garden City: Galilee-Doubleday, 1981), pp. 128–31, for a thorough overview of fundamentalist antagonism towards Billy Graham. While few question Graham's orthodoxy, some fundamentalists criticize him for not separating from the ungodly (i.e. Roman Catholics, some 'liberals', etc.). Ian Paisley, for example, calls for 'the complete rejection of Graham' and asks Christians to forgive Graham for 'sending converts back to the papal anti-Christ' (p. 247).

17 C. Henry, *God, Revelation and Authority* (Waco, Texas: Word Books, 1979) vol. 4, pp. 100, 122.

18 See D. Ford, 'Faith in the Cities', in C. Gunton and C. Hardy (eds), *On Being the Church* (Edinburgh: T. & T. Clark, 1989), p. 243.

19 The British Evangelical Alliance incorporates a broad cross-section of denominations and movements. Members include House Churches (Ichthus, Team Spirit, etc.), organizations (British Youth for Christ, Proclamation Trust, etc.) and representatives from denominations ranging from Anglicans to 'The Jesus Army' (formerly 'The Bugbrooke Fellowship'). The Evangelical Alliance represents fundamentalist, conservative evangelical and charismatic view-points. They organize annual public marches involving around one million people across the country (March for Jesus), annual conventions (Spring Harvest, attracting over 100,000 people per year), as well as organizing political and media-based campaigns. At present, the Evangelical Alliance is not a member of the new ecumenical instrument in England, 'Churches Together in England' (CTE). The reasons for this are unclear, but probably centre on their desire to keep their goals sharp and distinctive and a fear of colluding with 'liberals' and of being identified with a broad/pluralist expression of Christianity.

20 G. Lindbeck, *The Nature of Doctrine* (Philadelphia: Westminster Press, 1984), pp. 33ff.

21 *Ibid.*, p. 34.

22 An example of this would be the Universities and Colleges Christian Fellowhip's (UCCF, linked to IVP, Inter-Varsity Press) insistence on 'penal substitution' as being the only way of understanding the atonement. The notion of a variety of symbols and metaphors in the New Testament expressing what God has done in Christ on the cross, therefore leaving room for different concepts of what Christ's death means and achieves, is generally eschewed by UCCF. Members are required to sign a 'statement of faith' in which other possible interpretations are denied. For a fuller analysis, see S. Bruce, *Firm in the Faith* (1984).

23 See S. Sykes, 'Power' in *The Identity of Christianity* (London: SPCK, 1984), p. 11. See also S. Pickard, 'The Purpose of Stating the Faith' (Unpublished PhD thesis, University of Durham, 1990).

24 See M. Foucault, 'Space, Knowledge and Power' (interview). Transl. Christian Herbert, in P. Rabinow (ed.), *The Foucault Reader* (New York: Pantheon-Random, 1984), p. 247. For a similar, but more systematic perspective, see 'The Subject and Power' in H. L. Dreyfus and P. Rabinow, *Michel Foucault: Beyond Structuralism and Hermeneutics* (Chicago: University of Chicago Press, 1982), pp. 208–16.

25 Jane Rogers, *Mr Wroe's Virgins* (London: Faber & Faber, 1991), p. 210.

26 For a further discussion of charismatic leaders and power, see Anthony Storr's *Feet of Clay* (London: Harper-Collins, 1996).

27 C. Forbes, *The Religion of Power* (Grand Rapids: Zondervan, 1983), p. 54. See also R. Quebedeaux, *By What Authority?* (San Francisco: Harper and Row, 1982).

28 Forbes, *op. cit.*, p. 17.

29 *Ibid.*, pp. 58–9. Forbes has in mind here so-called 'possibility' or positive thinkers, who, she claims, influence American evangelicalism. An interesting example of this, although obviously not mentioned by Forbes, would be Roland Griswold's *The Winning Church: Church Growth and Evangelism for Today* (Wheaton, Ill: Scripture Press, 1986).

30 Forbes, *op. cit.*, p. 60.

31 *Ibid.*, p. 86. The experience of speaking in tongues is used by charismatics to inductively validate their own sense of the power of God. Extension of that experience to Forbes and others would further validate their sense of the divine

power, and ultimately provide 'proof' of their own charismatic power and capacity to witness.

32  see K. Barth, *Church Dogmatics* (Edinburgh: T & T Clark), vol. 4, bk. 2, chap. XV (1958), p. 648: 'The true growth which is the secret of the upbuilding of the community is not extensive, but intensive; its vertical growth in height and depth ... It is not the case that its intensive increase necessarily involves an extensive. We cannot, therefore, strive for vertical renewal merely to produce greater horizontal extension and a wider audience ... If it [the Church and its mission] is used only as a means of extensive renewal, the internal will at once lose its meaning and power. It can be fulfilled only for its own sake, and then – unplanned and unarranged – it will bear its own fruits.'

33  S. Sykes, *The Identity of Christianity* (London: SPCK, 1984), p. 208.

34  E. Farley, *Ecclesial Reflection* (Philadelphia: Fortress Press, 1982), p. 232.

35  This agenda was begun in a preliminary way by L. Gerlach, and V. Hines, *People, Power, Change: Movements of Social Transformation* (New York: Bobbs-Merrill, 1970). Gerlach and Hines analysed Pentecostalism and the black power movement, identifying how organization, recruitment, commitment and ideology functioned. Their thesis, however, lacks a thorough explication of power in its own right.

36  S. Hook, 'The Conceptual Structure of Power: An Overview', in D. W. Haward, (ed.) *Power: Its Nature, Its Use and Its Limits* (Boston: G. K. Hall & Co., 1979).

37  D. Wrong, *Power: Its Forms, Bases and Uses* (New York: Harper & Row, 1979), p. 2.

38  J. R. Silber, 'The Conceptual Structure of Power: A Review' in D. W. Haward, *Power, op. cit.*, p. 193.

39  S. Clegg, *The Theory of Power and Organisation* (London: Routledge & Kegan Paul, 1979), p. 45.

40  *Ibid.*

41  See S. Clegg, *Frameworks of Power* (London: Sage, 1989), for a more developed view of 'systems'.

42  Silber, *op. cit.*, p. 192. One could quote any number of other authors on power, but readers are also referred to the seminal 'The Restoration of Power and the Sociology of Religion' by James Beckford, in T. Robbins and R. Robertson (eds) *Church-State Relations* (New Brunswick: Transaction, 1987), also published in an earlier form in *Sociological Analysis* 44 (1983), 11–32. Beckford's careful exposition of power as a multi-faceted reality in socio-theological forms has many resonances with the paper. At a more practical level, some of the implications of Beckford's work can be traced in T. Robbins, *Cults, Converts and Charisma: The Sociology of New Religious Movements* (London: Sage, 1988).

# 5

# An anatomy of violence in established and new religious movements

A number of recent events suggest that there is a clear link between violence, fundamentalism and New Religious Movements (NRMs). This link is particularly apparent with the imminent dawn of a new millennium: names like Waco, Aum Shinrikyo, Jonestown, Solar Temple and Oklahoma City seem to be indelibly etched in the public memory because of their distinctive forms of brutality. The purpose of this chapter will be to explore, in some detail, the reasons for violence, fundamentalisms and NRMs being so inter-related. A combination of theological, sociological and psychological insights will be offered that will assist in the task of coming to terms with one of the most serious abuses religion can perpetrate: violence.

A good starting point, and I hope not too flippant, is to recount an oft-quoted joke from the Roman Catholic tradition that parodies the incident recorded in John's Gospel, Chapter 8, the story of the woman caught in adultery and Jesus' timely intervention. In the joke, the story is faithfully recounted up until the point of Jesus inviting 'any who are without sin to cast the first stone'.[1] Gradually, people drop their stones and begin to melt away, but before the crowd has dispersed, a large brick is lobbed from its midst, which hits the woman on the head, knocking her to the ground. 'Who threw that?', Jesus asks sternly, his intense gaze seeming to engage every eye in the crowd. No one owns up, and the crowd soon begins to look distinctly shifty. But then Jesus spots a small, sheepish face at the back of the crowd. He sighs, and then says, 'Mother, please go home.' Of course, the joke is not really aimed at the *theotokos*: it is directed at those who see themselves as being beyond reproach, and whose self-perception is tied up with perfection, rather than as one of the 'humble and meek'.

The joke is instructive here, because one of the most obvious reasons for fundamentalists and NRMs to engage in violence is to penalize the guilty for sin, from their standpoint as either (self-appointed) judges, or as instruments of God's punishment (conveying God's wrath). They throw stones precisely because they see themselves as largely 'without sin', whilst society or individuals deserve punishment because they are neither saved nor reformed. But there are other reasons for violence too. Some may involve motives that are attention-seeking, others may be apocalyptic or millennial, still others may be based on assessments of gender roles or sexuality. And who will ever know what the Solar Temple cult or the Aum Shinrikyo sect were trying to achieve?[2]

To consider why fundamentalists and NRMs might engage in violence, it is necessary to consider the context in which these bodies or groups operate. An anecdote may be helpful here. A young child belonging to a sectarian church was taken on a tour of an exquisite English cathedral and was told by the guide all about the history and architecture of the place. At the end of the tour the guide asked him: 'Who built your church?' to which the youngster replied: 'Jesus'. The child concerned belonged to a tiny branch of the Roman Catholic Tridentine Mass Church, and had been attending since birth. Most Christian fundamentalists essentially imagine their church or Christian body to be a near *perfect* body, and to be built by Jesus, and other Christian bodies outside their boundaries to be built by ordinary, mortal, human beings. The metaphor 'body' is significant: fundamentalism is a distinct body, but is an antibody against the body of society. It seeks to cure itself and all of society of the diseases of liberalism, secularism, pluralism, modernism and postmodernism, and like any antibody it inculcates a small amount of each disease in order to fight the wider diseases it identifies as enemies. So, for example, Christian fundamentalists might decry politics, and then nominate their own candidates for election, or then again, consistently campaign against media values, while vigorously engaging in tele-evangelism, operating Christian radio stations, and beaming satellite broadcasts to all and sundry in order to save souls.[3]

Before going further, we must note that NRMs and Christian fundamentalists are not the only groups engaged in aggressive activity: it is worth reflecting on the violent rhetoric and behaviour that can sometimes occur in more mainstream religious groups. I am not thinking so much of the language of crusading, a Christian motif that has led to some of the most appalling violence in the history of humanity, most especially in the European Great War of 1914–1918: that would be a subject for a separate paper altogether.[4] I am thinking more of ultra-conservative Christian groups who share with some NRMs and fundamentalists an interest in attempting to purge the body of society from liberal, plural and modernist trends. A few examples follow, which illustrate where the seeds of violence and oppression spring from.

In 1993, following the vote to ordain women to the priesthood being passed by the General Synod of the Church of England, The Additional Curates' Society polemically condemned '. . . modern, pagan notions of justice and peace' which they felt were supplanting real Truth.[5] Similarly, an Anglican priest in the Diocese of Lincoln, the Revd Anthony Kennedy of Holbeach, called for all 'priestesses to be burnt at the stake [as witches] because they are assuming powers they have no right to. In the medieval world, that was called sorcery. The way of dealing with sorcerers was to have them burn at the stake.'[6]

In the USA, extreme Roman Catholics and Protestant fundamentalists cleanse their country of 'abortionists', some feeling that it is morally justified to attack people who work in abortion clinics. In the wake of the murder of two receptionists at an abortion clinic in New York state in December 1994, one Roman Catholic archbishop called for a moratorium on picketing clinics. But in a calculated statement that implicitly condoned the killings, a neighbouring Roman Catholic bishop countered that the moratorium should only be obeyed if a similar one was placed on clinics opening. One Roman Catholic priest even went so far as to say that he felt unable to condemn the killings as murder: they may just be 'redressing the balance' – one guilty life for thousands of innocent ones.[7]

Nor should we discount Christian Evangelicals who campaign against gay rights, sex education and certain rights for women that allow freedom of choice. Some of these same people advocate the death penalty or severe physical retribution for moral lapses such as adultery, or homosexual orientation.[8] Within the Church of England the ultra-evangelical group, REFORM, openly discusses 'talking about peace while preparing for war' against liberalism.[9] Religion, we should note, attracts decent ordinary people who are sometimes persuaded to do or think extraordinary things that may have violent consequences. It is important to remember that violence and belief can be endemic and not just confined to extremists or fundamentalists.

But what is fundamentalism? Is it just violence against society disguised as religion? Assertiveness cloaked as evangelism? And what of NRMs: are they all pre-disposed to injure themselves and society by their implosion or explosion? Generalizations are problematic, since the terms 'fundamentalist' and 'NRM' map a rather spongy concept that is difficult to define because of the disparate and subtle nature of contemporary religion. But for our purposes here I would like to suggest a definition built around the following analogy: fundamentalist groups and NRMs can be likened to a diamond. It is intended to be bright and attractive to those outside the movement; it is intended to penetrate but not be penetrated; it is sharp and clear, and many-sided. Like a diamond, four qualities mark it out.[10] First, *clarity* – on selective issues there is no need to argue: the answer is in the Bible. One need look no further. Indeed, clarity is so valued that it leads to selectivity. For example, right-wing fundamentalists often defend their attacks on abortion clinics and legislation as 'defence of innocent life'. Presumably then, those same people, to be morally consistent, would be members of CND, anti-nuclear war, and maybe even anti-capital punishment. But they are not usually, are they? Their interest in being anti-abortionists lies in the area of controlling sex and pleasure, and restricting women's rights: defence of innocent life is usually, in my view, secondary.[11] Second, *certainty* – it deals with irreformable truth that is non-negotiable. Fundamentalists don't engage in dialogue, only in monologue. They have something to tell the world, but not much to learn from it. Third, and linked to the second point, their belief is often a form of *concretized* logic, which has a specific hardness about it, which can damage those who resist its impartation. Lastly, *colour* – to those inside the movement there is a complete world view that is packed with adventure and surprise. It is not a monochrome world, but one that is vibrant and alive.

Clearly, people have the basic human right to belong to or invest in naive or conservative beliefs. But what happens when that interferes with the rights of others? For example, in the debate over the priesting of women in the Church of England, an alliance developed between Anglo-Catholics and conservative Evangelicals. Generally, they have little in common. However, on the issue of women priests or women in authority, they can unite.[12] This is because they can agree about the controlling nature of revealed truth (although not about its substance). Both groups see the nature of truth as something unalterable, which is passed down from one generation to the next or, if you prefer, like a baton in a relay race, passed from one man to the next. (And it would usually have to be a man.) The 'faith of our fathers' must be passed on untainted to the next generation. The issue of control – keep women away from power – can be agreed upon in principle, although the two groups arrive at their conclusions from (and for) quite different reasons and presuppositions: one group fears male priesthood being compromised, the other group fears women in spiritual authority. The point of dealing with truth in this way is that fundamentalists like their truth to have the same amount of control and power as (it is said) it originally had.[13]

These preliminary remarks are important for our study, since we must ask what happens when power fails for conservative religious groups, fundamentalists or those within NRMs, control is lost, and the forces of modernity and liberalism seem to have the upper hand. Typically, the language of force or violence, or in some cases actual violence, is resorted to. This can be simply illustrated by focusing on some of the Catholic groups who protested against the Church of England General Synod's decision to ordain women to the priesthood. The ultra-conservative Catholic group Ecclesia resorted to rhetoric punctuated by violent 'Holy War' metaphors and images; talk of love, understanding and reconciliation was completely absent.[14] Equally, the rhetoric associated with so-called 'spiritual warfare' can become problematic. If mission or ministry fails, satanic forces may have the blame attributed to them. This is especially unfortunate if people or groups are then charged with being agents of the enemy, even if they are actually unconscious of that. Sometimes whole cities can be said to be demonized, and therefore the forces of evil are said to be offensive targets.[15]

Or, on a more personal level, divine retribution is frequently promised to those individuals who oppose the leadership of any given group: listening to the rhetoric of fundamentalist-charismatic Benny Hinn, following some (scholarly) undermining of his pneumatology, this is amply demonstrated:

> Now I'm pointing my finger with the mighty power of God on me . . .
> You hear this. There are men and women attacking me. I will
> tell you something under the anointing now, you'll reap it in your
> children. You'll never win . . . And your children will suffer . . .
> you'll pay, and your children will. Hear this from the lips of God's
> servant. You are in danger. Repent, or God Almighty will move
> his hand . . .[16]

These examples show, amongst other things, that a violent reassertion of power is often threatened by fundamentalist or sectarian groups, or NRMs, specifically against those who may have caused the 'power failure'. The power of God is appealed to, instead of motifs of love, toleration, dialogue or understanding. Love, by definition (cf. 1 Corinthians 13) gives freedom to respond, and does not seek to control. But if fundamentalists perceive that their control has been damaged, it is a reassertion of power rather than a commitment to love that will manifest itself. Ultimately, fundamentalists are guilty of loving the power of controlling truths more than the people they are supposed to serve. Their commitment to a God of power always precedes that of commitment to a God of love, and its consequent social, ecclesiastical and theological implications.

So, in the light of the theme of power, fundamentalism can be understood as a concentration of power, both in ecclesiology and theology. This is often read as sectarianism by sociologists, or as wilful religious naivety or bigotry by theologians. In fact, when one considers one of the main tasks of fundamentalists – defending omnipotence in the face of modernity – the phenomenon is better read as 'power concentrated for a particular task'. Quite often, this task can be defined as 'fighting', which requires the concentration of energy, resources, strategy and a degree of single-mindedness. Fundamentalists fight back (against modernity), fight for (a traditional worldview), fight with (doctrines or 'fundaments'), fight against ('the agents of assault on what they hold dear'), and fight under (God, or their 'sign of transcendent reference').[17]

## Violence Initiated by Fundamentalists and NRMs: A Brief Survey

In spite of the attention given to violence initiated by fundamentalists and NRMs in press and media coverage, little systematic effort has been made to analyse the data and to address the substantive questions raised. Commentators have often been content merely to list reported incidents in the attempt to support a prior conclusion that the level of aggression, whether rhetorical or actual, is sufficient to warrant suppression of nonconventional religions by society and government.[18] The cataloguing of reported acts of violence now allows examination apart from anti-fundamentalist polemic which has treated all violence as a symptom of a single phenomenon. Such previous amalgamations of data, gathered only as ammunition with which to assault the fundamentalists, have provided no useful assistance in, for example, locating potential pockets of future violence or preventing their occurrence.[19] The spectre of fundamentalist-initiated violence centres upon the possibility of a group, cult, sect or church, motivated purely by some religious ideal peculiar to itself, randomly attacking innocent people, or in some cases, groups of individuals that are perceived to be a threat to themselves or society (e.g. workers in abortion clinics). Occasionally, the spectre grows into an image of violent revolution and urban warfare. Of course, the Manson Family and extremist groups, ranging from the racially motivated Klu Klux Klan to the specious particularity of the urban guerrilla Symbionese Liberation Army, have supplied some verification of such possibilities.[20]

J. Gordon Melton, in his *Cults in America* (1986),[21] highlights some of the violence initiated by cults and sects as part of their rationale. He points out that during 1973 and 1974 for example, a series of random shootings occurred in San Francisco. The perpetrators turned out to be members of an informal group which had been organized within the Nation of Islam. Though the members of this small group kept their activities secret from the rest of the Temple, they assumed that they had been brought together on directives from the highest level of Muslim leadership in Chicago. Their mission: translate the violent anti-white rhetoric of the Nation of Islam into action by killing selected white victims. While there is no evidence that Elijah Muhammad and/or the formal leadership of the Nation of Islam either authorized or knew of the group, there is no doubt that the anti-white theology articulated by the Muslims provided the fertile ideological ground out of which the group could emerge. That is to say, the Nation of Islam created a group of people organized around their hatred of white oppression of blacks and a religious doctrine of divine disapproval of whites which justified action against them.

Interestingly, this dynamic may turn out to be the explanation for the nerve gas (sarin) attacks in Japan: it seems that Shoko Asahara has assembled a group of disaffected young people who, through the Aum Shinrikyo cult, may vent their frustrations on a liberal, secular and 'westernized' Japanese people.[22] The history of religion throughout the world is littered with examples of people who have called down divine sanctions to justify their anti-social actions. Historically, quite apart from warfare between rival religions, radical religious groups have committed robbery, rape, torture and even murder against non-members whom they define as evil, outside of God's chosen people or realm of law, or otherwise deserving of the violence inflicted upon them. Violence breeds violence as well. The handling of the Waco siege by the American Bureau of Alcohol, Tobacco and Firearms (ATF) may have been a disaster, but who would have predicted the Oklahoma City massacre as a response, which at least in part, was rooted in extreme right-wing fundamentalist militia?[23] This spiral of killing is wonderfully evoked in Cal McCrystal's poem:

> Here's your living dogma, there's your buried dead;
> Fundamental certainties . . . so who needs bread?
> Who needs mutton chops or flesh of any beast,
> If Lamb is God and Veal Calf revered High Priest?
> Flagellate dissenters whose caution is absurd;
> Let Borborygmus replace the Written Word.
> Preach in Oklahoma, in Yokohama too;
> If they won't give credence, take their blood in lieu.

> Holy-watered fingers plunging in our eyes,
> Theodicic bellmen timing our demise;
> Fulminating Islam, decomposing Marx,
> Zealots of the Talmud, and Christ in the Ozarks.
> Pulling up the drawbridge, drawing down the blind,
> List'ning for Al Daawa on the screaming wind.
> Hail the Millennium with miracles wrought,
> To unify all in a Commonwealth of Nought.[24]

But what is the actual cause of or justification for violence committed by fundamentalists? Melton suggests four reasons that immediately present themselves.[25] First, some fundamentalists have given and continue to give direct sanction to violent activity. Both the Black Muslims and the Church of the Lamb of God called upon the tradition of holy war to legitimize the killing of the group's (i.e. God's) enemies. The distinction between violent rhetoric and physical violence is but a hair's breadth. The justification for violence lies in the belief that certain times and situations not only allow but demand the faithful to take up arms in response to God's will. Of course, this was articulated powerfully in the Old Testament and from there was transmitted to Jews, Christians and Muslims alike. It has been used in this century to justify full-scale military operations, the assassination of political leaders, and the killing of random enemies of the faith. The way in which some American Southern Baptists support Israeli oppression of Palestinians because the Jews are 'God's Chosen' amply demonstrates this.

Second, while some groups and group leaders have given direct sanction to violence, more fundamentalist-related violence grows out of the indirect sanction of violence from belief systems which intellectually undergird group members' violent tendencies. For example, beliefs held by one group which stereotype another group and hence dehumanize its members are easily adopted by individuals as a rationale for action against members of the despised group. There is some evidence for this even in tolerant institutions like the Church of England. David Koresh built up his following out of a sense of apocalyptic conflict that would end in violence. The Church of Scientology, for many years, designated people as 'enemies', 'potential trouble sources', or 'suppressive'. It went so far as to suggest someone could be considered fair game. Within the Church and certainly in the literature, these terms are part of a vast body of technical language with specific meanings and correlative action guidelines. However, they are also highly emotive words which in the heat of controversy can convey, and undoubtedly have conveyed, their emotive charge in spite of the precise technical usage.

Third, much fundamentalist-related violence can be traced to the youthfulness of the following and leadership. Typically, first-generation movements draw leadership from among the early talented followers of the founder(s). If the organization spreads rapidly, young adults still in their twenties can find themselves the managers of a large national movement. Should that movement come under attack by elements in society or face severe tensions from within, they must guide the believers, often without any assistance from older individuals who have expertise in conflict resolution, public relations, or legislative lobbying.

Fourth, violence erupts, in most cases, only after a period of heightened conflict between either different factions of a religion or a nonconventional religion and the community. The controversy over Salman Rushdie's *Satanic Verses* is such a case: the playful postmodern posturing of the novel evoked reactions from the Islamic community that were reminiscent of fundamentalist Christian reactions to Monty Python's *Life of Brian*. All fundamentalists react badly to their truth being played with: it subverts their culture of certainty and challenges their identity, so they come out fighting. In such cases, both sides must bear responsibility when or if verbal violence turns to physical violence. Both sides will have inflicted damage upon the other, and each will have had multiple opportunities either to withdraw and refuse to perpetuate the conflict, or to seek a satisfactory alternative solution.

## Plotting the Anatomy

Because the occurrence of violence in relation to fundamentalisms and NRMs is polycausal and not monocausal, it is important to draw on a range of insights into the nature and causes of violence for the purposes of this enquiry. For example, in discussing violence and contemporary society, it is impossible to ignore the theories of Rollo May, René Girard and Hannah Arendt. Rollo May works mainly from a sociological perspective, Girard is an anthropologist, and Arendt, primarily, a political theorist.

Rollo May's sociology of power is an exploration of enabling and disabling power.[26] He proposes a five-fold typology – exploitative, manipulative, competitive, nutrient and integrative – which enables him to sift the sources of violence. Because May opts for a dispositional-functional notion of power, 'the ability to cause or prevent change', he is able to translate forms of power into modes of activity. Thus, integrative power is identified as a mutually empowering process, a sharing of resources and gifts that enables the other and the self. Nutrient power is the holding and offering of power for others, perhaps in the form of knowledge or skill. Competitive power is pivotal, and is a recognition that power is always dialectical, existing in opposition to other forms of power. Manipulative power is the holding of power over others, personally or politically (e.g. blackmail). Lastly, exploitative power is underpinned by the threat or possibility of violence leading to destruction: the Holocaust or any act of ethnic cleansing are its most prescient form.

In terms of violence and religious praxis, Girard's work offers an outstanding contribution to the field. His *Violence and the Sacred* (1972)[27] shows how violence is 'purified' through conceptualizing the sacred and profane. Thus, religious rites 'trick' participants: the spilling of blood, the surrogate sacrifice, and the righteous anger are motifs for reconciliation, justice and social order.[28] Violence, in effect, becomes an essential part of ritual in the interests of resolving conflicts. This is a kind of liminal theory, in which social or theological opposites such as God's mercy and wrath are resolved in the act of fresh sacrifice: violence becomes a means of atonement.[29] What emerges from Girard's theory is the proposition that 'the sacred is the externalization and transferance of a society's aggression on to a scapegoat'. In other words, this is a thoroughgoing projectionist view, suggesting that social violence has a divine referrent.[30] Moreover, the 'surrogate victim mechanism' is fundamental in explaining the differentiation of societies: crisis is resolved through ritual violence or scapegoating. Even in modern political life, in the most sophisticated societies, a scapegoat is required to explain a disaster. This disaster need not involve fatalities: it can be a matter of money, negligence or incompetence. It is almost as though society cannot bear mystery in relation to responsibility: *somebody* must be responsible for the aeroplane crash – machinery on its own cannot be entirely at fault. Once the scapegoat is located and punished, society may look forward again. Ritual violence is a recipe for coping with randomness.

Hannah Arendt is a political theorist. Her first major work, *The Origins of Totalitarianism* (1951), remains a classic historical study of Nazism and Stalinism as novel forms of oppressive regimes. Her subsequent works[31] present basic political concepts and distinctions in order to challenge existing interpretations of history. Through analysis of the dialectical relationship between power and violence, freedom and authority, space and privacy in public life, and work and labour, she emphasized their history as an evolution of concepts that gained their value from contemporary meaning and political relevance.

However, it is with Arendt's work on power and violence that we are chiefly concerned here, especially as she perceptively notes that, as a subject, it has not received the systematic treatment that it is due. In her three-part essay, *On Violence*,[32] Arendt offers a carefully nuanced explanation for the place of violence in contemporary society. Part one suggests that the amount of violence at the disposal of any one community is now a reliable indication of 'strength or a reliable guarantee against destruction' (p. 10). Related to this, and following Engels, Arendt also shows that violence requires implements to 'achieve [political] goals in the future world' (p. 4). In the case of Aum Shinrikyo, and also of North American apocalyptic or doomsday cults, the volume of armaments amassed is significant for the believers in the self-perception of their strength and their future capacity to influence or negotiate world events. Building on this, Arendt also shows how violence can then radicalize motifs that were initially non-violent, which in turn leads to a form of 'social control and persuasion' (p. 19). In other words, some groups may ultimately see violence as a progressive activity, not a destructive one (p. 29). Part two of the essay more specifically investigates the role of violence in the political realm. Arendt is more than conscious of the force that religion has had to play in the imposition of power through violent means (pp. 39, 41–5, 53ff.). Her conclusion (following Bertrand de Jouvenel and other theorists of power)[33] is that power, because it is linked with concepts of force, strength and authority, often justifies violence, yet ultimately fails (historically) to legitimize it. This subtle distinction is expressed in a way that has rich implications for our study: 'power and violence are opposites; where one rules absolutely, the other is absent. Violence appears when power is in jeopardy, but left to its own course it ends in power's disappearance' (p. 56). The intrinsic link with, yet dichotomy between power and violence forms the basis for discussion in the third and final part of Arendt's essay. Her conclusions are consonant with our earlier observations about violence, fundamentalism and NRMs, namely that when there is a 'power failure' in a given community, a rhetoric of violence or actual violence is often resorted to. As Arendt notes, 'every decrease in power is an open invitation to violence – if only because those who hold power and feel it slipping from their hands ... have always found it difficult to resist the temptation to substitute violence for it' (p. 87). Violence resolves disruptions of 'normative' power.

In a more detailed way, Guenter Lewy has carefully charted the history of religious revolution, especially focusing on millenarian revolts and related outbreaks of violence.[34] The seventeen case studies offered by Lewy allow a reasonable comparative analysis whilst preserving a discussion of the cases in depth. His taxonomy of revolution can be broken down into four main areas: (i) Millenarian revolts, ranging from Jewish Zealotism to pre- and post-Reformation revolutions up until the Mahdia of Sudan; (ii) Anti-colonial revolts, especially focused around emerging nationalist movements; (iii) Churches in response to revolution, with data gathered from Mexico, Spain and France; and (iv) Church-sponsored revolution, including Arab socialism, theologies of liberation and the Sinhalese Buddhist uprising in Ceylon. Lewy's basic thesis is that religious ideas, especially in the form of revolutionary millenarianism, function as an 'ideology'[35] that can inspire violence. In turn, this religious violence is sometimes inextricably linked with political activity which makes the discernment of sacred and secular motives a difficult task.

Lewy's conclusion is that religion 'integrates and also disrupts society', and as such, can either be the victim or perpetrator of violent activity.[36] In the case of millenarian revolts, religious groups can act in times of distress or social disorientation to attempt to create either an earthly paradise or an apocalypse: charismatic leadership is usually critical to such (new) religious movements. In a different way, militant nationalism often uses religion as a tool to awaken national consciousness: it becomes a symbol of self-assertion against oppressive regimes which are usually indifferent, if not hostile, to the native creed. Equally, religious groups, especially those that are established, may have a vested interest in suppressing or countenancing violence, depending on how their interests and ideology are best served. In turn, this can produce theologies of revolution and rhetorics of violence that will serve movements that are attempting to transcend the *status quo*. The overall strength of Lewy's argument is to demonstrate, by careful comparative analysis, the plurality and purpose of violence in the service of religious causes. Whether as a force for change or as a source of repressive stability, religion and violence are no strangers.

From a slightly different viewpoint, Leonard Berkowitz offers perspectives on violence from a socio-psychological standpoint. Berkowitz distinguishes between instrumental and irritable aggression: one is calculated, the other reflex. But in both cases, violence is propagated with the intention of seriously harming others for a particular end: motives include revenge, anger, punishment and vindication.[37] Yet Berkowitz is also careful to discuss violence as learned behaviour, a particularly pertinent point to note in relation to fundamentalism and NRMs. The dawn of the millennium, with an increasing 'global rhetoric' centred on apocalyptic motifs, ensures that copycat scenarios of violence will be perpetrated where and when sectarian religious groups perceive there to be a loss of power or control: events in Jonestown and the destiny of the Solar Temple cult bear testimony to this.[38]

In a more systematic way, the authors of *Violence and the Struggle for Existence*[39] show how polycausal religious and ideological violence can be. The authors offer theories of aggression and violence that stem from biological, psychodynamic, social and environmental perspectives. Their perceptive analysis of the currency of violence in the USA assesses the impact of the media, of violence as a means of conflict-solving, of the availability of instruments of violence (i.e. gun law controversies), and of mental illness and drug-related aggression. However, it is their conclusion on the place of violence in modern society that has the greatest ramification for our study: there are four main points. First, and following Freud, violence and aggression are a *primal survival reflex*.[40] Besides being fundamental, it is also adaptive, and individuals or groups who feel that their self, territory or belief are being threatened will justify offensive behaviour as defensive. The threat and use of violence will increase or decrease according to the perception of 'threat'. Second, violence and aggression are nearly always found where there is a failure to cope with change, perceived threats, intolerance or ambiguity. In this way, the authors see violence as a form of *coping mechanism*, which is operated by groups or individuals in response to frustration or violation, which can be physical, ideological or spiritual. Third, violence may be seen as a way of *resolving* issues. The mass suicides that litter sectarian religious history can be read, at least in part, as violent resolutions that terminate ambiguity and uncertainty. Fourth, violence can be a means of self and societal *transformation*: its use may have an intention that can only be realized in the future. Much aggression and violence in the name of religious revolution and Millennial activity fall into this category.[41]

At this point, mention should also be made of other relevant theories of violence. The rise of religious terrorism in the twentieth century – specific or indiscriminate targeting of individuals and groups – is analogous to that of political terrorism. Militant groups such as Hammas nearly always spring to mind when religious terrorism is discussed, but Christian groups have condoned or participated in terrorist acts in recent times: South Africa, South America and the Middle East have all played host to aggressive acts committed in the name of Christ and liberation. In his study of government and opposition,[42] Paul Wilkinson offers an element-ary typology of revolutionary and sub-revolutionary terrorism that is suggestive for religious motivation. The righteous assassin is clearly one distinct category of violence, which could include martyrdom for a cause that involved a form of suicide. Then there is a more general terrorism committed against liberal democracies or secular autocracies, the purpose of which will vary from group to group, but is primarily proactive. Yet violence, in the form of terrorism, may also be characterized as resistance against those same forces, a reaction against the perceived threats of modernity which might be regarded as evil, satanic or counterfeit. Much of the work undertaken by Wilkinson is paralleled by other studies. Edward Hyams offers a theory of terrorism based on the relation between theorists and practitioners of violence as a means for social change.[43] For Hyams, terrorism is a kind of hermeneutic, a translation of ideology into reality which in turn feeds back into the ideology. Brian Crozier, however, sees conflict as a revolutionary mechanism for challenging contemporary states, a form of subversion that is calculated to bring justice through the perpetration of some injustice: the ends justifying the means.[44]

Finally, sociologists of religion have also made pertinent observations about the place of violence in NRMs and fundamentalist communities. Thomas Robbins has collated information and analysis in response to the People's Temple sect and subsequent mass suicide at Jonestown.[45] Robbins points out that one of the major reasons for violence is the 'precariousness of charisma' which is endemic to extreme groups. Because the groups we are considering are essentially 'world-rejecting', a 'sharp break with the world around them can only be legitimated by extraordinary authority'.[46]

In saying this, Robbins is hinting that the leadership of groups determines the amount and type of violence in relation to the charisma and authority the leader(s) might enjoy. Robbins is also aware of the Durkheimian processes at work in religious violence: these include internal cohesion, boundary clarity, projected hostility and aggression, and paranoia. In short, the underlying system dynamics of a given group can account for the psychopathology of violence: millennial cultures may produce violence precisely because of their inculcation of apocalyptic motifs, rhetoric, expectations of persecution and a charismatic ideology that is centred on struggle and fight.[47]

These observations begin to tie up with earlier remarks about political terrorism in Robbins' conclusion. Robbins sees cult violence as a relational phenomenon arising out of volatile charismatic leadership. Part of the price of this form of leadership is its innate inability to engage in dialogue – with other more moderate voices from within the group, or opposites – with the result that violence seems to be a 'spiralling process'. Following Melton, and the political theorists previously discussed, it is possible to see violence as a potential hazard for many NRMs and fundamentalist groups. When dialogue or monologue fails, groups may wish to 'step up their action': this is common to extreme Roman Catholics and Protestants on issues like abortion, and white Mormons on race or marital issues. Violence is a way of resolving conflict, and vulnerable groups with volatile charismatic leaderships can either explode or implode at the very point of catharsis, when they feel most threatened by exterior forces: this is the socio-theological dynamic of Jonestown and Waco.

One weakness of the approach of Robbins is the oversight of movement ideology. Although charisma is a vital element in equations of violence as a phenomenon in its own right, it often requires an ideological base to relate to: the question is, what kind? Numerous studies of movement ideology that are relevant to NRMs and fundamentalisms do exist, and it is not possible to survey them all here. However, following the seminal work of Gerlach and Hine,[48] the following points are worth noting. First, violence emerges when the relationship between dogmatism and certitude on the one hand, and adaptive ambiguity on the other, is disturbed. This leads to a 'party line' being developed (say against new dissidents), with the group appealing to sources of power that overcome the opposing forces. Second, there is a rejection of the ideal–real gap, which in turn requires positive or robust reinforcement when threatened. Third, fundamentalists and NRMs often share a 'dichotomous world view which is used to define the opposition', which can then lead to a spiral of activity resulting in retribution and violence.[49]

## Summary

The perspectives that have been deployed from political, historical and sociological disciplines can be synthesized in such a way as to allow a tentative conclusion. In offering this, I am not going to make predictions about future locations of violent activity within fundamentalist groups and NRMs. However, my observations will have important implications for the next millennium within the context of postmodernity.

First, violence can be resorted to by some fundamentalists in a postmodern society, if truth claims are mocked, their rights are infringed, or as a means for hastening an apocalypse. Violence is an abuse that is a reactive response to a perceived abuse initiated against the group by society. The associational rhetoric and culture of 'Holy War' provides a permanent linguistic canopy under which the conditions for violence are always germinating.

Second, oppression of oppositional forces is justified on the basis that it is defence of truth, belief, or true community: aggression can always be justified by the self-righteous. The violent form that this can sometimes take is a religious 'sacralization' of the principle, that 'the ends justify the means'. One of the characteristics of fundamentalism, revivalism and NRMs in the postmodern age is the sheer pragmatism and selectivity of their movement ideology.[50] For example, some fundamentalists can claim that workers in abortion clinics are legitimate targets for violence, even though the underlying principle of the group perpetrating the violence might be 'defence of (innocent) life'. This is justified on moral, social and theological grounds, and depends on literal and naive interpretations of religious tradition and social history.

Third, fundamentalists seek to concentrate their power in the world in order to verify their beliefs. Sometimes that concentration of power needs to be measured or demonstrated by testing the implements of violence. Most commonly this is done spiritually and not physically. Rhetoric that encompasses images such as the 'tools of spiritual warfare' found in Christian Charismatic communities, or the 'weapons of truth' (sword, helmet, shield, etc.)[51] found in other religious groups are good examples; but the tools need not be 'spiritualized' in other faith communities. If their power is in any way dissipated or threatened, they will not love, forgive or discuss: they will most likely fight, and, if necessary, die for their faith, taking others with them.

Fourth, the socio-religious situation in the postmodern, western hemisphere, may actually be creating the very conditions under which violent behaviour will flourish. Noam Chomsky regards the USA as being more like Iran or other fundamentalist Middle Eastern countries than akin to

Europe. And where America leads, Europe often follows. Noting that 47 per cent of Americans believe the world is only 6,000 years old, that only 8 per cent believe in Darwinian evolution, that the popularity of secular and sacred cults and of urban myths is rising, that many support punitive methods for dealing with crime, including the death penalty, Chomsky concludes that the times ahead could be ugly. The collapse of industrialized society and the alienation and de-professionalizing of the middle classes has turned many people to beliefs that fit 'real pre-Enlightenment times': the social and religious situation in the West is more akin to Europe in the wake of the Black Death. Under these conditions, powerful charismatic figures may well emerge and be able to evoke violent crusading mentalities that will seem to make sense of the chaos in contemporary society, bringing order through retribution and hegemony.[52]

Fifth, violence in religion is always related to the infringement of territory. This territory does not have to be geographical; it can be ideological, spiritual or moral. John Bowker perceptively points out that it is the 'borderlands' of religious belief that provide the most 'flashpoints'. It is the extremities of religious expression that resort to violence, since extremes are more likely to provoke clashes with other territories, than regions of belief that are central and settled.[53] This prompts Bowker to suggest that religion can become a form of 'licensed insanity' in which the believers' violence and madness is vindicated by 'the just cause', perceptions of truth, a crusade, or charismatic and apocalyptic motifs. Insanity becomes rationality, and Foucault's warning that 'religion is what we do with our madness' is suddenly very apposite.[54]

Lastly, the occurrence of violence in NRMs and fundamentalist communities must be seen against a background of teleology and eschatology.[55] Teleology (following Fukuyama)[56] assumes that developments are shaped by an overall purpose or design – a kind of 'Grand Narrative'. So history is not open-ended, but is rather increasingly focused towards its own end: under these conditions, violence can be justified as 'hastening the end', fulfilling history and destiny. The place of violence at this point is doubly secure because of eschatology, the belief that a transhistorical, spiritual kingdom will come into being that will complete the end of history and initiate a new beginning. In that new kingdom, violence will not be needed, since only the righteous will inherit.

## Notes

1 John 8:1–11. The quip is neatly re-told in a poem by Andrew Hudgins, 'An Old Joke'. See A. Hudgins, *The Never Ending*, Houghton Mifflin Publishing, 1991. In

the poem, the brick kills the woman: it is thrown by her fellow adulterer to silence her.

2 Damian Thompson hazards a guess in his exemplary *The End of Time: Faith and Fear in the Shadow of the Millennium* (London: Sinclair Stevenson, 1996).

3 For a fuller discussion of contemporary fundamentalism, see my *Words, Wonders and Power: Understanding Contemporary Christian Fundamentalism and Revivalism* (London: SPCK, 1996).

4 See Alan Wilkinson's *The Church of England and the First World War* (London: SPCK, 1978). The material on the then Bishop of London, Arthur Foley Winnington Ingram, and his 'just war' theory makes for particularly disturbing reading.

5 See the *Magazine of the Additional Curates' Society* (January 1993), p. 3.

6 *The Times* (9 March, 1993), p. 3.

7 *The Tablet* (14 January, 1995), p. 56.

8 The history of Christians defending the death penalty is extensive. One of the best treatments of the English situation is Harry Potter's *Hanging in Judgment: Religion and the Death Penalty in England* (London: SCM, 1993). Potter points out that as late as 1810, the Bishops in the House of Lords were voting *against* the abolition of hanging for the offence of stealing five shillings. The history of Christians and the death penalty in the USA is still being made, thanks to pressure from 'New Right' Christian coalitions.

9 *Church Times* (14 January, 1995), p. 3.

10 Although I offer three hallmarks here, I have written up a more systematic definition that is available in two articles. 'Fundamentalism: A Problem for Phenomenology?' in *The Journal of Contemporary Religion*, vol. 10, no. 1 (1995), and 'Power and Fundamentalism' in *The Journal of Contemporary Religion*, vol. 10, no. 3 (1995).

11 A good insight into this dynamic can be found in Jacques Pohier's provocative book, *God in Fragments* (London: SCM, 1985), translated from the original French *Dieu Fractures* (Paris: Editions de Seuil, 1985).

12 An apposite verse from Scripture that reflects this alliance might be 'from that day on Herod and Pilate became friends, for before that day they had been at enmity with each other' (Luke 23:12).

13 Space does not permit a detailed discussion of gender and violence in relation to fundamentalism and NRMs, but readers are referred to the following works: *Violence Against Women*, ed. Elisabeth Schussler Fiorenza and Mary Shawn Copeland; *Concilium* (1994), issue 5 (London: SCM); *Refusing Holy Orders: Women and Fundamentalism in Britain*, ed. Gita Saghal and Nira Yuval-Davis (London: Virago, 1992); *Fundamentalism and Gender: 1875 to the Present*, Margaret Bendroth (New Haven: Yale University Press, 1994).

14 Although it is technically a separate issue, we might want to press the question of how theological language was used in this debate to mask deep psycho-sexual angst about women being allowed to share in priestly power. A number of the male bishops who voted against the legislation in November 1992 have since been exposed by the pro-gay group 'Outrage' as homosexual in orientation. Although I am personally supportive of the Lesbian and Gay Christian Movement, I am sure that some discussion about how women have been kept from holding authority in the Church needs to relate to the origins and ethos of some gay sexualities.

15 See C. P. Wagner, *Territorial Spirits: Insights into Strategic Level Spirit Warfare from Nineteen Christian Leaders* (Chichester: Sovereign Publishing, 1991). Wagner borrows rhetoric from the socio-political situation of the 1980s to talk of 'bringing

down' reigning spirits as though they were like enemy aircraft. We should also note the violent rhetoric in New Christian Movements: 'blitzing' describes evangelism in the London Church of Christ, and 'love-bombing', the process of attempting to recover lost converts in the Jesus Army.

16 *Christianity Today* (March 1992). Even within more 'mainstream' charismatic renewal, I have uncovered numerous examples of leaders threatening dissident members of churches with God's wrath. For further discussion, see my *Words, Wonders and Power* (London: SPCK, 1995).

17 See the Preface in M. Marty and R. Scott Appleby, *Fundamentalisms Observed* (Chicago: University of Chicago Press, 1992).

18 Of course, I am excluding studies done by cultural and social anthropologists here, which tend to approach the subject with more openness. Mary Douglas' *Purity and Danger* (London: Penguin, 1966) and Robert Girard's *Violence and the Sacred* (New York: Johns Hopkins University Press, 1977) both link sacredness and place together, with violence. Although we are more concerned with the ideological factors that give rise to violence in this chapter, the influence of places should not be forgotten. Religious and ethno-nationalist fanaticism can often prompt violence. The Middle East is constantly providing examples of clashes, but other more recent incidents of violence have included the disputed ownership of the temple at Amritsar in India, a mosque in Luton, Bedfordshire, and churches being bombed in Northern Ireland.

19 Exceptions to these generalizations are few, but there is some good discussion of violence and NRMs in E. Barker, *New Religious Movements: A Practical Introduction* (London: HMSO, 1995), pp. 42–57, 102, 158. Mention should also be made of John Saliba, *Perspectives on New Religious Movements* (London: Mowbray, 1995), pp. 118ff; J. Gordon Melton, 'Violence and the Cults', in *The Encyclopedic Handbook of Cults in America* (New York: Garland, 2nd edition, 1992), pp. 361–93; and Robert Hicks, 'Cult Label Made Waco Violence Inevitable', in *From the Ashes: Making Sense of Waco*, ed. James Lewis (Lanham, MD: Rowman & Littlefield, 1994), pp. 63–5. Although this chapter does not really have space to consider suicide as a form of violence, interested readers are referred to the following articles: R. W. Maris, 'Suicide', *Encyclopedia of Sociology*, ed. E. Borgotta and M. Borgotta (New York: Macmillan, 1992), vol. 4, pp. 2111–19; 'The Historical Antecedents of Jonestown: The Sociology of Martyrdom', *New Religious Movements, Mass Suicide and the People's Temple: Scholarly Perspectives on a Tragedy*, ed. R. Moore and F. McGehee (New York: Edwin Mellen Press, 1989), pp. 51–76; and *Violence and Religious Commitment: Implications of Jim Jones's People's Temple Movement*, ed. K. Levi (Philadelphia: Pennsylvania State University Press, 1982).

20 Of course the SLA were not specifically religious. But the 'cult-like' status of their guru/leader, Cin(que) Mtume (aka Donald DeFreeze) transformed the SLA from a protest group into a revolutionary group fighting against the nascent secularity of modern society. In doing so, they possessed an almost 'postmodern insanity' (Nicci Gerrard, *The Observer*, 21/01/95): they are chiefly remembered for their kidnapping and subsequent recruiting (through brainwashing?) of Patty Hearst, a young American heiress, in February 1974.

21 *Garland Reference Library of Social Science*, vol. 213 (New York: Garland Publishing, 1986).

22 See Abigail Haworth, *The Observer* (14 May, 1995), p. 16. This kind of scenario has historical precedents: Henry II's rhetorically violent question ('Will no one rid me of this turbulent priest?') persuaded a small group of schismatic noblemen to kill Thomas à Becket, an action Henry II probably did not intend.

23 See Phil Reeves, 'Living with the Bomb', *The Independent* (13 May, 1995), p. 32.

24 Cal McCrystal, *Out of Fundament*, unpublished poem, used with permission. An intriguing book that, for me, similarly evokes the spiral of violence within a fundamentalist community as it competes with other communities and consistently purges itself of dissidents, can be found in Margaret Atwood's *The Handmaid's Tale* (London: Virago Press, 1987).

25 J. G. Melton, *op. cit.*, pp. 241ff.

26 R. May, *Power and Innocence: A Search for the Sources of Violence* (New York: Norton, 1974; London: Collins, 1976).

27 R. Girard, *Violence and the Sacred* (1972) (Baltimore: Maryland, Johns Hopkins UP, 1977).

28 *Ibid.*, Chapters 1 and 2.

29 For a discussion of liminal theory, see Victor Turner, *The Forest of Symbols* (Ithaca: Cornell UP, 1967); for a discussion of theological legitimization of penal violence (such as the death penalty in 19th-century Britain and its relation to theological concepts such as substitutionary atonement), see T. Gorringe, *God's Just Vengeance: Crime, Violence and Rhetoric of Salvation* (Cambridge: CUP, 1996).

30 For further discussion, see Paul Dumouchel (ed.), *Violence and Truth: On the Work of Rene Girard (1985)* (London: Athlone Press, 1988).

31 *The Human Condition* (1958), *Between Past and Future* (1961) and *On Revolution* (1963).

32 Hannah Arendt, *On Violence* (London: Penguin, 1969).

33 See Bertrand de Jouvenal, *Power: The Natural History of Its Growth* (London: Heinmann, 1945).

34 Guenter Lewy, *Religion and Revolution* (New York: Oxford University Press, 1974).

35 *Ibid.*, p. 539.

36 *Ibid.*, p. 583. See also Peter Berger, *The Precarious Vision* (Garden City, NY: Doubleday, 1951), p. 156.

37 L. Berkowitz, *A Survey of Social Psychology* (New York: Holt, Rinehart and Winston, 1980), pp. 336ff.

38 Readers are also referred to the illuminating discussion of sociobiology and religion in John Bowker's *Is God a Virus? Genes, Culture and Religion* (London: SPCK, 1995), especially chapters 3–5 and 13–18.

39 *Violence and the Struggle for Existence*, ed. David Daniels, Marshall Gilula and Frank Ochberg (Boston: Little, Brown and Company, 1970).

40 See S. Freud, *The Ego and the Mechanisms of Defence* (New York: International Universities Press, 1946).

41 Daniels, Gilula and Ochberg, *op. cit.*, pp. 405ff.

42 Paul Wilkinson, *Political Terrorism* (London: Macmillan Press, 1974).

43 E. Hyams, *Terrorists and Terrorism* (London: J. M. Dent & Sons, 1975).

44 B. Crozier, *A Theory of Conflict* (London: Hamish Hamilton, 1974), pp. 22–4.

45 T. Robbins, *Cults, Converts and Charisma* (London: Sage Publications, with the International Sociological Association, 1988), pp. 7–8, 116ff., 182ff., etc.

46 *Ibid.*, p. 117.

47 *Ibid.*, pp. 188–9. For a slightly different perspective on 'fighting' in fundamentalism and NRMs, see T. Robbins, W. Shepherd and J. McBride, *Cults, Culture and the Law: Perspectives on New Religious Movements* (American Academy of Religion), (Chico, California: Scholars Press, 1985).

48 Luther P. Gerlach and Virginia H. Hine, *People, Power, Change: Movements of Social Transformation*, (New York: Bobbs-Merrill, 1970).

49 *Ibid.*, p. 182.

50 See James Hopewell, *Congregation: Stories and Structures* (London: SCM, 1987), pp. 23ff., for an illuminating discussion of pragmatism.

51 For a discussion of 'fighting rhetoric', see my 'Falling Out of Love: The Ordination of Women and Recent Anglo-American Anglican Schisms Explored', *Journal of Contemporary Religion*, vol. 12, issue 1, 1997, pp. 35–50.

52 See Noam Chomsky, *Keeping the Rabble in Line – Interviews with David Bausamian* (Edinburgh: Academic Press, 1994), pp. 124ff.

53 See John Bowker, *Licensed Insanities: Religions and Belief in God in the Contemporary World* (London: Darton, Longman & Todd, 1987), pp. 14ff.

54 M. Foucault, *Madness and Civilisation* (New York: Random House, 1961).

55 A range of studies on this theme will be published soon. See for example, J. Zulaika and W. Douglass, *Terror and Taboo: On the Fables and Follies of Terrorist Discourse*. This is an anthropological study of the social construction of terrorist discourse, including analysis on Timothy McVeigh, the principal perpetrator of the Oklahoma City bombing in response to the Waco siege. T. Robbins and S. Palmer (eds), *Millennium, Messiahs and Mayhem: Contemporary Apocalyptic Ferment in the USA and Canada* is a sociological study of contemporary religious violence. J. Brink and J. Mencher (eds), *Mixed Blessings: Gender and Religious Fundamentalism Cross Culturally* contains a couple of relevant articles on violence and women. All the above are to be published by Routledge, USA.

56 For an introduction to Fukuyama's work see Jacques Derrida, *New Left Review*, no. 205 (1994). The complete text of this lecture appears in *Spectres of Marx* (London: Routledge, 1994).

# 6

# Theories of exchange for the
# Toronto Blessing

Generally, there can be no question that charismatic renewal involves forms of exchange at many different levels. Ritual exchange is easily identified, as is the personal and cathartic. There is also a sense in which the communal enthusiasm operates as a kind of sacrament. In exchange for expressing and configuring the activity of praise in excitable and passionate ways (i.e. a celebration), the group is rewarded with a sense of God – God is said to 'inhabit' the praises of his people, so if they praise, he will be present. This is a form of pseudo-mystical, mechanistic religion, where enthusiasm is eventually exchanged for presence.

The Toronto Blessing is a phenomenon that was initially particular to the Toronto Airport Vineyard Church, in January 1994. As a church in the Vineyard tradition (fundamentalist–revivalist),[1] the community had already experienced many of the things that would be typical for Christians in this sort of ecclesial setting: healings, an emphasis on deliverance, speaking in tongues, and a general sense of the believers being in the vanguard of the Holy Spirit's movement towards the 'end times'.[2] What appears to mark out the Toronto Blessing (TB) for special treatment is the more unusual phenomena that occurred. There was an unusually high reportage of people being 'slain in the Spirit'. A number would laugh uncontrollably, make animal-like noises, barking, growling or groaning as the 'Spirit fell on them'. Others reported that this particular experience of God was more highly charged than anything that had preceded it. In view of this, the 'blessing' became known by the place where it was deemed to be concentrated. In just two years, over one million 'pilgrims' have journeyed to Toronto to taste the blessing for themselves.[3] Many of these pilgrims report dramatic healings, substantial changes in their lives, and greater empowerment for Christian ministry.[4] As we shall note at the end of this chapter, the Toronto church is more of a shrine than a church, its adherents more like pilgrims than members of a congregation.[5]

Yet in spite of the extraordinary success of the church, John Wimber, a founding pastor of the Vineyard network, excommunicated the Toronto fellowship for '(alleged) cult-like and manipulative practices'.[6] Some evangelical critics of the TB cited the influence of the Rhema or 'Health and wealth' movement through its connections with Benny Hinn and Rodney Howard-Browne, as another reason for Vineyard-led secession.[7] In January 1996, the Toronto Vineyard became independent, forming itself into the Toronto Airport Christian Fellowship (TACF). Under the leadership of its pastor, John Arnott, it continues to exercise an international ministry in the fundamentalist–revivalist tradition so beloved of its followers. It should be said that the influence of TACF is mainly international (through the revival 'circuit') and *not* local; so far as I can tell, few in Toronto who operate outside the revivalist circuit actually know of the blessing. As Steve Bruce notes, this is not unusual for revivalist and New Age Movements in late modernity or postmodernity, namely, the failure of a given community to be 'engaged' with its immediate environment.[8] Thus, the TB represents a significant, typical form of contemporary revivalism which can be legitimately identified as a focus for research. In the summer of 1996 I was fortunate to be able to spend just over a week at TACF. This may not seem much, but I should point out that I attended 16 meetings of praise, discussion and worship, and was given fairly reasonable, informal access to the leadership and to the pilgrims. In all, I spent more than 50 hours at TACF events, and was able to talk to a wide variety of people from various countries who had experienced the TB for themselves.

The reasons why social exchange theories might help assess the TB will become apparent as the analysis proceeds. For the moment however, we should note that the discipline has not really been systematically applied to religion, unless it has come through an anthropological sieve, which is another way of configuring social exchange theory.[9] Yet Marx, in his sociology, was alive to religion being a system of exchange in which producers, consumers and commodities played a part.[10] Moreover, what is implied by religion being the 'opium of the people' is not just an exchange of present material paucity for future spiritual gains, but the actual provision of 'pain relief' in return for obedience now, this world for the next, and reality for fantasy.[11] This is an early exchange theory, of sorts: religion as a compensator, the wistful 'sigh of the oppressed'. The immediate question to ask of TACF therefore, is 'what is on offer'?

Initially, and in terms of the rhetoric used by TACF, close scrutiny of the metaphors used to describe the blessing is helpful. These metaphors tend to revolve around concepts of water and fire, and then bodily intimacy as a means to personal and communal empowerment. When the TB first 'broke', British leaders in charismatic renewal were careful to 'position' the commodity in the 'charismatic market'. It was variously described as a 'spiritual top-up', 'in-flight re-fuelling', 'refreshing, not revival', 'latter rain', and the like.[12] In other words, the TB was a form of resource for a tired or flagging movement. TACF, in its own journal (*Spread the Fire*), tends to adopt the same line. For example, Roger Forster, a British House Church leader and convert to the TB, speaks about the 'soaking (which) refreshes vision', whilst others see the TB as learning to 'turn on the faucet (tap)', which imagines God's blessing as a type of reservoir.[13] TACF has expressed the desire to see a network of pastors who will 'be permanently wet with renewal'.

Allied to the watery metaphors, there are also analogies concerning drunkenness. Because one of the distinguishing features of the TACF/TB is 'holy' and 'uncontrollable' laughter, some within the movement have inevitably linked their experience to the account of the outpouring of the Holy Spirit described in Acts 2, where the apostles are accused of being drunk.[14] Again, the desirability of non-control is suggested by the rhetoric: 'don't rationalize – just let go'.[15] Randy Clarke, one of the revivalist leaders closely associated with the TACF, talks about dispensing the Holy Spirit like a drink: pilgrims are encouraged to 'have a double, not a single'. Clarke is known within the TB movement as 'God's bartender'. As with the watery metaphors, we find the Holy Spirit being referred to as a resource or thing: a parcel of power which can be disposed and dispensed.[16]

The metaphors of fire are generally used to describe the purging and refining that charismatic movements bring, as well as the passion and excitement that revival ensures. Fire is also, like water, uncontrollable at first; and it is going to 'increase' in such a way that few can stand. The TACF sees itself as a movement that comprehends that power, can receive fire, control it (to an extent) and then direct it. Yet there is an irony for individuals who wish to access this power: they must renounce their self-control to gain power. Many of those who report being overcome by being 'slain in the spirit' are prepared for this ritual by a careful 'grammar of possibility' that is in place, and the provision of carpets and people that catch those who fall; those who succumb then often go on to describe an associated burning sensation.[17] The intimacy (with God) is located in the rhetoric of worship, and is sometimes quasi-erotic. Believers are to know Christ's nearness, and even to experience the 'kisses of his mouth'.[18]

Thus, the task of the individual and church, which is simultaneously soaked with water and on fire (!), as well as uncontrollably drunk, is to strive for greater intimacy, which will lead to the acquisition of power: 'seeking, even cultivating an overwhelming hunger and desperation for intimacy with the Lord . . . enjoyment of the Lord . . . through intimate worship . . . embrace(ing) the cross . . . walking in continual, child-like dependence.'[19] Individuals, as part of the celebrating community, are being asked to acknowledge their hunger and desperation for God, and then to become hot, wet, powerless and passionate, as a prerequisite to *knowing* power.[20] Thus, what is on offer is reified (spiritual) power in the form of personal religious experience. This could simply be *charismata*, but it might also be a form of primal ritual therapy that deals with unresolved stress or profound cathartic crises.[21] In exchange for questing, obedience and soaring to new heights of worship, the pilgrims perceive that they gain 'power from on high' in particular forms, which, generally, address the need for refreshment, excitement, greater power, identity and security.[22] Fire and rain are falling from heaven: those who are intimate (or drunk) with God can catch it for themselves, personally. Indeed, the TB/TACF suggests that they can learn to tap it when they like: revival is no longer a surprise, but is now a ready and available resource, constantly accessible.[23] The mighty river is flowing, and Toronto is its source. Once this is grasped, they can spread the revival floods and fire themselves if they wish, becoming God's instrument of empowerment for others. For this reason, TACF events are often geared to attract church leaders.

As a site of pilgrimage as distinct from a church, TACF's location is significant: less than a mile from the main international airport at Toronto. It is a large conference centre, nestling amongst hotels, restaurants, industrial estates and criss-crossing freeways; the area is completely non-residential, and all TACF members must have access to a car. The building is modern and purpose-built as a trade centre; although not aesthetically attractive, it is functional, well lit, spacious and open. It has an impressive reception area, a small restaurant, seminar rooms, offices and a main auditorium that can seat over 5,000.[24] There is also a bookshop on site which carries a large stock of charismatic literature: Benny Hinn, Leonard Ravenhill, John Wimber and Bill Surbritzky seem to be the most popular authors there, after TACF's own staff. You can also purchase T-shirts, videos, CDs, audio-tapes and other products that are synonymous with charismatic culture, such as car bumper stickers, cards, pens and the like. The church advertises weekly social activities such as 'Spirit-led aerobics', a Christian rambling club, creches, bowling and 'work with the poor'. The atmosphere was pleasing and friendly – the church is obviously used to visitors. Adjacent to the church is a sizeable two-storey office block that houses more offices for pastors, and is the main administrative site.[25] TACF also has its own School of Ministry, a building nearby the main church. Employees of TACF, including volunteers from the School of Ministry, exceed 80 persons. Income in 1995 was more than $7 million (Canadian), which is about 3.5 million pounds sterling. Much of this income is from visitors, although TACF points out that the budget would not be so large if it were not for the volume of pilgrims.

The weekly pattern of religious meetings is carefully regulated. There are nightly renewal meetings (except Monday) which attract many visitors. These begin at 7 p.m. or 7.30 p.m. and can run until midnight, although many have left by 10.30 p.m. There are daily workshops for pastors which run each weekday morning, covering the same themes week by week. Monday – pastoring renewal; Tuesday – the biblical basis; Wednesday – the historical basis; Thursday – worship; Friday – prayer. In the afternoons there is intercessory prayer for revival. The form of these meetings – in a more intimate, but nonetheless large seminar room – is testimony, encouragement, prayer and praise. They generally last about two hours, and seemed to me to be less controlled than other meetings: anyone who felt led to speak, pray, exhort or prophesy could do so. In addition to these meetings there is Sunday morning worship and various extra workshops and conferences run throughout the year. In a normal week in July, between 750 and 1,000 people attended each weekday, spread across the various events. Sunday is for 'church members', but their actual numbers (about 1,200) account for only a fraction of the total number attending TACF in any one year.

Whilst it is not possible to record all that has been observed at TACF, it does seem that the TB is distinguishable from other forms of revivalism (at present) by its distinctive and relentless appeal to specified concepts of love and power, and its rejection of God–Satanic dualisms. There is, I think, a clear relationship between the rhetoric deployed and the subsequent phenomenology. Believers sing about the power and intimacy of God, hear testimonies of it, listen to it preached, and then finally get to experience it for themselves. In effect, they reap what they sow.[26] Believers who attend TACF clearly imagine that 'the power of (dead or dry) religion' is being broken, and that they are being given direct access to the awesome power of God. The screaming, shaking, and almost banshee wailing are comprehensible only when one listens to the grammar of possibility that prepares the ground of actuality. In a more modest way, this is sometimes described as refreshment, renewal and revival. Yet there is also a sense in which this behaviour is already developing into a form of routinized religion.

As with other charismatic groups in history, the Arnotts' group members cannot resist the lure of denominational association to 'spread their fire'. In spite of claiming, as British Restorationists once did, that they were not a denomination, but rather a restoration of God's kingdom, TACF announced a new umbrella of churches whilst I was there called 'Partners in Harvest', which would cater for and safeguard this particular brand of revivalism.[27] In some ways, I think this marks the beginning of the end for the TB, namely its routinization, in the full Weberian sense. TACF will only survive if it can continue to 'market' the blessing, or improve upon it for existing and new consumers who are hungry for this kind of God.[28] As Margaret Poloma candidly admits, '[this] Renewal is about satisfying the desire of the human heart'.[29] Precisely. If it fails to do that, its peripatetic clientele will take their business elsewhere.

## Social Exchange Theory and the Idea of Blessing

Exchange theories view social order as the unplanned outcome of acts of exchange between members of a given group. Given that it is so difficult to read or get a handle on what is taking place in the TB/TACF, and that participants appear to think the outcome of the TB is unplanned (at least by its leaders), social exchange theory may offer a way forward here. There are two major variants of the theory to note. First, rational-choice theory locates the source of order in the personal advantage individuals gain through co-operative exchange. Second, anthropological-exchange theory claims that both order and the pursuit of individual advantage are *effects* of the underlying ritual and symbolic nature of the thing that is exchanged. Both strands of social exchange theory have something to say about religion as an exchange process, although we should note that the second tradition, especially through the work of Mauss, is the more dominant. Mauss, in his observation of what he called 'primitive or archaic types of society' understood that if God was 'blessed' in certain ways, God would 'bless' in return. For Mauss, the notion of 'gift' was central: in return for worship, the gifts of the spirit are given. In return for the gifts being exercised, more gifts are added. Charisma, *charismata*, power and empowerment are all inextricably linked.[30]

These two traditions of social exchange theory offer different perspectives on what is exchanged in religion, and to what end. Rationalists such as Peter Blau stress the structural nature of society as being guided by exchange: the basis of belief lies in its ability to deliver on desires. Individuals, in this configuration of the theory, weigh extrinsic benefits within a system of reciprocal exchange.[31] Anthropologists such as Mauss take a different line, arguing that orderly collective life is a pre-condition, not a consequence, of self-interested choice. A key to this configuration of the theory is the role of obligation, and the rules and commands that must be followed in order to belong to society, as well as to benefit individually. Both theories, critically for this analysis, share interests in power and collective behaviour. They provide an account of what individuals and groups give and gain by belonging, perhaps suggesting that the 'mystique' of the TB may actually involve some quite rational or embedded assumptions on the part of individuals and groups which are sociologically accountable.[32] What I shall be mainly attempting to show in this section is that both the rationalist and anthropological approaches to exchange theory are right in different ways when it comes to the TB. Some pilgrims definitely come seeking a specific blessing: a return for their investment. Others come in a more enquiring mode, but nonetheless find themselves surprised or blessed by the apparently unplanned outcome of the obligations and gifts that configure the movement.

Two additional distinctions in exchange theory also need noting before proceeding further. Peter Ekeh, in his work, describes the traditions as being 'collectivist' and 'individualist', which are derived from Talcott Parsons' categorization of British and French orientations in sociology.[33] For Ekeh, the correlation is individualistic–Protestant and collectivist–Catholic, and modern sociological theory is a 'marriage' between these strands. From the point of view of this analysis, this is significant since the TB movement is undoubtedly Protestant in one sense, namely its origin from a neo-Pentecostal and fundamentalist background. Yet there is also a Catholicity about this movement too: it is less textual and more symbolic than conventional Protestantism.[34] Also, it has a place for the *nouveau-sacramental*, namely the identification of *charismata* and certain types of celebratory worship as pivotal points of instrumentality through which God is encountered and blesses. Thus, in Blau's definition of exchange theory, there is a place for collective, organic emotionalism (Catholic) alongside individualistic, atomistic rationalism (Protestant), and the possibility of movements as well as theories that have managed to merge the two in late modernity.[35] With this in mind, we shall now look at three areas of exchange theory in relation to the TB/TACF movements: the structure of group relations, power and exchange, and finally the nature of gifts. This will indicate some suggestions about individuals and the community formed around the 'blessing'.

In terms of the structure of group relations, exchange theory has shown that group size is important.[36] Of particular note is Blau and Schwartz's observation that 'as group size increases, the probable rate of outgroup relations decreases'. A number of considerations arise from this. First, the sheer scale of TACF and the TB movement offers pilgrims the possibility of exchanging their present world for a new world configured in charismatic terms. There is sufficient culture in the TB movement – clothes, books, conferences, media, etc. – to offer a sustainable alternative world to those who opt in. The size of the operation is a crucial factor here: believers must see that they are opting into a world (or world-wide network), not just a micro-group such as a cult or sect. Second, the decrease in outgroup relations needs careful handling. The TACF is profoundly unrelated to its immediate environs: members drive in and drive away, just as pilgrims fly in and fly away. Yet the absence of outgroup relations is masked by the popularity and size of the TACF. Third, the sizeist aspirations of TACF are deeply embedded in its cultural roots through the American-led 'Church Growth Movement' (CGM) founded by Donald McGavran and developed by Peter Wagner. In CGM thinking, there are three sizes of groups and each performs different tasks. The cell is for intimate, in-depth personal work. The congregation is a collection of local cells – a small church, perhaps. And finally, there is the celebration, a collection of congregations that is intentionally sizeable in order to impress believers and attract new followers. Whilst the congregation is to be somehow 'earthed' locally, the celebration simply exists anywhere for the sake of its size and what that connotes about God and the community of believers. Its purpose is to demonstrate God's power in a concentrated form to a sizeable group.[37]

However, the TACF has gained its size through slightly different means: social association and the mobility of pilgrims are primary factors in promoting a permanent resident community of celebration. The TB movement marks a change in the heterogeneity of contemporary charismatic renewal. For the first time in its history, there is now a place which hundreds of thousands are visiting as a source of blessing, rather in the way that pilgrims in other religious traditions visit shrines or sites. Mobility is a key to understanding the success of the TB, since it has enabled the blessing to be carried, transported as it were, back home to the places from whence the pilgrims came. The sense of size is enhanced by the ever-expanding network of followers who are linked by common bonds of faith, but have also tasted the blessing for themselves at source.[38] Put crudely, some see the mobility around the TB as a legitimate exchange for getting God to act: 'when God moves, the people move'.[39]

Naturally, this movement or mobility has implications for structures and group relations within contemporary charismatic renewal. Effectively, it creates classes or subdivisions between those who have been willing or able to go to Toronto or one of its satellite 'filling/refreshing' meetings, and those who have not. An obvious area to highlight is the equation between financial means and sacrifice. Going to Toronto, or to one of its key satellite conferences, is a costly business. Those who do go are looking for value, or are charged by a supportive sending group with bringing back the blessing. So far, this means the movement has not moved much beyond the European, American and Australasian middle classes.[40] In short, inequality and differentiation have crept in at many levels.[41] Structurally, there are now distinctions to be made between pro-TB and anti-TB revivalists, between Wimberites and Toronto followers, and so forth; typically, these groups have quickly developed their own cultures, complete with requisite merchandise. And, as I remarked earlier, size is a factor here. The larger the size of a community, the greater the increase in the rate of overt conflict between competing groups. It would not be unreasonable to suggest that Wimber's excommunication of the TACF was more to do with its growing size than its doctrine. However, both groups have yet to address the 'consolidated [or perhaps consecrated?] inequalities' that are present in their respective groups through hegemonic structures and authoritarian leadership, although the split between the two groups has something to do with this.[42]

Ultimately, what is governing structure and group relations in the TB movement is the realm of cultural symbols and meanings centred around power, coupled with the rhetoric of choice. This gives rise to the configuration of 'overlapping circles' of interest and belief in contemporary revivalism which encourages mobility, heterogeneity and consolidation. So, structurally and relationally, there is both harmony and difference in revivalism, although the same story about God's power is basically being told everywhere. The believers have obligations to the power, namely to receive it and reify it in appropriate forms. In some cases, they may choose how this is done. But in others, the underlying revivalist culture might determine the mode of receiving, as for example in being slain in the Spirit. Either way, size emerges as proof of power and enables the group concerned to adopt its collective representations of power as organizing principles of social structure.[43]

Power is already beginning to emerge as a pre-eminent feature of exchange theory. Theorists such as Emerson, Homans, Thibaut and Kelly have all noted that power relations lie at the basis of exchange.[44] The simple yet elegant proposition is this: one person's power resides in the dependency of another. If two persons are unequally dependent, the less dependent person acquires a power advantage over the other, and an imbalance of exchange arises, with the more dependent person giving or losing more than he or she receives.[45] We shall turn to the implications of this for the TB in a moment, but two characteristics of the power theorem need to be noted initially. First, the determinants of power are structural characteristics of the relation between persons rather than (just) individual characteristics. Second, 'power' and 'power use' are conceptually distinct: power is a function of the structural position, whereas power use refers to the actual method of control that might determine behaviour. How does this affect the TB?

The dependency in power relations for the TB is linked to the focus of divine power being located (or poured out) in one place: Toronto. This delivers power into the hands of the leadership, who naturally become power-brokers, or the main agents/interpreters of the manifestations. Even in spite of some believers' insistence that the TACF does not hype-up the TB, and is not that charismatic (in the Weberian sense), its structural position in the power equation automatically creates a hegemony. The fact that the type of power the TB/TACF offers is novel and particular further stresses the imbalance of power. Thus, pilgrims wishing to receive must 'let go of themselves' in a TB context in a way that would not be required of them were they to step into an average Episcopalian or Anglican service of matins for example. In short, to receive anything, almost everything in the cognitive-rational sphere has to be given up, including critical faculties; we have already noted the accompanying rhetoric – 'don't rationalize – just let go'. So, independent of the charisma of the leader, the power-relation context requires obedience to the prophets, leaders or bringers of the blessing.[46] Second, and linked to this, it should be obvious that power only becomes something when it is used. A belief in an inerrant Bible is useless unless there is an interpreter: it is not the Bible-as-power that rules in ecclesial settings, but the one who controls its use.[47] It is in the use of power that the behaviour of another is determined. Thus, the carefully prepared grammar of assent that surrounds TB meetings is actually quite significant. In appealing to certain revivalist phenomena of the past, using a selection of testimonies from the present, as well as suggesting what is about to happen in the immediate future once the Holy Spirit has been 'invited to visit' ('some of you may fall over, others weep or laugh . . .', etc.), adherents are actually being controlled. This is partially, but not wholly with their consent, since the inequality of the power-relations in the first instance renders complete freedom of choice impossible for those who want this blessing.

Exchange theory, at this point, cannot know how structural advantage is actually translated into behavioural control. However, in terms of power relations, we have the first indication that a power structure is also a power process.[48] Another way of expressing this would be to say that the suggestion of determination, interpretation and conversion of power outcomes ultimately leads to behaviour control. Thus, the responsiveness of someone to power is key. Those who wish to receive will most likely become high users of power; those who are more passive may well give and gain less. Variations and reinforcements in the power process may reconfigure individuals, but the essential point to grasp is that those who want power are part of a process that will, to some extent, deliver it. Foucault, in a slightly different way, was alive to this when he noted that power only exists in reciprocal relations, and then again in the intentions and gaps that form the structures and processes of power.[49]

Given that networks, processes and structures are important for describing power and its use, it is now necessary to turn to the issue of heterogeneity. Any consideration of heterogeneity needs some comprehension of how membership boundaries are determined. Peter Blau makes a distinction between nominal and graduated types of discrimination for groups.[50] The nominal forms of discrimination may be age, sex, race or religion. In the case of TACF, and, in fact, many churches on the revivalist circuit, there is little serious nominal discrimination. Whilst it is true that there are few women in senior pastorship positions, this is probably an artefact of evangelical or fundamentalist views on the role of women in Christian leadership and ministry that has survived in revivalist churches. The graduated form of discrimination takes into account such characteristics as charisma, power, education, rhetorical ability, lucidity and the like. Here, a clear power shape begins to develop in revivalist churches; salience is acquired here for a group like TACF. How, though, does the separation of nominal and graduated affect power relations? There are a number of issues to consider.

First, the division of labour in any given religious group will be shaped by perceptions about who has most or least charisma, giftedness, *charismata* or other desired qualities. In short, the division of labour is configured in terms of ideals or ideology. This takes us into the heart of Weber's notion of ideal types:

> An ideal type is formed by the one-sided accentuation of one or more points of view and by the synthesis of a great many diffuse, discrete, more or less present and occasionally absent concrete individual phenomena, which are arranged according to those one-sidedly corporate viewpoints into a unified analytical construct. In its conceptual purity, this mental construct cannot be empirically anywhere in reality ... it is a utopia.[51]

Whilst Weber might have understood ideal types to be abstract, they are becoming reified in the idealized or idolized revivalist community. So, although groups like TACF are heterogeneous, they should be seen as converging communities in which horizons of desire and possibility are gradually being shaped, moulded, narrowed, focused and concentrated into a form of idealism.[52] Blau confirms this shape to power, when he notes that inequality of power goes hand in hand with heterogeneity, since there is always, somewhere, a concentration of power.[53] In the case of TACF, and its special access to the TB, it is obvious what is going on. Those outside the community are deemed to be impoverished, starved of power, as it were. TACF however, knows and owns the power in a concrete, concentrated form, so is wealthy. An exchange or redistribution of wealth depends on being willing to 'reduce diversity' in order to gain equality.[54]

Second, Blau suggests that the shape of power is pyramidal. From the top, there is absolute power; this is supported by proportionate power which immediately relates to the absolute; lastly, there is relative power, which although experiencing inequality can nonetheless relate to the absolute, albeit solely through the proportionate. This shape is the shape of social power relations in exchange theory. It assumes a hegemony that actually provides a heterogeneity, albeit one that is converging to its absolute point or focus. This shape has space for collective action to be undertaken, conflict to be allowed, an elite to emerge, and has time for interpersonal relations. In other words, the model for power turns out to be a paradigm for exchange. The group history that knows one or two people are especially anointed, and are the harbingers of a unique blessing, provides a social account of the relationship between TACF and the TB, between leaders and pilgrims, and between the absolute authority – the interpreter and chief imparter of the blessing – and his followers. This requires a little more clarification. The leadership structure at TACF is rather flat when the TB is benign: there appears to be no one obviously in sole charge. However, when the TB is exported to other churches, it is the chief importer who acquires prophetic charisma over others within their own context. This immediately creates a pyramidal shape. Increasingly, as TACF stresses the prophetic more and more, the routinized charisma of its leaders emerges (offering checks, controls, balances and the like), culminating in the creation of hegemonic apostolic authority for a few over the many. Wimber's relationship to the Vineyard movement offers a nearly identical historical paradigm.

Third, and given these remarks, it is also worth pressing the question of why religious power is able to operate like this in an essentially pluralistic society. How does a group like TACF hold the attention of its followers? How does it avoid routinization or adverse bureaucracy? To some extent, the answer lies in seeing the TB as offering a competing commodity within a spiritual market, rather than setting up an alternative spiritual bureaucracy: 'power accrues to those having the tools with which to maximise efficiency outcomes'.[55] Coupled with this, Weber's notion of bureaucratic transition is now in reverse flux: there is declining attachment to organization, and an expectation of products being tested by the vicissitudes of market forces. This elevates a characteristic like charisma, and novel derivatives of it, in a way that was not possible when modernist organizations and metatheories were in the ascendancy. But the new postmodern celebration of difference only works if it is understood that the language of power is now the language of *efficiency*.[56] TACF, for all its explicit power language, is, in common with other revivalist groups, rather shy of that. What is preferred is talk of 'what God has done' or is doing, and testimonies that demonstrate the reification of power in return for (perceived) legitimate exchange.

Finally, in this section there needs to be some consideration of the nature of gifts or commodities, and the individual and community that is formed around the blessing. I have been suggesting that power and charisma are gifted and exchanged in a dynamic relational structure that is gradually converging towards an absolute point of reference. The grammar of assent – metaphors of water, fire, intimacy, force (the Spirit falling) and drunkenness – are all descriptions of the social control that is engendered by the leadership. In other words, to distort Peter Berger, the 'theological construction of reality' has direct *ecclesial* consequences.[57] The valued behaviour becomes intimate-enthusiastic, which is offered in return for a deeper experience of what this is said to deliver.[58] The TACF leadership remains in the power structure, but as leaders they acquire the status of brokers or interpreters: they are themselves partly sacramental – God's pivotal point of instrumentality which directs and disposes of blessing. The hegemonic structure of TACF is necessarily so, since access to power must always be controlled, especially when it is deemed to be in such a concentrated form. Correspondingly, leaders emerge who are variously described as 'God's bartender' or 'God's instrument of laughter/ wind/blessing'.

Thus, rather than describing the Toronto phenomenon as a blessing, the application of exchange theory seems to point in a slightly different direction, at least for the individuals who appear to gain from being involved in the TB movement. What appears to be occurring is a complex form of social abreaction, which is then ascribed religious significance. Abreaction describes a therapeutic process – conscious or unconscious, group or individual – wherein repressed feelings, desires, traumas or negativity are allowed to be expressed and perhaps resolved.[59] Typically, the process involves a high disposal of emotional discharge; when the feelings are expressed, psychological, social or spiritual insights into conditions may be gained and behaviour modified. For many, this is a religious interpretation of a 'natural event', a sense of being 'healed', or of being 'touched by God'. Hypnosis,[60] primal therapy, psychodrama and enthusiastic religion can all play a part in any abreactive process, which is gained through catharsis.[61] What is clear from the ecstatic religious experiences that characterize the TB/TACF movement is that there are constituent gains in releasing rationality, control, emotions and the like. What. the believer gains by yielding to the powers can vary: an altered state of consciousness, social integration or re-integration, increase in conviction, or relief from stress are all possibilities.[62] Thus, the TB/TACF movement operates as a system of exchange. In order to benefit, it is necessary to learn the cathartic processes before abreaction can be reached.[63] This makes the movement profoundly individualistic, which is of course, exactly what it is. In spite of the numbers involved, the sizes of groups and the shared perceptions, everybody is gaining something that is mainly of a personal nature, and will remain so.

## Summary

The phenomena of jerking, barking, shaking, dancing and falling in revivals is not new,[64] although there are some phenomenological differences between the kinds of manifestation occuring in the late twentieth century and those of the eighteenth and nineteenth centuries.[65] What can be said with some clarity is that there are behavioural traditions in revivals which arise out of certain social conditions. For example, the turbulence and displacement of frontier life in the early nineteenth century appears to have encouraged community camp meetings that indulged in religious fervour and enthusiasm in response to preaching: religion, in the original sense of the word, was a force for binding the disparate. The new religiosity was both a compensator for social displacement and a reflection of the newly emerging optimism of modernity. Like the present revivalist conferences, these meetings lasted for days at a time, with the organizers knowing that, within reason, the more believers had to travel and sacrifice of themselves, the more rewarding the meeting was.[66] Believers reaped what they sowed. The more they personally sacrifice in worship, the more they perceive they will be blessed. Abrogation of rationality leads to acquisition of spirituality.

Following Stark and Bainbridge, it does seem, at least sociologically, that the TB is a profound example of 'gaining rewards or avoiding costs and is lodged in exchange relationships'. The power that is present in the TB/TACF movement controls the exchange ratio, with 'the consequence that the more powerful, the more favourable the exchange ratio'.[67] The exchange ratio is the net rewards or ultimate compensators over costs in an exchange; power is simply the degree of control over the exchange ratio. Stark and Bainbridge are suggesting that religious sects or schisms are evidence of demand for religious rewards or compensators that will combat the alienating affects of modernity. Indeed, secularization actually stimulates the growth of sect movements through the pressure it brings to bear on religious belief.[68] They further suggest that a new religious group, schism or sect that can offer a low-tension environment (i.e. a relatively easy relationship with the world that is non-separatist), alongside high rewards (healing, wealth, social cohesion, elevated spiritual insight, family values, etc.), will be avoiding the fate of cults and the failures of mainstream churches.[69] TACF is a good example of the ideal they have in mind: an undemanding body, configured via power relations, in which rewards or compensators are gained through the exchange of inhibitions, rationality or other forms of personal power. Thus, this 'revival' is mainly about personal renewal: it is an expansive survival reflex, and emerges as 'the staging of episodes of increased religious affect to sustain compensators'.[70] The more believers invest in the blessing, the higher the rate of return: it is a virtuous circle. In reality, TACF is not so much a church as a centre of pilgrimage. It has developed into an evangelical shrine at which God's power is deemed to be specially manifest. As a place where God works, there is less stress on charismatic leadership, and more on exchange relations. To receive the TB, congregations pay up to send an emissary. In turn, this person gives by investing in TACF worship and its grammar of assent: the emissary is then blessed, and returns home to give the blessing back to the investors.

In this chapter there has been some sort of attempt at assessing the complex phenomenology of the TB and TACF through theories of exchange. In turn, any insights gained through exchange theories have implications for the study of power in the Church. What is clear is that the grammar of assent that is peculiar to TACF, conceived through notions and analogies of passion, power and passivity, not only describes the TB but actually helps create the situations that configure it. However, it must be emphasized that sociological method and theological reflection cannot provide a completely comprehensive account of religious experience. It is a complementary description and, as such, still requires careful theological and ethnographic support for any findings that may emerge.

# Notes

1 Some struggle with this definition of the church, arguing that a movement that is clearly so experiential cannot be fundamentalist. However, the church, largely for pragmatic reasons, defines itself as both. Its recent statement of faith published on the Internet confirms the description as apt: http://www.grimi.org/TAV/ – 'we believe that the Bible is God's Word ... speaking to us with authority and without error'.

2 Some call this the Third or Fourth Wave of the Spirit. For a discussion of the Vineyard church, see my *Words, Wonders and Power: Understanding Christian Fundamentalism and Revivalism* (London: SPCK, 1996).

3 These figures are based on Michael Mitton's assessment in *The Heart of Toronto* (Cambridge: Grove Spirituality Series, no. 55, 1996), p. 3.

4 See M. Poloma, *By Their Fruits: A Sociological Assessment of the Toronto Blessing*, published by the church. Poloma is a lecturer at the University of Akron, Ohio, and a supporter of the Toronto church, even though she remains an Episcopalian. Her account is highly sympathetic to the TACF. Poloma's sociological method in this article is based on quantification of data from questionnaires, slanting the sociology towards science rather than art.

5 Many who have journeyed to Toronto speak of themselves as pilgrims coming to a Holy place. For a discussion of this in the context of postmodernity, and related issues, see Virgil Elizondo and Sean Freyne (eds), *Pilgrimage: Concilium 1996:4* (London: SCM, 1996), especially Paul Post's essay, 'The Modern Pilgrim', which identifies a new 'post-traditional' pilgrim emerging.

6 Although according to TACF staff pastor, Ian Ross, it was because the 'tail was wagging the dog': TACF staff still claim to be hurt by Wimber's exclusion of them from the Vineyard network (taped interview: 09/07/96). A fuller account of this is available in my 'City on a Beach', in *Charismatic Christianity: Sociological Perspectives*, ed. S. Hunt, M. Hamilton and T. Walters (Basingstoke: Macmillan, 1997).

7 See Mark Smith, *Testing the Fire* (Cambridge: St Matthew Publishing, 1997); B. J. Oropeza, *A Time to Laugh* (Peabody, Mass.: Hendrickson, 1995); Jim Beverley, *Holy Laughter and the Toronto Blessing* (Grand Rapids, Michigan: Zondervan, 1995).

8 See S. Bruce, *Religion in the Modern World: From Cathedrals to Cults* (Oxford: OUP, 1996). Bruce notes that globalism produces tribalism and, eventually, ghetto religion. Much New Age religion, including its Christian forms such as the Toronto Blessing, indicate a trend towards esoteric, personal religion, that is generally unrelated to social contexts or questions. Bruce cites the Findhorn community as an example.

9 The most notable example of this is still Marcel Mauss, *The Gift: Forms and Functions of Exchange in Archaic Societies* (published in 1950) (trans. from the French by Ian Cunnison) (London: Cohen & West, 1966).

10 See *Capital*, 1867; extract in K. Marx and F. Engels, *On Religion* (Moscow: Foreign Languages Publishing House, 1955), pp. 135–6.

11 See *Contribution to the Critique of Hegel's Philosophy of Right* (1844), in *On Religion* (1955), pp. 41–2.

12 I am indebted to Peter Berger for the notion of this phenomenon being 'something' to 'sell'. See his 'A Market Analysis of Ecumenicity', *Social Research*, vol. 30 (1963), pp. 75–90. The phrases used above belong to Nicky Gumbel, Curate of Holy Trinity, Brompton, a leading supporter of the Toronto Blessing. They appeared in various editions of the *Church of England Newspaper* in early 1994.

13 See *Spread the Fire*, vol. 2, issue 1 (February 1996).

14 Acts 2:13. The story is being read by TACF inductively, namely the tracing back of present experience into the past in order to validate contemporary praxis. However, 'drunk' is an insult to the apostles, not a prescription for behaviour. Furthermore, the story is almost certainly (in part) a construction or myth, designed to signify the universal nature of the Spirit of Christ now available, reversing the story of the Tower of Babel in Genesis 11. Contrary to popular belief, Acts 2 does not present a paradigm for neo-Pentecostal behaviour.

15 Cf. Dr Roy Clements, 'What should we make of the Toronto Blessing?', Spring Harvest, Word Alive, 1995 (cassette tape no. 55, ICC, W. Sussex). Clements notes, as one might expect from an ultra-conservative evangelical critic, that many aspects of the New Age are mimicked by the TB. He points to the touching and anointing for blessing, and the obsession with excitement, fulfilment and 'drunkenness with God'.

16 The appellation of 'bartender' applied to Clarke is more usually used of Rodney Howard-Browne, a revivalist also linked to TACF.

17 See G. Chevreau, *Catch the Fire* (London: Marshall/Collins, 1994), p. 33.

18 This might sound a bit tendentious, but I am not alone amongst sociologists of religion in articulating ideas like this. Max Weber suggested that gnosticism within Christianity compensated for the lack of orgiastic indulgence that had once been prevalent amongst converts. He believed certain kinds of religion could provide 'sublimated masturbatory surrogates' for believers. Similarly, Rollo May has argued that certain contemporary religions amount to a search for Eros and the erotic, which the rational religion of post-Enlightenment lost. I should make

it clear that I am not arguing against appropriate inculcation of Eros in worship and religious experience. The issue here is clustered around concepts of control, space and freedom. See Paul Avis, *Eros and the Sacred* (London: SPCK, 1989).

19 See TACF homepages on 'Partners in Harvest' and 'Prophecy': http://www.tacf.org/etc/html.

20 See my forthcoming essay 'Sweet Rapture: Sublimated Eroticism in Contemporary Charismatic Worship' in *The Body and Theology: Gender, Text and Ideology*, ed. Jan Jobling (Leominster: Gracewing/Fowler-Wright). There is some discussion of the claim made by some revivalist leaders that worship is 'making love to God', and the claim by Paul Cain (Vineyard) that 'Jesus is turned on by our desire for him' and then rewards that with power, especially prophetic revelation.

21 Clements, *op. cit.*, side 2.

22 For a discussion of reification in revivalism, see my *Words, Wonders and Power* (1996), pp. 49ff.

23 Inevitably, one should see this as the legacy of Finney, whose *Lectures on Revivals of Religions* (1835) provided Free Churches with a handbook on how to organize a revival. Finney's *Principles of Revival* (1836 etc.) provide a marvellous example of religious exchange theory, especially his writing on conversion as both obligation and gift (ed. L. G. Gifford Parkhurst, Minneapolis, Minnesota: Bethany House Publishers, 1987).

24 The original building for the Toronto Airport Vineyard was much smaller, but the advent of the Blessing in January 1994 forced the leadership to seek larger premises. The present building is 71,000 square feet, and is owned by TACF, as are the other buildings. (Source: Ian Ross, TACF).

25 There is also a Seventh Day Adventist Church opposite TACF, and a certain amount of sharing of buildings takes place, especially during busy conferences.

26 A difficult thesis to prove, but one that merits testing. If meetings began with different hymns, the testimonies had a different focus, and the sermons covered other themes, it would be no surprise if the pneumasomatic phenomena suddenly underwent a marked decrease.

27 A conference for 'like-minded' pastors to augment the new federation was planned for October 1996.

28 See Peter Berger, 'A Market Model Analysis for Ecumenicity' in *Social Research*, vol. 30 (1963), pp. 75–90.

29 M. Poloma, *By Their Fruits*, p. 21.

30 Marcel Mauss, *The Gift: Forms and Functions of Exchange in Archaic Societies* (trans. Ian Cunnison) (London: Cohen & West, 1966), pp. v-x, 1–4ff.

31 Peter Blau, *Exchange and Power in Social Life* (New York: John Wiley & Sons, 1964).

32 See for example Gustave Le Bon's *The Crowd* (New York: Viking, 1895/1960): Le Bon argues that people surrender their individuality in crowds, and find their rational-moral powers suspended by the hypnotic effect of leaders and the consequent mass behaviour. However, writers on collective behaviour since Le Bon have shown that crowds are much more mindful, rational and socially organized than Le Bon first thought: see R. H. Turner and L. Killian, *Collective Behaviour* (Englewood Cliffs, NJ: Prentice Hall, 1987).

33 P. Ekeh, *Social Exchange Theory: The Two Traditions* (London: Heinemann, 1974); Talcott Parsons, *Theories of Society* (New York: The Free Press, 1961), pp. 85–97.

34 Although a different perspective can be found in R. Spittler, 'Are Penecostals and Charismatics Fundamentalists? A Review of American Uses of these Categories' in Karla Poewe (ed.), *Charismatic Christianity as a Global Culture* (New York:

Columbia UP, 1994), pp. 103–16. Spittler argues that the roots of fundamental-ism are different from those of revivalism (pacifist, Quaker, Shaker, etc.). Whilst I agree that Pentecostalism has a richer history than fundamentalism, I do not really see pressing historical or phenomenological reasons for driving a wedge between the two movements now. They share interests in power and certainty, are ecclesiologically similar, and are both, at present, like-minded in their pluriform responses to modernity and postmodernity. Without being fully fundamentalist, they may be fundamentalistic.

35 Ekeh *op. cit.*, 1974, pp. 5–17.

36 See P. Blau and J. Schwartz, *Crosscutting Social Circles: Testing a Macrostructural Theory of Intergroup Relations* (New York: Harcourt Brace Jovanovich, 1984).

37 *Ibid.*, pp. 28ff. See also my discussion of the Church Growth Movement in 'How to Win Congregations and Influence Them', *Contours of Christian Education*, ed. J. Astley and D. Day (Great Wakering: McCrimmon, 1992), pp. 174ff.

38 Blau and Schwartz, *op. cit.*, pp. 55ff. See also Michael Mitton, 'Pilgrimage to Toronto', *Anglicans for Renewal* (Winter 1995), and P. Richter and S. Porter, *The Toronto Blessing* (London: DLT, 1995).

39 David Pytches, 'The Toronto Blessing' (Video), (Chorleywood: Kingdom Power Trust, 1995).

40 This is not an unusual feature of contemporary revivalism. See M. McGuire, *Ritual Healing in Suburban America* (New Brunswick: Rutgers University Press, 1988) for a treatment of middle class American healing groups. See also Anthony Archer, *The Two Catholic Churches: A Study in Oppression* (London: SCM, 1986), p. 220: 'Typically, then, a Catholic who came to take part in the charismatic renewal movement was ostensibly successful, economically and otherwise, but conscious, if only vaguely, of being deprived of other sorts of satisfaction'. Archer describes renewal as 'charismatic chicanery' – the enthusiasts' response to modernity, which reflects middle-class values and success, whilst alienating the working class and poor.

41 Blau and Schwartz, *op. cit.*, pp. 161ff.

42 *Ibid.*, p. 177. The discussion between TACF and John Wimber on the Internet prior to the excommunication supports this thesis. TACF argued that Wimber's jealousy of the TB was analogous to Saul's envy of David, recorded in 1 Samuel 16ff.

43 For a fuller discussion, see P. Blau and R. Merton, *Continuities in Structural Inquiry* (London: Sage, 1981).

44 See R. M. Emerson, 'Power-dependence Relations', *American Sociological Review* (1962), vol. 27: pp. 31–42; G. C. Homans, *Social Behaviour* (New York: Harcourt Brace Jovanovich, 1974); H. Kelly and J. Thibaut, *Interpersonal Relations: A Theory of Interdependence* (New York: John Wiley, 1978).

45 See Linda Molm, 'Linking Power Structure and Power Use' in Karon Cook (ed.), *Social Exchange Theory* (London: Sage, 1987), pp. 101ff.

46 For example, Paul Cain, a prophet of the Vineyard Church and one of the 'Kansas Six', had little in the way of endearing charismatic qualities. Yet his position as a prophet ensured a whole series of power-dependent relations. Once outside the Vineyard, his charisma and any personal power he might have largely failed to give him the public platform he once enjoyed in revivalism.

47 See K. Boone, *The Bible Tells Them So: The Discourse of Protestant Fundamentalism* (London: SCM, 1990).

48 K. Cook, *op. cit.*, p. 102.

49 See M. Foucault, 'Space, Knowledge and Power' in *The Foucault Reader*, ed. Paul

Rabinow (New York: Pantheon Press, 1984), p. 247. However, I wish to add that I do not entirely share Foucault's belief that there is nothing to power apart from space and relationships: this would amount to a capitulation to non-realist views of divine power, based on projectionist theories of religion (Feuerbach).

50 P. Blau, *Inequality and Heterogeneity: A Primitive Theory of Social Structure* (New York: The Free Press, 1977), pp. 7ff.

51 See M. Weber, *The Methodology of the Social Sciences*, ed. E. Shils and H. Finch (New York: Free Press, 1948), p. 89.

52 As I have noted in my *Words, Wonders and Power* (SPCK, 1996), the ideology expressed in worship is a crucial factor here.

53 Blau, *op. cit.*, 1977, p. 13.

54 Blau, *op. cit.*, p. 73.

55 See M. Meyer, 'The Weberian Tradition in Organisational Research', in *Structures of Power and Constraint: Essays in Honour of Peter Blau*, eds M. Meyer and W. Scott (Cambridge: CUP, 1990), p. 211.

56 See Stewart Clegg, *Frameworks of Power* (London: Sage, 1989), for a discussion about the 'forgetting of power' as a subject, in spite of the fact that it persists in a postmodern context. Peter Morriss, from a more purely philosophical perspective, makes the same point in *Power: A Philosophical Investigation* (Manchester: Manchester UP, 1987), Part I, where he suggests that we should see power in dispositional terms – something that we create conceptually, in order to comprehend the episodic. For a discussion of episodic and dispositional forms of power, see Steven Lukes, *Power: A Radical View* (London: Macmillan/British Sociological Association, 1974).

57 Peter Berger (with Thomas Luckmann), *The Social Construction of Reality* (Garden City: Doubleday, 1966).

58 R. Knox, *Enthusiasm: A Chapter in the History of Religion* (Oxford: Clarendon Press, 1950).

59 See D. Benner, *Encyclopedia of Psychology* (Grand Rapids, Michigan: Baker House, 1985), p. 9; I. Cotton, *The Hallelujah Revolution: The Rise of the New Christians* (London: Little, Brown & Co, 1995), pp. 114ff.

60 My observation of hypnotists like Geno Washington suggests that phenomena like speaking in tongues and religious experience can be induced through any medium that delivers an altered state of consciousness.

61 See M. P. Nichols and M. Zax, *Catharsis in Psychotherapy* (New York: Gardner Press, 1977).

62 See W. James, *The Varieties of Religious Experience* (1902) (Garden City, New York: Image Books, 1978): 'Incursions from the transmarginal have a peculiar power to increase convictions' (p. 372). See also E. Bourguinon, *Possession* (San Francisco: Chandler & Sharp, 1978); A. Aylland, 'Possession in a Revivalistic Negro Church', *Journal for the Scientific Study of Religion* (1962), 1, pp. 204–13.

63 See W. Samarin, 'Glossolalia as Learned Behaviour', *Canadian Journal of Theology* (1969), 15, pp. 60ff.

64 See the account of Barton Stone's 1847 autobiography in *Christian History*, vol. XIV, no. 1 (1995), p. 15.

65 Nowadays, the attribute of God focused on is power, with people tending to fall down after preaching, and during ministry, and resting on their backs. In the eighteenth and nineteenth cenutures, the attribute of God mostly focused on was holiness, with falling occuring during preaching, believers resting face down.

66 *Christian History*, vol. XIV, p. 2.

67 R. Stark and W. Bainbridge, *A Theory of Religion* (New York: Peter Lang/Toronto Studies in Religion, 1987), pp. 33ff.
68 *Ibid.*, p. 304.
69 *Ibid.*, pp. 122ff. A high tension/low-reward sect would have a poor relationship with the world, low recruitment, and also offer few compensators for belonging. A church, according to Stark and Bainbridge, is low-tension and low-reward – schisms that are variants of mainstream religion therefore often present the most attractive formula for some. Some high-tension religious groups offer high rewards, but these tend to be communitarian or cultic.
70 *Ibid.*, p. 273.

# 7

# Bureaucratic ideology in established religion

One of the oldest jokes about the Church of England goes like this. 'How many Anglicans does it take to change a light-bulb?' 'Five – one to put in the new one and four to admire the old one'. Typically, the joke is used to lampoon almost any institution beholden to its past and is almost infinitely adaptable. For Anglicans, however, there is an irony in the quip: admiration of the past is an important and necessary feature of their ecclesiology and theology. Without tradition, structure, history and liturgy, the Church of England would not be. Its rootedness in the past is part of its fabric and value. Consequently, anything that transforms the past or dispenses with it is bound to raise questions about identity for the Church of England.

This is the main issue to be addressed in this chapter. It will be an examination of how the introduction of management techniques to the Church can be read as a 'polity of oppression'. The first part of the chapter addresses itself to a critique of the Turnbull Report, *Working As One Body*,[1] which is designed to reduce bureaucracy in the Anglican church and streamline it. The very existence of the report presupposes a bureaucracy that needs dismantling, in much the same way that Margaret Thatcher's government once attacked public services and turned them into private industries. Efficiency for the common good is the aim of the agenda, but its actual goals remain unclear. The second part begins to tease out some of the political problems in relation to power that the Turnbull Report raises, and then explicates some alternative visions. The relationship between ecclesial government and secular sociality is often one of tension. The recent Roman Catholic report, *The Common Good*,[2] spoke up for the minimum wage, trade unions and equal opportunities. The Catholic Church was, in effect, offering a Christian blueprint for a fair and just society. Yet its own internal machinations are far from perfect in this respect. Its priests are poorly paid and treated like serfs by bishops; the laity often have fewer rights than a servant. What the Catholic church prescribes for a liberal democracy does not seem to carry forward into its own self. This is because it sees itself as a theocracy, in which individual rights are necessarily subjugated to the common good that is defined and controlled by prelates. As we shall see later, the way the Church governs itself has implications for its witness to society. The way it holds power and disposes of it offers a model for others. Attention to power within ecclesiology is therefore vital.[3]

*Working as One Body* is the outcome of the Archbishops' Commission on the organization of the Church of England. The Commission was headed by Michael Turnbull, Bishop of Durham, and is intended to offer a blueprint for ordering the governing and consultative bodies of the Church of England. The Report is, in its own words, 'a more comprehensive review of the national institutions of the Church than has ever before been undertaken ... if implemented, it would radically change the ways in which the Church of England operates ... [redefining] Episcopal leadership and synodical governance'. The Report comes in twelve chapters, the first three of which outline the main theological basis for advocating change. The remaining nine chapters cover areas such as finance, restructuring the Church and the task of Episcopal leadership.

The proposals include swallowing up a variety of long-established committees that have very particular social and ecclesial tasks (e.g. the boards of social responsibility, education, etc.), and streamlining their breadth and diversity under one Board of Mission, presided over by one Chairman.[4] The Chairman would be a member of a new National Council which would consist of some bishops and leading managers from business and government.[5] The Report was noted by the General Synod in November 1995, and was due to be debated and promulgated in 1996, although further progress continues to be delayed. There is even a rationale for the haste and speed with which it might be adopted ('A time for swift action', pp. 44ff.), and some directive suggestions as to how it might be appropriated: 'Most of the changes outlined ... are essential to an integrated package of reform ... we do not believe they could be implemented piecemeal ... they are urgent, and [failure to assent to them] will damage staff morale' (p. 43). At present, it does not look as though the people and parishes of the Church of England will get much (if any) opportunity to debate the Report. Understandably, there is some concern about this in Synod and beyond.

## A Brief Critique

So, what are the principal problems with a report like this? There are a number of preliminary observations to be made. Any restructuring proposed by such a report may potentially pave the way for undermining existing bodies such as the Anglican Consultative Council. Traditionally, this body 'true to the Anglican Communion's style of working . . . has no legislative powers'.[6] The concentration of power in a National Council, suggested by the Report, makes the task of liaison and consulting more difficult, since the National Council is largely accountable to no one but itself. Some people may be puzzled as to why concentrating more power in the hands of the bishops is seen as a peculiarly English-Anglican problem. Yet it is prudent to remember that the methods for selecting bishops are unique in England; the processes are not as democratic in the way that other parts of the Anglican communion experience them.[7] Furthermore, enhanced episcopal power in England necessarily magnifies the profile of the Archbishop of Canterbury. One of the dangers the Report leans towards is imposing the Archbishop of Canterbury as the *de facto* head of the Anglican Communion, imitating a form of papal leadership and its consequent authority structures. At present, members of the Anglican Church world-wide are in communion with Canterbury: authority and power are shared and equivocal, and locally based. *Working as One Body* may turn out to be the first step towards ruling an international church, not just a national one. Indeed, I am tempted to say that the genesis of the report appears to arise out of the Archbishop's correct perception that he does not in fact have very much authority and power: the role is that of a convenor and co-ordinator, not an executive chairperson. It may well be his wish to change this, which presumably accounts for all the rhetoric about leadership, authority and management. These are all serious allegations, yet they pale into insignificance when one begins to appreciate the deeper impulses that drive the Report. There are three main areas of concern.

First, the way ecclesial power is handled as the basis for the Report is at serious fault. The members of the Commission were almost entirely male and bourgeois; so too, is to be the proposed National Council (pp. 118ff.). This is socially unjust, and quite startling when one considers the good work of reports such as *Faith in the City*, and their efforts to consult with a wide cross-section of society.[8] As such, *Working as One Body* is not reflective of society, and signals a retreat from the Anglican faith in comprehensiveness and its capacity to reflect the diversity of God's people, and for those same people to reflect God and so help society transcend itself. *Working as One Body* also proposes the concentration of ecclesial

123

power in the hands of the bishops (or just a few of them?) and a small bourgeois power elite (pp. 47ff.). Whilst this might make the Church sharper it may also make it narrower, since the guiding philosophy seems to be 'let the managers manage'. There is an irony here for Anglicans: it is not quite congregational enough in its polity to 'let the people manage the people', because it is an episcopal church. At the same time however, it is not episcopal enough to devolve power to just a few: the *via media* rules. Generally, Anglicanism may be said to have an endemically compromising ecclesial habit. The intention of this is not to be woolly; rather, it places a liberal hermeneutic (following Ricoeur, one that is constructive or one of restoration – not one of suspicion[9]) at the centre of its ecclesial polity, which is monitored by an inclusive heart. Thus, one of the major problems for *Working as One Body* is that it posits power in the hands of an elite class: the thinkers, or those with certain kinds of managerial skills. This has been successfully argued against by a number of Anglican theologians as being contrary to the true Anglican ethos, besides being an abuse of power.[10]

Second, the vision for episcopacy can be said, in some sense, to be distorted. *Working as One Body* is littered with phrases such as 'the Bishop-in-Synod', 'leadership' and 'authority'. There are serious problems with the way the episcopate is treated here. For example, by using Hooker in a selective manner, *Working as One Body* conflates bishop with the (biblical) metaphor head of the body, which is Christ. But Hooker uses head mainly to describe the supreme Governor of the Church of England (namely the King or Queen), which he then deliberately conflates with Christ.[11] Students of late sixteenth- and seventeenth-century history will recall that the monarchs enjoyed the privilege of governing by 'divine right' and over-ruling an elected and representative Parliament when they saw fit, which partly led to the English Revolution of the 1640s. The Report's use of head could lead to a form of divine right being established in the contemporary episcopate in a similar way to the Stuart monarchs. This may not be the intention of *Working as One Body*, but it is the likely result. In terms of ecclesiology, one would begin to see a kind of papal authority being invested in the Archbishop of Canterbury, and the authority of the Curia being invested in the National Council. We should also note here that Hooker took a more subtle view of the power of monarchs, and to some extent, felt that their power over the people was a consensual matter, not a divine prerogative.

Related to this second point, and underlining the basic theological and ecclesiological concerns, there are some general sociological questions about the proposed nature of the new ecclesial polity. Sociologically speaking, and following writers such as Weber and Sohm, it does seem that *Working as One Body* might unintentionally invest too much in the *charism* of the individual bishop. Concentrating power in the hands of a few requires a degree of charisma if the power is to be held responsibly (or authoritatively) and shared dynamically. If this does not happen, severe routinization of charisma and over-management of people and resources can lead to fissure. Or it can render the ecclesial community permanently cautious and conservative. In spite of the Report's use of Hooker (pp. 64ff.), I suspect his vision of bishops in relation to synodical government is one of mutuality and dispersed power that is held in trust by the laity and the threefold order of priests, deacons and bishops. It is doubtful if Hooker could assent to *Working as One Body* as it stands.[12]

Third, there are some wider ecclesial perspectives that need deeper consideration. Almost since its inception, Anglicanism has worked with a quadrilateral pattern in its moral reasoning and for arriving at provisional theological truth claims.[13] The fourfold relationship between scripture, tradition, reason and experience (or culture) is sacred to the ecology of Anglican identity. *Working as One Body* would disturb the delicate balance of this ecology by adding a fifth dimension – namely enhanced episcopal authority – or it would place the bishops over the quadrilateral as its presiders. Ironically, either of these positions could allow the Church to become hostage to congregational or ultra-Catholic forces. It is a path that potentially leads to a capitulation to conservatism. (There is already some evidence of this in the bishops' treatment of *Something to Celebrate*, which was deemed to be too liberal in its theological values and too accommodating of contemporary cultural norms.)[14]

Added to this, and following Hooker, primacy must be mutual and consensual. The erosion of clergy and laity rights implicit in *Working as One Body* – bishops or council as head, the rest the subservient body – transforms the Church of England into an Episcopalian denomination. If you like, the Church of England now becomes a church *in* England. If this vision becomes reality, English Anglicans risk marginalization and the loss of their often unarticulated socio-ecclesial horizons. More serious however, is what the combination of marginalization under the governance of a small power elite might bring. Schism is certainly one option, over a range of theological, moral or personal issues, which in turn could lead to the break-up of the National Church Service (p. 105).[15]

One of the issues that the report seems to miss is Hooker's broader vision of the 'body of Christ', which extended beyond the gathered congregation. The 'commonwealth model' was his preferred mode of socially describing the mystical nature of the Church.[16] *Working as One Body* works with a limited notion of body, and a distorted notion of how the parts of the body or commonwealth relate to each other. Who defines the head, and in what sense is that part of the body superior to the others? Can the commonwealth be presided over by the weak and powerless, with the bishops as nominal heads, mirroring the British Commonwealth? Thus, there is an inversion of Paul's vision in 1 Corinthians 12 in the Report as a whole, which is very curious, given its title. It is essential to remember that Hooker and Paul agree on the need for the body of Christ to be a *body of power*, not a passive association that only receives its power from or through the head: that is no kind of body. Indeed, we can go further here and ask why body and head occur as the choice metaphors to describe the Church in the Report? There are many other images and metaphors in the New Testament to choose from (bride, vine, etc.). The notion of a body always invites deferment to a head in contemporary thinking, since we are used to imagining our personal centre as somehow being cognitive – in the mind. Thus, a hegemony naturally arises when this image is overplayed or used exclusively: perhaps other metaphors might counteract this?

Another issue that the Report appears to miss is that management and efficiency are not at the heart of leadership as portrayed in the New Testament. Instead, service and sacrifice are presented as models, mirroring the *kenosis* of Christ on the Cross (Philippians 2:5ff.). The head or manager of the early disciples was the one who, according to the fourth evangelist, took a towel and washed his disciples' feet (John 13:1–11). The Son of Man who came to serve (*diakonesai*, Mark 10:45) is the one who calls Christians to do likewise. In terms of leadership and a hegemony of power, Jesus rebukes his disciples thus: 'it shall not be so amongst you' (Mark 10:43). What, in effect, seems to be the problem here is the use of biblical language and metaphors, yet in contexts and with meanings which have been detached from those in the New Testament's own self-understanding. Bishop, body, head, power and authority are indeed all words that occur in the New Testament, yet mostly in the context of service and suffering. Not so in the Report, where the words have been linked with management and efficiency.

In short, *Working as One Body* attempts to offer a mechanistic blueprint – 'the rationalization of congregational process and the animation of social will to achieve results' that lacks a symbolic, organic or contextual vision.[17] The first three chapters do not actually inform the Report, and in spite of their periodic genuflection to a symbolic and organic blueprint, they are surpassingly weak in their ecclesiology. The irony of *Working as One Body* is that its bold vision necessitates a restriction of ecclesial horizons in the interests of concentrating and managing resources. The Report is right to deconstruct the history of Synod (pp. 61ff.), and question the working arrangements for boards, dioceses and deaneries; but the basis of the document still feels aggressively dialectical, failing to comprehend the mystical, dispersed nature of Christ's body on earth. Thus, although a rationalizing document, it is not a document of faith: this is no *Lumen*

*Gentium*, but a bourgeois-management-led bid for the centralization and control of power. In effect, we are looking at a document that is pure ideology, with a theological gloss.[18] And like all ideologies, some will be liberated by it, but many will be oppressed. The report suffers by beginning with a capitalist-managerial ideology, and then attempting to fund that theologically. The consequence of this is that the ecclesiology looks thin, even alienating. The defence of a *nouveau* hegemony amounts to the creation of a *kyriearchy*, in which feudal lords, their leadership uncritically mapped and projected on to biblical concepts such as Head, with the serfs as the Body, will rule and dominate in the name of the Lord. This will be done through a crude rationalizing, efficiency-based and capitalist ideological dogma that oppresses the weak, powerless and (allegedly) inefficient, but rewards the loyal. Laity, parish clergy and those who are beyond the body but who are served by it ought to be deeply concerned about the implications of the Report if it is implemented.[19]

In *Working as One Body*, we are possibly witnessing the first steps in disestablishment, the actual break-up of the National Church Service, and a collapse into systems of ecclesial management that borrow their ethos from a culture of privatization, local (and often non-accountable) trusts and a small, supreme central authority that can govern at whim or will.[20] Indeed, the Report actually proposes a regionalizing scheme (p. 105) which implies a twin strategy of decentering the people's power on the one hand, whilst at the same time consolidating central and ultimate power in the hands of a few. Politically, this model has already been imposed on local government, the health service, and education, but it is a debatable point as to who gains from these reforms.[21] The report is justly concerned about financial costs and managerial effectiveness; but the counter-costs in terms of ethos should also be weighed – more may be lost than gained. If there is to be a new kind of head, the price should be fully costed in terms of human resources, not just financial expediency.

I have described the report as a mechanistic blueprint because its focus is programme effectiveness. James Hopewell, in his excellent analysis of different types of ecclesiology based on structural critiques of narrative, points out that mechanistic approaches to the Church occur when contextual visions are lost.[22] Typically, a contextual ecclesiology is concerned with how it relates to its environs. It sees the Church and world as a woven fabric that shares a variety of strands, yet also has an obligation to somehow stand apart from society, yet not in a way that removes it from its deep and implicit social inter-connections. Closely allied to this vision is the organic perspective, which is also concerned with 'style, grace and social cohesion'. Hopewell notes that these liberal-incarnate visions have given way to mechanistic and image-led (symbolic) ecclesiological blueprints. This is partly due to the specialization and particularity encouraged by postmodernism, but also because many religious responses to pluralism and secularization are in fact quite pragmatic. (Indeed, as we have already noted, few are genuinely theological; most are ideological, with theology added for legitimization.) Of course, it is necessary to consecrate this pragmatism so the Church can adopt it, but this often amounts to little more than the sacralization of marketing, management and communicative techniques. Critically, the supporting philosophy of the agency or tool being used is left unaddressed.

In spite of these major reservations, it is important to stress that there is a need for some reform. The governance of the Church of England is far from perfect, and some sort of rationalizing is certainly required: the question is, what kind? There have been some signs recently that other critics of *Working as One Body* are hoping to adapt and improve the report. Chairs of Diocesan houses have been meeting regularly, and have registered concerns about 'a stampede towards legislation', and asked for space to consider the 'roots of our discomfort'.[23] Hugh Dickinson has raised questions about the vision for episcopacy in the Report and the underlying models of leadership. Oswald Clark has pointed to the tensions that might emerge in an episcopally 'over-egged' National Council.[24] The *Framework for Legislation* [25] has attempted to deal with some of their objections and some of mine, but substantial problems about faith and vision remain.[26] What model of management is being proposed, and what are its underlying political and social assumptions? How can one be sure that a heavy hegemony will not develop, driven by a mechanistic (even capitalist) vision of individuals and the Church? If sharpness and efficiency are the desiderata of the Report, what will be lost in achieving that goal? How is the Report a document that inspires faith? In what sense is the ecclesiological vision faithful to Anglican tradition, true to the Gospel, true to boldly leading society? A number of considerations arise at this point, and they are worth considering in the light of my earlier remarks.

## Some Alternative Visions

First, it is vital that the Church consider the advantages and disadvantages of restructuring. Whilst restructuring may be necessary, swallowing the current organizational assumptions that are present in society may be unhelpful. Taking the 'Turnbull tablet' will not actually get the Church of England 'sorted', let alone 'high': the remedy is not the curative it seems, since the underlying symptoms and side-effects the Report presents are left unaddressed. For example, the Church of England has experienced a recent shift in transforming its sense of mission from something relatively benign into something far more proactive. What was once an ecclesial habit is now the focus of a decade. There are some advantages in this, yet in defining itself more sharply as a body, to cope with plurality and postmodern culture, it has created a gap between itself and society. The function of this is to maintain distinctiveness, but it also risks alienation: social or established religion can quickly move from being public religion to being private belief.[27] Correspondingly, the Church loses its sense of being a national service in exchange for a body that offers service, but as an option alongside other things or products. This is not a new situation at the end of modernity and the advent of postmodernity. Sociologists of religion such as Peter Berger and Thomas Luckmann have been describing and analysing 'the privatization of religion' for over thirty years. Berger, in particular, is alive to the 'demonopolization' that is occurring: the pluralistic situation creates a market situation in which religions compete. Thus, 'the religious tradition which previously could be authoritatively imposed, now has to be marketed – "sold" to a clientele that is no longer constrained to "buy".'[28] The modernist response to this is ecumenicity – reducing competing units through amalgamation and cutting resources, dividing up the market between the larger units that remain, and engaging in a form of ecclesial cartelization.[29] This can have definite benefits for the institution concerned, not least because the organization itself benefits from the impetus of a sharper identity; ironically, the adjustments made, even if they are a scaling-down, convey a sense of relevance to the group. However, it probably has as much to do with a loss of nerve and identity as it has to do with a desire to reform. Frequently, many people resent the shift, because they detect the distance that has been created between themselves and what was once their church, their health service or their public utility. This is what Sara Maitland describes as 'the Church of England plc . . . stress the 'l' for limited'.[30] It is the logical end of all mechanistic blueprints.

Second, it follows that the perceptions of its employees might also change. *Working as One Body*, because it lacks an organic dimension to its interpretation of embodiment, effectively creates the machinery in which decisions and people are processed in the interests of efficiency. The lack of humane, alternative-symbolic and mystical visions of the Church plays into the hands of capitalist philosophies and rhetoric that have done so much to dehumanize our society.[31] In terms of mission, phrases such as audit, action-plan, effectiveness (again!), strategy, target and accountability riddle discussions about evangelism. The assumption is that the Church of England is engaged in some sort of evangelistic accountancy, always looking to numbers, being geared up to be sent out to the world, as though it wasn't there already. Yet Anglicans are not primarily called to be re-located as a church (even if they do feel profoundly dis-located), nor are they called to draw people away from society into an exclusive church. In England at least, and certainly in the Church of England, Anglicanism affirms that all belong to the body unless they choose not to do so. Christians are baptized to be different, but to stay where they are: it is not that the Church has something to offer, but simply that it is the offering church. The price to pay for this is a profound lack of definition, a blurring of boundaries between Church and world, which risks losing the public attention as much as it has rights in gaining it. This may seem a tangential point in respect of the Report, but it is actually quite central. The 'body' of *Working as One Body* assumes a cultural and moral gap between the established Church and the world. By definition, an established church has no right to create or assume such a gap; rather, it is constantly attempting to obviate it, knitting together heaven and earth, the sacred and the profane. The impoverished notion of mission that underlies the Report provides a mirror to some of the other underlying assumptions that are uncritically inculcated. Sharper definitions may raise profiles and rationalize the ecclesial processes. Yet the same strategy also risks marginalization by society, alienating constituents and sounding a general retreat from a comprehensive service.

Further dangers lie in wait at exactly this point. A smaller service is more easily dominated by a single group of people, or single rationale or agenda. It is interesting to note that the notion of the location of 'governing power' seems to have shifted from theologians to bishops, and then finally to the National Council. 'Governing power' it seems, lies wherever the main theological resourcing for the Church of England is coming from. Of course, this radically robs the *plebs Dei* of their right to power, since power is constantly concentrated, never dispersed. As we noted earlier, this is faithful neither to Hooker nor scripture: the body is to be a body of real power, not the main agent of the head.[32] This is so for good theological reasons: the incarnation of Christ, like the Church, is primarily a risk of embodiment and a negation of power – it only acquires its authority through that action. Any attempt to concentrate or conflate power in the agency (e.g. head) inevitably marginalizes Christ and society, leading to a form of introspective congregationalism.[33] Recognizing that the body has power leads to an appropriate directional plurality for the Church and the realization that the dispersed nature of the Church's power is only really focused in the dynamic and economic Trinity.[34] In other words, development comes in mutual and open relationships that empower by gift, sacrifice, trust, service and otherness. The Turnbull Report seems to have lost the Anglican vision for directional plurality which almost defines the Church of England, and replaced it with a form of managerial sharpness – backed by the usual theological discourses – that exorcizes power, authority and leadership from the *plebs Dei* and into the hands of a few. A good analogy would be this. After years of faithful service, I take my trusted Morris Minor into the garage for its annual MOT. Alas, I am told the repairs and restoration needed to maintain the vehicle now outweigh its value, and the garage owner then attempts to sell me a motor scooter in its place. 'It's cheaper to run', he says, 'and you won't be bothered by giving other people lifts any more.' That is the issue: to renew and restore, or to replace? And what do you lose by choosing the latter?

Third, and in response to the two points above, it therefore follows that there needs to be some evaluation about how the Church might turn this agenda around: how does religion make society, instead of simply copying it? Scholars such as Charles Davis have attempted to sustain the contextual and organic approaches of 'political theology' in the 1960s which have now largely fallen into disfavour.[35] Davis is suspicious of the postmodern exaltation of the local, defined and different: he sees this as anti-universalist, and therefore a retreat from truth. In place of this he proposes a universalism of love (socialism or sociality as a moral and religious ideal) as the rationale for the Church in relation to society – loving reasoning in praxis. Perhaps the best way to illustrate the implications of this for *Working as One Body* is to highlight the basic differences between a shareholding and a stakeholding society.[36] The shareholding society, as many will now be aware, has proved to be profoundly disappointing: it has failed to deliver on its promise to give people a say in their public utilities and a share for all in its success. People know that after the launch or sell-off, the new uniforms, corporate logos[37] and first dividends, comes streamlining: redundancies; suddenly no longer being able to supply all the public but only those who can pay; and massively concentrated power, with salaries to match in the hands of a very few, quickly follow. The rationalizing process turns what was once a possibly weak, but at least definitively comprehensive service, into a business.[38] By contrast, a stakeholding society follows the lead of Davis and others, by giving everyone a stake in the economy, not just those with capital, expertise or advantage. Significantly, employees have a say in what their organization stands for; there is order and mutuality, with power deliberately dispersed. Perhaps the difference between the two can be seen in terms of employment. Shareholders believe in contracts and short-termism, which are governed by results. Stakeholders are orientated by the more biblical concept of covenant, in which results only play a part in configuring the bonds of commitment.[39] Here, as has been noted before, *Working as One Body* fails to be inclusive and progressive: the wider sense of participation and belonging which the Church should bring is dominated by the managerial class. A stakeholding society does not place effectiveness before people, treating them as resources, products or units. It recognizes that institutions often exist for the wider good of all society, not just itself. In short, the Church works for one body (society), but it is not necessarily the case that it works as one identifiable homogeneous unit. An incarnate, ambiguous and susceptible body that risks failure may be able to serve society far better than a clearly defined community that is rationalized, strong and sharp.[40]

I should add a discursive note here. The absence of the feel-good factor for the last Conservative government – in spite of low interest rates and falling unemployment – had to do with the issue of security in relation to work and human valuing. Society is now seeing a profound shift away from the rationality, 'management-speak' and materialism that dominated the 1980s. The free market traded the covenant for the contract in the interests of greater wealth and efficiency, but in so doing lost graces such as trust, good-will and loyalty that are implicit in covenants, but largely absent in contracts (except as a thing to be rewarded). Many workers, as individuals, soon discovered that they were now mainly valued as units within a process of production or consumption: work and worth were subordinate to profit and a certain kind of rationality. Furthermore, contracts tended to become more short-term, in the interests of competition or in response to the economy, which further undermined trust and security at every level, thus fostering individualism, and perhaps even selfishness. Often, the stress of this new rationale was borne personally by workers and their families. Divorce rates increased as the promise of the economy went wrong: 'when poverty comes in through the front door, love leaves by the back door'.

The Church of England has not been immune to this shift, with the gradual erosion of clerical freeholds in favour of contractual arrangements, usually with bishops. In terms of social bonding, the results are only just beginning to emerge. Long-term loyalty to a company (or church) no longer guarantees value in the workplace, so workers can consequently experience profound loss of motivation and self-worth. The (allegedly) inefficient are marginalized or unemployed, whilst the managers gain greater power and wealth, provided they perform. (This is not yet true for bishops, of course, who unlike many of their clergy, are always consecrated into a secure job instead of being ordained into a short-term contract.) Thus, individualism rises directly in proportion to organic deconstruction. This is famously encapsulated in Mrs Thatcher's remark that 'there is no such thing as society', it being just the sum of its individuals – a phrase that emerged in an interview with *Woman's Own* magazine in 1987.[41] A parallel proclamation would be 'there are no buildings, only bricks'. The discursive point being made here is about belonging and valuing: people, like bricks, are made for togetherness, mutual support and interdependence. When this is deconstructed by an over-emphasis on management or efficiency, the individual components lose their power, and sense of purpose, order and belonging. At this point, management either becomes exploitative or totalitarian, or then again, can simply fail to manage meaningfully over a fearful and disenfranchised workforce. The public also tends to demand much more from any organization claiming to prioritize efficiency, as many privatized public utilities will testify. In turn, this often further undermines an under-resourced workforce that cannot cope with the new demands. The workers are effectively caught in a pincer movement: experiencing over-demand from public and management alike, yet without enjoying security of tenure due to the short-term nature of the contract, since it is linked to their performance. An over-rationalized workforce will always struggle with issues of security and value. In turn, this can make employees resentful and cautious. The final end is ironic, since true individualism is ultimately quashed in the whole process, since nobody risks stepping out of line. An ideology of individualism leads to a culture of conservatism.

Next, an ecclesiological vision of the Church which fails to take seriously the Pauline model of Christian leadership at the very least runs the risk of failing to hear the Gospel. Paul had his moments of authoritarianism and bullying,[42] but also knew that secular notions of power and authority simply embodied what we might call 'the management-speak' of his day. The scandal of the cross meant that human actions and institutions were to be remodelled and even perhaps made independent of human skill and advantageous attributes. A true mediation of Christ's resurrection power in Christian ministry could only be by an inculcation of Christ's obedience, weakness, suffering and humility. The point the report misses is that it is not the structure which matters, but the extent to which ecclesial leadership models and mediates the scandal of the cross, and then adopts the pattern of Christ's own ministry.

Finally, and related to the point above, the Church needs to live as a fully transcendent and fully engaged social ethic, not just function as a unit that has such an ethic. If the call of the Church is partly about being possessed by the truth rather than assuming that it possesses it to hand on, this raises real questions over which managerial vision owns *Working as One Body*. George Ritzer invites us to reflect on the franchising processes in society that are turning individualized bodies into homogenized corporations on a par with beefburger chains. The complaint, as before, is that the 'market-driven economy' with its accompanying managerial strategy is profoundly dehumanizing. I am not suggesting that the Turnbull Report will turn the Church of England into a sort of 'God-U-Like' franchise. Yet the erosion of individuality and rights that its implementation could lead to is disturbing.[43] Here we face an irony. On the one hand, hoping for a form of corporateness in the Church, and on the other hand, arguing against the vision outlined in *Working as One*

*Body*. The difference between the Turnbull Report and myself lies in concepts of service, notions of 'body' and how difference and weakness are to be valued. In other words, what I have earlier termed the necessary 'directional plurality' of Anglicanism. If the Church lives as social ethic, some of our greatest evangelists and leaders will not be managers, but made of the same material that formed the group around Jesus known as 'the disciples'. They will be workers, labourers, those used to being the voiceless, or those disempowered by society. If the Church believes itself to be one body, it will use all its members in assisting in the task of self-definition under the power of the Holy Spirit, not just those it is accustomed to using as consultants.[44]

Richard Hooker picks up some of these themes of equivocal relations in his own writings. 'The Church of Christ is a bodie mysticall. A bodie cannot stand, unless the parts therof be *proportionable.*' Equally, it must also recognize that the conduct of its affairs is submitted 'unto the general triall and judgement of the whole *world*',[45] not just the Church. The dilemma the Turnbull Report faces is this: does it give us a model for the Church (a community of faith that is a conscious reflection and critique of society) that is appropriately Christian? Or does it rather assume too much about what any structural body in our contemporary culture might look like? After all, the body of Christ only really exists when gathered around the eucharist and animated by the Spirit. Beyond that activity, it ceases to be a programme or a real society in itself. The Church is the body of Christ only by the gift of the Holy Spirit: that Spirit is clearly not under our control. Therefore, any attempt to seriously rationalize the congregational process risks domesticating (and to some extent privatizing) God. My guess is that this kind of vision for society, although clearly endemic at the moment, is beginning to wane as people look for more hopeful, profound and transcendent forms of living. *Working as One Body*, if it is to be implemented at all, must be quite self-conscious about the type of society it is proposing, not just its model for the Church. The Church that marries the spirit of the age always risks rejection or divorce in the next.[46]

## Summary

Some final points. *Working as One Body* is struggling with at least two possible futures for the Church of England in a time of pluralism, postmodernity and financial constraint. It is beginning to own its place as the institution that represents the God whom many believe in yet they choose not to belong to it. Consequently, Christianity retains its dominant social profile, whilst at the same time losing its depth and breadth of articulation.[47] One response to this is to retreat and consolidate into an associational pattern, where questions of effectiveness constantly arise. As I have already said, the problem with this vision is that it assumes a gap between the Church and England that is not necessarily there. Another response is to rehabilitate the communal vision that is both parochial and universal rather than congregational, and is deeply concerned about the context of religion as much as its content. This would be expensive and time-consuming, but may have the advantage of being more expansive in the long-run. For example, at a time when there is considerable tension and competition between European government, Parliament and local government, any established church is quite well placed to facilitate the (re-)building of communities by acting as mediator, agent or initiator. If the Church took seriously its obligation to address all needs, it might find that its body was not so small, and that its boundaries were not so obvious. Furthermore, that it was needed by society, because it offers a hopeful vision of community in a competitive and fragmented world, as the social form of the Truth.[48] The Poet R. S. Thomas puts this much better than any theologian can:

> It's a long way off but inside it
> There are quite different things going on:
> Festivals at which the poor man
> Is king and the consumptive is
> Healed; mirrors in which the blind look
> At themselves and love looks at them
> Back; and industry is for mending
> The bent bones and minds fractured
> By life. It's a long way off, but to get
> There takes no time and admission
> Is free . . .[49]

What is ultimately so unsatisfactory about *Working as One Body* is that the approach it takes to itself, to the body of Christ, and to individuals, amounts to little more than 'consecrated pragmatism'. I say consecrated, because the Report is an episcopally driven agenda: more and more power is slowly but surely being concentrated in the office of bishop. A shapely pyramid of power is developing, and it is clear what sits atop. Paradoxically, perhaps, this impetus seems to be coming from the evangelical prelates, who allegedly have a high doctrine of the *plebs Dei* and the priesthood of all believers. Yet it is amongst this group of bishops that most anxiety and need for action is expressed about their own leadership and authority. Consequently, 'directional plurality' is slowly being lost to the forces of imposed unity: the age of the informal Anglican *imprimatur* has arrived. Thus, clergy or diocesan conferences are now becoming known as 'bishop's conferences'. In one diocese, budgeting for sabbaticals for clergy is minimal due to lack of funds. Yet instead of a properly structured system for allocating what time and funds there are, the bishop holds the power by 'rewarding initiatives' from clergy who approach him with interesting proposals for study. As for pragmatism, the term 'pragmatic' has a sliding scale of definitions. At its most basic, it simply means being 'skilled in affairs'; but at its more developed, it can mean 'interfering, meddling, opinionated, dictatorial and dogmatic'.[50]

The creation of a *kyriearchy*, backed by a theologically-resourced ideology, is a highly problematic development for the Church of England, and it represents, potentially, a defining moment in its identity. It could signal a retreat from being the Church for all to becoming an episcopal denomination that serves loyal and faithful members. (Those who are not and avail themselves of services such as occasional offices presumably become customers by default.) In an era of (postmodern) constitutional reform, this may be inevitable, but the Church ought at least to begin to ponder the costs and future implications of this. Furthermore, it ought to be arguing for a more profound view of society, individuals and the Church that begins with a theology and an appropriate sociality, and not some borrowed, transient ideology.[51] Ultimately, one cannot derive a satisfactory ecclesiology from a secular ideology, any more than one can conjure up a satisfactory doctrine of the Church from an emphasis on one branch of missiology. First and foremost, one would have to begin with God, not a managerial pragmatism painted over with a theological gloss.

What *Working as One Body* demonstrates is the desire to routinize, control and stabilize divine and human power in an age of uncertainty. Priests who dissent from prescribed morals or doctrine are more easily dealt with in a rationalized, efficiency-driven body. Targets, goals and aims suddenly replace the ambiguity of sacraments and the dangers of prophetic contemplation. The hazards ahead however, are all too obvious. Turnbull's church is profoundly safe – it doesn't rock the boat or question authority. It is comfortable, secure, down-sized and maximized, and it speaks with one voice. Therein lies its problem. For bureaucracy brings with it the suffocation of diversity, the emasculation of prophecy, and the dubious gift of a tightly controlled denominationalism to what was once a national church.

## Notes

1 *Working as One Body* (London: Church House Publishing, 1995).
2 *The Common Good: Report by the Roman Catholic Bishops of England and Wales* (London: CIO, 1996).

3 Or more specifically, conflation between the Godhead and the unchosen but ruling earthly agents. A marvellous example of this is featured in the principal stained glass window of the Chapel at Christ's College, Cambridge. It shows Christ presiding over the College (on a cloud), attended by Bishop Fisher and Lady Margaret. What is significant about the depiction is the clothing the characters are given. Christ is adorned in red and purple robes – the colours in art for monarchy and divinity. As his earthly representatives, Lady Margaret wears red (monarchy), with the Bishop dressed in purple, signifying divinity. The stained glass window seems to be saying that if you cannot see Christ for the cloud, you can always turn to his chosen instruments of government on earth.

4 I do mean 'Chairman' here. The Report lacks any finesse in the direction of political correctness.

5 However, one wonders quite how the Secretary of State for Education and Employment will respond to letters from the established Church headed 'Mission': is that really how the thousands of church schools in England primarily perceive themselves?

6 *The Church of England Yearbook* (London: Church House Publishing, 1995), p. 257.

7 Thus, the problem is twofold. First, the National Council does not appear to be that accountable to Synod. Second, the bishops sitting on it, as individuals, are not as accountable as they could be to their constituents, because they are not elected.

8 *Faith in the City: The Archbishop of Canterbury's Report on Inner City Areas* (London: Church House Publishing, 1985). One might say the same of *Faith in the Countryside*.

9 See P. Ricoeur, *Freud and Philosophy* (New Haven: Yale University Press, 1970), p. 27.

10 See for example R. Roberts, 'Lord, Bondsman and Churchman: Power, Integrity and Identity' in *On Being the Church: Essays on the Christian Community*, ed. D. Hardy and C. Gunton (Edinburgh: T. & T. Clark, 1989).

11 See R. Hooker, *Of the Laws of Ecclesiastical Polity*, ed. A. McGrade (Cambridge: CUP, 1989), pp. 158–76.

12 See McGrade, *op. cit.*, pp. 201–7.

13 See *The Anglican Tradition*, ed. G. Evans and J. Wright (London: SPCK, 1991), pp. 343, 355, 387 and 450. Of course, the actual Quadrilateral is Scripture, Creeds, Sacraments and the Historic Ministry.

14 See *Something to Celebrate: Valuing Families in Church and Society* (London: Church House Publishing, 1995).

15 See my paper 'Falling Out of Love: Recent Anglican Schisms Compared', *The Journal of Contemporary Religion*, vol. 12, no. 1 (1997), pp. 35–50. See also *The Encyclopaedia of American Religion*, ed. J. G. Melton (Washington DC: Gale Publishing, 1994).

16 McGrade, *op. cit.*, pp. 129ff.

17 See J. Hopewell, *Congregation* (London: SCM, 1987), for a severe critique of mechanistic approaches to ecclesiology. A sharper sociological critique of the dynamic I am describing can be found in George Ritzer's *The McDonaldization of Society* (revised edition); (London: Sage Publishing, 1996).

18 For a discussion of the difference between an ideology with a theological gloss, as opposed to a proper, constructive theology, see my *Farmington Paper* (Oxford: Harris Manchester College, 1997), 'Is There a Modern Charismatic Theology?'.

19 For a discussion of *Kyriearchy*, see David Nicholls, *Deity and Domination: Images of God in the Nineteenth and Twentieth Centuries* (London: Routledge, 1989), p. 30. See

also Daniel Hardy, *God's Ways with the World: Thinking and Practising Christian Faith* (Edinburgh: T. & T. Clark, 1996), p. 184: 'the (distorted) *monarche* of God is transferred to states and individuals ... social structures (become) arbiters of social coherence ... by contrast, the complexity, pluralism and changeability of society are regarded as alien ... justice is seen as conformity.' In other words, ideology is dictating 'theology', blotting out appropriate diversity.

20 See my 'The Churchgoer's Charter', *Signs of the Times* (January 1993), pp. 5–8. Indeed, the Synod has been warned about the link between the Turnbull Report and 'disestablishment ... by stealth', Michael Alison, MP, *The Independent* (14/02/96), p. 6.

21 For a discussion of the ambiguities of privatizing utilities in the public domain, see Will Hutton, *The State We're In* (London: Vintage, 1995), pp. 217ff.

22 J. Hopewell, *Congregation: Stories and Structures* (London: SCM, 1987), pp. 19ff.

23 *Church Times*, (09/02/96), p. 3.

24 *Ibid.*, p. 12.

25 *General Synod Paper* (GS 1188) (February 1996).

26 Indeed, the assumption of General Synod Paper GS 1188 (Framework) is that the Turnbull Report will still be a controlling document. Noting that the lack of accountability was a problem in the original report, Alan McLintock, Chairman of the Board of Finance and member of the Turnbull Commission still says 'what we must go for is control and ordered change' (*Church Times*, 16/02/96).

27 The problem lies in the exaltation of the individual over the corporate as a 'market'. The most accessible discussion of this dynamic is Robert Bellah's (ed.) *Habits of the Heart: Individualism and Commitment in American Life* (Berkeley: University of California Press, 1985) (2nd edition, 1996). Following Alasdair McIntyre (*After Virtue*, London: Duckworth, 1981), Bellah makes helpful distinctions between expressive, ontological and utilitarian individualism, which each hold public religion to ransom for private gain in slightly different ways.

28 Peter Berger, *The Sacred Canopy* (Garden City: Doubleday, 1967), p. 138. In terms of the Church of England and mission, the most obvious area where this shift is located is in Baptismal policy. The rise of groups like MORIB – with their desire to restrict and delimit the availability of sacraments – implicitly embraces disestablishment and congregationalism.

29 Peter Berger, 'A Market Model for the Analysis of Ecumenicity', *Social Research*, vol. 30 (1963), p. 87.

30 S. Maitland, *A Big Enough God? Artful Theology* (London: Mowbray, 1995), p. 150. See also *Tomorrow is Another Country: Education in a Postmodern World* (London: Church House Publishing, 1996), pp. 58–9, for a distinction between 'Church of England and Son', 'Church of England plc' and 'Church of England Enterprises'. The Turnbull Report offers an ecclesial vision somewhere between those last two.

31 Cf. W. Hutton, *The State We're In* (London: Vintage, 1996). As Hutton notes, this often just compels employees to compete with each other rather than working together (pp. 27ff.): the rhetoric divides, then conquers.

32 Cf. J. Bowker, *Licensed Insanities: Religion and Belief in God in the Contemporary World* (London: DLT, 1987), p. 142. Bowker writes: 'The systematic nature of systems is undoubtedly open to abuse and exploitation. All too easily the system becomes the end in itself, instead of the means towards an end which lies beyond itself. The responsibility of all Christians, in any generation, is to transform – or allow God to transform through them – the dry bones of the system into a living presence which in turn touches, heals, restores, sustains many lives far beyond its own.'

33 See my *Words, Wonders and Power: Understanding Contemporary Christian Fundamentalism and Revivalism* (SPCK, 1996), p. 155: 'The creative way forward in solving the dilemma of identity is to ensure that all churches attend properly to their borders and margins. All too often churches live as though they are central to salvation, making Christ peripheral; the agent displaces the source at the centre of itself ... we are not called to be places of concentrated power, but to be open, incarnate communities that risk weakness, and even death.'

34 This directional plurality is, it seems, slowly being eroded in the episcopacy, as it adopts a monotheistic model of God rather than a Trinitarian one. The bishops seem to be obsessed with agreeing with each other on issues of contention, so as to present a united front to Church and society. Like contemporary British politics, this very activity is profoundly suffocating. Instead of being offered two or three tracks of truth, in which people can live, move and journey, the laity are all too frequently offered one episcopally-backed line to walk on. Debate and dialogue are freeing and progressive, encouraging participation. Monological unity feels imposed and restraining, and is alienating.

35 C. Davis, *Religion and the Making of Society: Essays in Social Theology* (Cambridge: CUP, 1994). The point is that an established sociality promotes differing opinion, whereas individualism ultimately becomes conformity.

36 For a fuller discussion, see W. Hutton, *The State We're In* (London: Vintage, 1996), Chapter 12.

37 At the time of writing, Lambeth Palace has just announced that it has acquired such a logo – a 'gift' to the church from a marketing company that was given at 'cost price'.

38 I am not suggesting that the report is an anti-service document *per se*. As Hopewell (*op. cit.*) notes, 'mechanists are not opposed to the intentions of service ... but they argue that unless basic structures are sound and dynamic, any sort of parish *goal* is in jeopardy ... the primary need of churches today is the rationalization of the congregational process and the animation of social will to achieve *results*' (p. 26 – italics mine).

39 See Robert Whelan, *The Corrosion of Charity: From Moral Renewal to Contract Culture* (London: Institute of Economic Affairs, 1996), and W. Hutton, *The State We're In* (London: Vintage, 1996), p. 282.

40 See my 'How to Win Congregations and Influence Them' in *Contours of Christian Education*, ed. J. Astley and D. Day (London: Mayhew-McCrimmon, 1992).

41 The seeds of this philosophy, incidentally, are outlined by her as early as 1975. See her address 'Let Me Give You My Vision', reprinted in *The Penguin Book of Twentieth-Century Speeches*, ed. B. MacArthur (London, 1992), pp. 402ff.

42 See, for example, G. Shaw, *The Cost of Authority* (Philadelphia: Fortress Press, 1982).

43 See also footnote 39. We should note that one of the earliest concerns of the present Archbishop of Canterbury was the removal of clergy freehold in exchange for job contracts. This policy was ostensibly driven by the desire to weed out (inefficient?) clergy who had been in one place too long and thus perhaps protect the interest of parishioners. The rhetoric to justify this was strangely resonant with Margaret Thatcher's demonizing of trade unions as 'barriers' to growth and efficiency. As we have seen, the assault on unions has led to chronic abuse of workers by employees: short-termism, part-time, low-wage jobs, with little recourse to justice. If clergy continue to lose freehold (covenant exchanged for contract), they also lose one of their very few power bases which allow them to retain a living whilst not necessarily getting on well with their bishop. Once again, concentration of power is an issue here.

44 See G. Ritzer, *The McDonaldization of Society* (London: Sage, 1996). On the Church as a body, see S. Hauerwas 'What Would it Mean for the Church to be Christ's Body? A Question Without a Clear Answer', SST paper (1992), and Anthony Dyson, 'The Body of Christ has AIDS' SST paper, also 1992.

45 R. Hooker, *Laws*, Book 1, pp. 23 and 58, Folger Library – emphasis in italics is mine.

46 Actually this is not strictly true. Churches are very adept at continually marrying the spirit of any age: the real issue is over what is lost and gained by such cultural liaisons.

47 See G. Davie, *Religion in Britain Since 1945: Believing Without Belonging* (Oxford: Clarendon, 1995).

48 Politically and spiritually, this is well-expressed in Christopher Bryant's *Possible Dreams: A Personal History of the British Christian Socialists* (London: Hodder & Stoughton, 1996). See also Donald Reeves, *Down to Earth: A New Vision for the Church* (London: Mowbray, 1996), Chapters 2a, 3 and 9.

49 R. S. Thomas, 'The Kingdom', *Later Poems* (London: Macmillan, 1983), p. 35.

50 *The Shorter Oxford English Dictionary on Historical Principles*, Vol 2. (Oxford: OUP, 1984), p. 1646.

51 We should note that David Nicholls (*Deity and Domination*, London: Routledge, 1989), shortly before his sad and untimely death, was alive to many of these issues. His own unpublished critique of *Working as One Body* was to have been humorously entitled *Turnbullshit* (*The Independent*, Obituary, 18 June, 1996, p. 14).

# 8

# Erotic ideology in experiential religion

Christian charismatic communities and churches are extremely diverse in their theology and ecclesiology. So any attempt to suggest a core ideology that might be generic for the movement would be rightly treated with some suspicion. Indeed, ideology itself has a career as a concept that is equally diverse, so one might be doubly cautious. However, in this chapter, I want to suggest that ideology expressed in and through contemporary charismatic renewal is in some ways configured around concepts that represent sublimated eroticism. In turn, this ideology – a grammar of assent, if you like – is a partial explanation for the actual religious experience that constitutes much of charismatic identity. The genesis of this thesis lies in the acceptance of Lefebvre's 'Logos–Eros dialectic' as a condition within modernity. The former is rational, cognitive and bureaucratic (as we saw in the previous chapter); the latter delivers space, and is the birthplace of needs and the sating of desires.[1] This is undoubtedly a contentious, even controversial thesis. Yet I will be attempting to show how worship, packed with images and analogies of intimacy, immediacy, power and eroticism, lead to the particular forms of embodiment and somatic experience that is particular to aspects of contemporary charismatic renewal.

Let me first briefly clarify how the term ideology might be understood to operate in this essay. David McLellan sees ideology as a product of pluralism, or rather as a reaction to it. Following Habermas, McLellan sees ideology emerging as a legitimization of powers that serves competing sectional interests in an increasingly fragmented world. As 'universal dogmas' disintegrate and traditional myths begin to lose their social currency, ideologies are born to replace them. Therefore, in a postmodern world, it is appropriate to speak of a pluriverse of ideologies that all convey different types of vision and argue for different forms of normal behaviour, even if that turns out to be 'alternative'.[2,3]

In speaking of an ideology, I mean a kind of 'social system'[4] that is regulative and transforming: it is a unity of language, science and ideas that provides a form of coherence. In this respect, it is close to Geertz who sees ideology as a 'cultural system',[5] and again close to McLellan who more systematically describes it as 'a system of signs and symbols in so far as they are implicated in an asymmetrical distribution of power and resources'.[6] The approach here will be to consider some of the forms of sublimated eroticism in charismatic communication that partially constitute its overall ideology. I have chosen to look at how charismatic authority is established in the 'latent' messages present in some forms of postmodern worship. This analysis will be mainly focused on material emanating from John Wimber's Vineyard Churches, the Toronto Blessing movement, and the like. (Wimber died in 1997, but the Vineyard Churches are still very much his.) They have been chosen because of their pre-eminent status in contemporary charismatic renewal: their songs have affected styles and concepts in worship that have touched virtually every denomination in every corner of the globe. Wimber, indeed, could even lay claim to being the 'founding father' of 'intimate worship' in a charismatic genre. Yet all the remarks have wider applicability. The substance of what we shall be assessing is the postmodern church, which in a strange way can evoke 'a state of pre-political, undifferentiated human affinity, which dissolves tensions and [binds] people together despite the differences between them in the non-ritual space and time'.[7] In such an environment, an appreciation of the place of power will ultimately be essential.

Given that many people who attend a Toronto Blessing meeting often report that as a result, 'they are more in love with Jesus', or 'more intimate with the Father', or 'have been touched by the Spirit', we are immediately presented with an analytical problem.[8] Just how do you measure and assess the presence (or sense of the presence) of God? Indeed, can it be shown that what one person claims is a moment of divine intervention does in fact have another, possibly better, explanation? Ideological analysis cannot provide a complete and alternative frame of reference for assessing such issues. What can be said, with some certainty at the outset of this essay, is that contemporary revivalism provides its adherents with a tactile experience of the presence of God, partially derived from the ascriptions to God that are present in the (ideological) worship.[9] I do realize that defining an erotic context is a highly subjective and potentially problematic exercise. Part of the problem here lies with a category such as 'eroticism'. Indeed, it lies with categories generally.[10] What contemporary culture understands by the terms 'sexual', 'erotic' or 'gender' are not universal frames of reference that can be applied to all times and in all places.

## Eroticism in Enthusiastic and Ecstatic Religions: Past and Present

The religion of ancient Greece was a legitimization of the dominant philosophical and social dualism that was prevalent in its time. Just as body and spirit were separated, so was the 'balanced, rational' from the 'intoxicated, irrational'. The god Apollo represented the rational, the cult of Dionysius the irrational. Dionysian religion, with its roots in the pre-Aryan devotion to Shiva, has always been linked to sexual performance: a horned god, with worship typified by music, dance, prophecy and ecstatic rites.[11] According to legend, Dionysiac religion induces a form of temporary 'madness': the ecstasy that Dionysius embodies is alien to normal, rational life. Those who 'catch' it are possessed by it; those who resist are threatened with extinction. As Walter Otto notes in his *Dionysius: Myth and Cult* (1933), Dionysius was the god who satisfied demands for immediacy with the divine, was received socially, in rapture and ecstasy, then responded to personally in 'insanity': he was 'the god of the most blessed ecstasy and the most enraptured love.' Other scholars of the cult point to the Dionysian capacity to induce abrogation of social and personal responsibility.[12] This was a god who allowed the worshipper, for a brief time, to 'let go and let God' – to actually stop being oneself for a moment. Sometimes known as Lusios (the Liberator), the function of this religion in modern-day psychological terminology was to provide processes for catharsis and abreaction.[13] These seem to have been achieved through certain rituals and a rich grammar of assent that stressed intimacy, abandon, ecstasy and sacralized eroticism.

Following Alain Danielou's work, it can be suggested that the actual techniques of this ecstatic inducement included certain musical rhythms and beats, a high level of sound, particularly bass, drums, dancing, an emphasis on immediacy and ecstasy, an interest in the erotic, and the creation of a sacred space in which the worshippers were immunized from the ordinary, namely the rational, mundane world. The worship created a sort of spiralling staircase to the god, in which the journey upwards was as exciting as the free-fall following the blissful encounter. Small wonder that Danielou calls these believers 'the delinquents of heaven'.[14]

Those who inhabit the world of contemporary Christian revivalism would naturally wish to claim that their religion is not of the same spirit, in spite of worship songs that encourage believers to imagine the kisses of Christ's mouth, a God who takes, comes and consumes, and believers who melt, and are moulded and pass out in ecstatic desire.[15] And then added to this, the ecstatic cries of revivalist gatherings, the body language of believers, and the social and theological stress on intimacy. Even so, many in revivalism would be appalled at the suggestion that their religion involved eroticism, sublimated or otherwise. The evangelical roots of revivalism ensure deep suspicion of anything that is sexual, or emotionally expressed in embodiment.

Yet recent writing has hinted at phenomenological and ideological similarities. For example, James Hopewell's insightful analysis of narrative in contemporary ecclesiologies, using the work of Northrop Frye, describes revivalism as being configured around the 'romantic genre'.[16] Hopewell notes that the language, stories and structures of contemporary revivalism stress adventure, immanence, providence and power. In short, an exciting religious narrative that rewards adventuring beyond convention, leading to a new kind of knowing of God and a higher level of (fluctuating) happiness. The grammar of assent here, is, to an extent, a grammar of possibility, created by the dualities present in the language. Thus, believers are empty, dry and hungry for God: the revivalist resolution is to offer a God who fills, waters and revives, and who satisfies desires.[17] Admitting the former beckons the latter. In terms of eroticism, Hopewell's notion of the romantic genre being synonymous with charismatic ideology stresses the *enthousiasmos* of the indwelling spirit, rather than the *ekstatis* of exteriority. Believers know what it is like to have the 'liquid love of God' poured through them: they gain 'power and love, joy and peace . . . there is more out there and we want more'.[18]

Harvey Cox gives historical and ideological support to the notion that contemporary revivalism, to an extent, depends on accepting the Appollonarian–Dionysian duality of ancient Greece. Cox suggests that one of the reasons for the growth of experiential religion is the exhaustion-point that has been reached between the over-rationalism of the debates between 'fundamentalists' and 'liberals'.[19] In saying this, Cox is arguing that revivalism may be, in fact, a kind of creed for the third millennium: cognitive religion has had its day – the future lies with feeling. Cox may be right here, but his thesis is, in places, chronically under-developed.[20] He fails to note that the stress on experience will also, necessarily, be a move towards the subjective. In turn, this will be a translation into individualism. This is not actually a surprising observation for scholars of enthusiastic or revivalist religion. Its very function, as Knox and others have noted, is to take people out of the world, creating a sacred-social space that is undeterred by routine, rationalization or the rapacious forces of relativism.[21] True, this happens to occur in group contexts; but the prize is usually a personal experience of knowing God, which can then be shared, magnified and reconstituted for benefits that are largely individualistic in orientation.

The supreme irony of this, which again Cox fails to note, is that the historical-cultural linkage between Pentecostalism and contemporary revivalism is not one of continuity, but dislocation. Pentecostalism was an experiential response to modernism – it produced a limited number of denominations and a relatively homogeneous identity that only later became racially divided. It was also born out of holiness and piety movements (Methodist in origin), and a cultural context that had experienced severe racial oppression. Contemporary revivalism, on the other hand, holds up a mirror to postmodern trends: it copies and competes with healing movements, the New Age, materialism, pluralism, and, as I shall suggest later, contemporary eroticism. It is a more avowedly therapeutic, personal, sectarian and ultimately individualistic religion than Pentecostalism. It is postmodern revivalism that has produced the most mood-enhancing, emotive kinds of worship of recent years, some of which could almost be described as 'smoochy'. Mark Noll has traced this same development in evangelical hymnography. Nineteenth-century hymns beseeching God's Spirit tended to lead to a deeper engagement with the world, taking the 'dimness' of the soul away. In contrast, the equivalent in contemporary revivalism see 'the things of the earth grow strangely dim, in the light of his glory and grace'. Here we have the echoes of Dionysian abrogation.[22]

That said, it is surely time to recall that Christian spirituality has a rich and indulgent history of erotic language in its ascription to God. A quote from the thirteenth century mystic Hadewijch will suffice:[23]

> Then he gave himself to me in the shape of the sacrament, in its outward form, as the custom is; and then he gave me to drink from the chalice ... After he came himself to me, took me entirely in his arms and pressed me to him; and all my members felt his in full felicity, in accordance with the desire of my heart and my humanity. So was I outwardly satisfied and fully transported.[24]

Caroline Walker Bynum, in her analysis of such material, uses, although not uncritically, the liminal theory of the anthropologist Victor Turner.[25] Symbols have an 'orectic' quality about them; that is to say they have a sensory dimension wherein their power lies. Thus, whatever words, wonders or rhetoric are used, whatever symbols emerge from whatever sources, they are experienced in the body. All religious language and symbolism ultimately 'opens out beyond itself to an intractable physicality'.[26] In this embryonic theory, a phenomena like worship becomes a social drama or processual unit whose function is to provide liminality. Turner means by this, generally, a moment when normal rules and roles can be suspended, boundaries crossed, norms violated, and conflictual elements inculcated or rejected. In short, symbols condense and unify a variety of disparate elements into a focus of *significance*. Typically, two opposite poles of meaning will be brought together: the normative and the emotional, or dominating power with liberating love. In turn, these can help form a *communitas*, which hitherto was comprised of competing personal and social elements – out of apparently unresolvable paradox, comes praise.[27]

This is a liminal theory of religion. But what would it mean for something like eroticism to be *sub*liminal? If the eroticism is somehow below the surface of agreed meaning in a given community, can we be sure it is there at all? The answer can only come through due and appropriate attention to the language, metaphors and analogies about God. In particular, it is likely that one will locate these cores of meaning in worship, rather than anywhere else. Sermons, teaching, articles of faith and the like are didactic, and can be the focus of assent or dissent. But worship is in a sense the basis of community for believers. The activity of praise assumes a community that is focused and together: dissent in worship is usually a community at war with itself.

Bynum suggests that the erotic elements in mysticism or praise were orectically significant, especially for women. Visions were sometimes known as 'sensual (or erotic) ticklings;'[28] bodily stirrings were a form of 'proof' that the religious experience was genuine. Physical union with Christ, because it could be symbolized in terms of marriage and sexual consummation, often resulted in ecstatic behaviour. Furthermore, the more women religious (nuns) became marginalized from even minor clerical tasks in the Middle Ages, the more physical union with Christ in the eucharist became romanticized for women. Here, the eroticism was a vehicle of spirituality, which no doubt owed some of its power and popularity to its implicit exclusion of the male imagination. As Bynum notes, erotic, eucharistic ecstasy was a means of reclaiming power for women, and of bypassing male authority. It was also a way of personally embodying religious experience for themselves, that was beyond the reach of conventional male-dominated lines of interpretation. Thus, women regularly speak of tasting God, kissing him deeply, of going into his heart, being covered, smothered and embraced by Christ.[29] Thus, Bynum is arguing that women in the Middle Ages had to stress the charismatic somatization of their religious experience in direct proportion to their loss of clerical power. The gradual romanticizing and eroticizing of relationality with Christ created an exclusive, orectic category of symbols that kept women's access to the humanity of Christ largely free from male domination.[30] If medieval religion was thus embodied, with erotic-ecstatic experience playing an important role in liberating individuals and groups, are there parallels in the contemporary world of revivalism?

The cultural context of postmodernity suggests that this is at least possible. If it is correct that modernist metanarratives are dissipating, then we should be alert to what replaces them, including the religious response to and inculcation of this moment. One strategy that Giddens, Chomsky and Connor, amongst others, suggest is a sort of return to pre-Enlightenment thinking in some religious groups.[31] I say 'sort of return' here, because there is no real attempt to recover the past in postmodernity: only copy, mimic and echo it. And then perhaps to develop a phase that is more commonly understood as a fashion: disposable, but also recyclable. Thus, we find an explosion of interest in angels and demons in contemporary revivalism perhaps not seen since the seventeenth century, accompanied by an angelology and demonology that resonates with some medieval scholastics, although the postmodern version lacks that serious theological resourcing. I want to suggest that the re-kindling of eroticism in experiential worship, albeit sublimated, is part of the same cultural trend; in other words, the restoration of romance and eroticism to worship. The prosecution of this thesis depends on observing pre-eminent forms of contemporary revivalism, such as the Toronto Blessing. In terms of erotic language and the significant symbols that are present, there is plenty to note.[32] Although the Blessing is better known for its epiphenomena such as laughter, animal noises and people being slain in the Spirit, the sublimated eroticism is all too apparent. The question is, where does it occur? The places are numerous, but lie chiefly in the rhetoric of ascription, testimony and worship.

## The Grammar of Assent

First, the metaphors used to describe the (ideal) revivalist church reveal an interesting fascination with passion. Typically, the blessing of God is described as being channelled through water or fire. Thus, revival is rain, a river, wave, refreshing and the like: the task of the church and the individual believer is to become soaked in this. As one Toronto pastor expresses it: 'we want to create a network of pastors and churches who will be permanently wet with renewal'.[33] Alongside the metaphors of wetness are those of heat. Revival is also a fire, the people burn to be touched, and the presence of God is often described as a sensation of hotness or burning bright heat. There are then a further series of metaphors that value temporary loss of control. A believer who is 'under the anointing' may often describe the experience as being akin to being pleasurably drunk or drugged. The supporting rhetoric for this puzzling phenomena encourages people to 'let go', release themselves, and to enjoy the occurrence, without rationalizing it. Some believers even talk of getting 'all blessed-up' at meetings, in much the same way that some people might describe using soft drugs at a rave. Finally, believers are encouraged to be passionate with God: intimacy with God is the path to empowerment. Thus, and to summarize, believers and their churches are to become hot, wet, passionate and open, subject to temporary loss of physical and rational control, then intimate with God, in order to receive the blessing.

Second, the consequent expressive physicality that emerges from this rhetoric is remarkably akin to sexual behaviour. There are sighings and groanings, ecstatic yelps of delight, piercing screams of ecstasy, an abundance of assorted rhythmic movements, passing out, shaking and quaking. Yet these phenomena, we should note, do not produce any orgiastic displays. Believers assent to this grammar of possibility and receive their experiences largely on their own: there is remarkably little inter-group touching.[34] The church encourages believers to join in what they call 'carpet time': falling backwards, resting on the floor, or being 'slain in the Spirit'. If this happens to those who volunteer for this ministry, recipients are encouraged to soak in prayer, or even marinate in God's Spirit. Perhaps Max Weber and Rollo May are therefore correct in hinting that we are dealing with 'sublimated masturbatory surrogates' here: the experience of a personal moment of Eros compensates for the otherwise arid diet of rational religion.[35] Indeed, those wishing to receive the blessing are asked to '[seek], even cultivate an overwhelming hunger and desperation for intimacy with the Lord . . . through intimate worship . . . embrace(ing) the cross . . . walking in continual and childlike dependence'.[36] Admitting your need is a prerequisite to receiving.

Third, the grammar of intimacy is highly developed beyond the implications of being hot, wet, passionate and open. There is a distinctive vocabulary of sexual consummation. Worship is described as 'making love to God', Jesus is 'turned on by our desire for him', the Spirit a 'brooding lover' who woos and courts.[37] According to Carol Arnott of the Toronto Airport Church, the 'purpose of intimacy with Jesus is marriage'. Furthermore, Jesus is quite particular about the type of bride he desires: he 'wants a passionate bride . . . to be a disciple is to be a love slave of Jesus'.[38] As one might expect with an ecclesial community that has fundamentalist roots, yet is primarily identified as belonging to postmodern revivalism, the metaphors of marriage in relation to God, based on texts in the New and Old Testaments, are literalized and individualized. Thus, a significant spiritual vision for Carol Arnott, and shared with her congregation, is of 'Jesus meeting all his brides at the wedding feast . . . and then coming over to me, out of all of the brides, and asking me for the first dance'.[39] This 'prophetic revelation' is delivered with accompanying somatic signs. Carol Arnott frequently groaned, sighed or almost passed out as she spoke: the explanation for this is that it is the 'intense power (of the Spirit) on her'. In the congregation during this speech, the sighs and groans emanate voluntarily from the audience, especially the women, although they sound more obviously romantic and sexual than those of the speaker. Other 'visions' shared include heads being stroked whilst resting in the lap of Jesus, Jesus 'putting me to bed' when special care was required in a time of stress (this is probably more about parenting than sexual intimacy), and the Gospel as a fairy tale like *Cinderella* – 'we are all looking for a Prince Charming who will save and protect us'.[40]

Fourth, whilst the use of marital motifs clearly does have scriptural echoes, the underlying definitions of love in the church remain distinctively romanticized. Many of the pastors in the church describe 'ideal' love in rather immature terms. The most frequently used configuring scenario to describe the ideal form of relationship with God is that of a teenager in love. Thus, 'wearing a stupid grin', 'starry-eyed' expressions, 'unable to speak properly', 'uncontrollable feelings' of elation or ecstasy, 'a rosy glow', 'not able to concentrate' or 'helpless laughter' are seen as ordinarily symptomatic of receiving the blessing – they become desired behaviour. Jesus, the congregation is told, 'is the greatest lover you will ever have': the Toronto Blessing is simply restoring that sense of first-ever-love to the Church. Correspondingly, valued behaviour ceases to be 'adult' and is replaced by something approximating 'soppiness'. Indeed, many women in the congregation can become quite giggly when this rhetoric is being used, and will describe themselves as 'feeling quite gooey'. Love then, is being translated into the pre-critical obsessionalism that can sometimes infatuate young teenagers: concepts such as rationality or maturity are therefore obviated, and sometimes even named as 'blockages' to real spiritual love.[41] As Niklas Luhmann notes, 'the dominant semantics of a given period becomes plausible only by virtue of its compatibility with social structure'.[42] What is being preached here is a subtle call to romantic regression, under the guise of restoration. As we have already noted with postmodernism, this is not actually a recovery of romance at all, but rather a mimic of it, in which all the stress, anxiety and confusion of first love has been obviated and replaced by a reconstructed emotional certainty. Thus, believers are being asked to forget or abrogate complexity and temporarily embrace an exciting and soothing form of simplicity. This is why such preaching frequently incites believers to 'receive like children': only then can Jesus emerge as the romantic super-hero, who will sweep the believers off their feet.[43]

Finally, something should be said about the rhetoric of parenting in the Toronto Airport Christian Fellowship. The average person attending this church is white, middle-class, North American, aged about 47, with some college education.[44] It is perhaps inevitable that there will be some conflation between the desired images of God and the actual concerns of this social group. The messages are complex and conflictual, reflecting the contemporary confusion amongst this group of Christians about roles within family identity. Women attending the church also use maternal imagery to describe their spirituality. Thus, the groanings are like 'birth-pangs', Jesus' nurturing 'just like a good mom'. Some women go further, and talk about giving birth to a new church, and carrying Jesus' seed inside them. Men attending the church, who might have some difficulty with intimacy and marriage with Jesus in terms of the homosexual reson-ance, seem to be particularly struck by the stress placed on what I would term 'intimate patriarchy'.[45] At one prayer meeting I attended, a visitor came forward to speak towards the end of the session, but then appeared to be 'struck dumb'. When he did finally speak, his revelation was that God had asked him to give his prophetic word last of all today, but being frightened of missing his chance, he had disobeyed the prompting, and moved forward early. God had silenced him, but the revelation was that 'instead of Daddy spanking me, he filled me with joy' so speech was impossible.[46] God, the intimate father who disciplines with love, is of course mirrored in ecclesial relationships in the Toronto church. But beyond that, the rhetoric taps in to a frequently expressed angst in north American evangelicalism about poor, distant or absent fathers. Healing is often offered to men and women who feel they may have suffered from this, and might then be projecting their disillusionment onto God. Indeed, even if a believer has been sexually abused by his or her father, the Toronto church stresses unconditional forgiveness and reconciliation as a means to greater intimacy with the heavenly father.[47] Many of the men who attend also belong to the 'Promise Keepers' organization, which emphasizes male bonding, emotivity and fathering.[48] John Arnott, leader of the Toronto church, prefers the Toronto Blessing to be known as the 'Father's Blessing'. Arguably the chief benefit of this rhetoric is to once again stress the need for child-like dependence in the congregation, whilst at the same time securing a degree of intimacy and expectancy. After all, the father is benevolent, giving gifts to his children: all believers need to do is lie back and receive the love and power that is to come.

## Worship as Ideology

Much has been written about the ideology of certain movements in order to explain their power and appeal. There is no doubt that familiarity with the theology or the ideological formulations of a specific movement is essential to an understanding of it, especially in the study of revivalism. The question therefore necessarily arises: How might we locate an ideology, particularly if it is subliminal? Most studies of revivalism tend to suggest that the ideology of a given group can be located in the dogmatic creeds, principles and formulations that it advances to the world. At least one consequence of this reading is a tendency to perceive revivalist ideology as either a reductive or deductive theological stratagem. However, if the recovery or restoration of certain experiences somehow lies at the centre of revivalism, then it is likely the core ideology will in some way be inductive.[49] Many songs from the revivalist tradition are intended to evoke romantic feelings whose power is enhanced by their erotic overtones:

> *Jesus take me as I am,*
> *I can come no other way.*
> *Take me deeper into you,*
> *Make my flesh life melt away . . .*[50]

If postmodern revivalism is to be partly understood in terms of power, passion and romance as Hopewell suggests, then the ideology needs to be traced to the actual religious experience itself, not to the principles or dogmas derived from it. It is my contention that 'core' ideology can be located in the worship of revivalism: it is the worship of a community that provides it with its primary religious experience, and thus its certainty and ideology. As Eric Hoffer remarks, 'the effectiveness of a doctrine does not come from its meaning but from its certitude'.[51] Nowhere is that certitude more keenly expressed than in the arena of worship, where God is both met and meets, is addressed and addresses. The diet of 'smoochy' worship that precedes preaching effectively creates the believers' ground of actuality. In worshipping a passionate God, through quasi-erotic grammar, believers are reaping what they sow – they obtain the passion they subscribe to in God.

Analysis of ideology always needs to take account of the social situation in which language functions, and a history of such social situations may provide clues as to the origins of such rhetoric. Space does not permit the charting of the history of revivals here, but most scholars of revivals appear to hold to the view that the place of feelings and affections in social or public religion was prevalent in America by the early nineteenth century.[52] The roots of the ideology may lie in many places: Puritan stress on 'conversionist language' and Methodist emphasis on 'personal testimony' may have contributed to the new phenomenon that Sandra Sizer describes as a 'community of intense feeling' in the context of revival.[53] Individuals underwent similar experiences that tended to centre on conversion, and thereafter united with others in matters of moral and social orientation. The language adopted and employed in such contexts created and sustained both the community and its feelings. With respect to Wimber, similar concerns are at stake over the place of emotions in his worship meetings. It is people's feelings that are to be changed first (by the experience of worship), before their minds are changed (by teaching and subsequent somatic phenomena). The mind and emotions are to be fixed on the object of worship until a response is discerned. All this is framed within the context of a God whose heart can be touched by our own yearnings:

> *Your prayers are very precious,*
> *They reach the heart of Jesus,*
> *Like a sweet, sweet perfume.*[54]

The stress on feeling leads to a stress on unity of feeling ('agreement'). If worship is to flow (in the Spirit), and prayer is to be rewarded, it is vital that the affections and minds of the audience are as united as possible. In part, this is achieved through emphasizing an aspect of God. For example, in early Restorationist music (*circa* 1975–85), the metaphors of God were often monarchial or military. God was 'baring his holy arm'; the church was the 'army of the Lord', 'terrible as an army with banners' or 'trampling down the enemy under our feet'. Frequently, this millennial militarism led to tribalism, with Restorationist churches identifying more with Old Testament tribes than with any New Testament ecclesial concepts.[55] However, in the late 1980s and 1990s, the emphasis has turned from tribalism to the therapeutic, and from aggressive power to emotions and passions:[56]

> *I will be Yours, You will be mine*
> *Together in eternity*
> *Our hearts of love will be entwined*
> *Together in eternity, forever in eternity.*

> *Father I want You to hold me*
> *I want to rest in Your arms today*
> *Father I want You to show me*
> *How much You care for me in ev'ry way . . .*
> *You love me as I am*
> *I know I am Your child,*
> *I feel Your arms holding me, I'm not alone.*

> *Do it again Lord, do it again Lord,*
> *Cause us to see. Do it again, Lord,*
> *And set us free. Let Your fire fall in power,*
> *Let Your joy come with laughter, Do it again . . .*
> *We desire Your presence, as never before.*
> *Lord, come in power, as we ask for more . . .*
> *Do it again, Lord, do it again . . .*[57]

In the case of contemporary revivalism, especially in Wimber's songs and those of that genre, the metaphors of 'You' and 'Lord' are now the dominant modes for addressing God: God 'the warrior' has been lost, and been replaced with something suspiciously narcissistic. 'You' and 'Lord' are both models of God, as well as ideological tools, in that they mediate an immediate framework of power and passion to the worshipper.[58] In short, this is how the social and theological construction of reality comes to be. 'You' brings intimacy: healing, passion and passivity. The 'Lord' brings power: domination, authority and order. By focusing on the metaphors of 'You' and 'Lord' in worship, Wimber and his fellow song-writers create a romantic yet hegemonic ideology that guides the communication of selected essentials, via a fixation on concepts of love and power. Many in contemporary revivalism are happy to declare this quite openly in worship, singing 'more love, more power, more of You in my life'.[59] The ideology consists of symbols and metaphors that connect deeply with the emotional realm and offer a framework in which individuals can find identity and power, and see it magnified in their own language about God. It is irresistible passion encountering passivity.

## Summary

Worship, as a grammar of assent in the kind of revivalism we have been discussing, offers a romantic and semantic framework to believers which ties in with the visions and analogies outlined earlier. Jesus emerges as a sort of romantic super-hero; God as father is portrayed in intimate, idealistic terms; the Spirit as a source of immediacy. Several things need to be noted here.

First, this type of revivalism seems to appeal especially to white, middle-class, middle-aged women. Colleagues of mine who have visited host churches for the Toronto Blessing have made some remarkable unsolicited observations. One said: 'it looked like a lot of women having orgasms, led by a man at the front'. Another that it was 'well-heeled, normally well-buttoned up ladies releasing a lot of pent-up sexual energy'.[60] Crudely, one could suggest that these epiphenomenal mani-festations, brought on by the worship and actualizing of the grammar of possibility, are just creating a sacralized version of a secular culture steeped in erotic imagery.[61] One could also simply argue that an emphasis on eroticism is an essential component in ecstatic religion. Getting in touch with the body, its desires and its needs is profoundly releasing.[62] In addition, one could say that the subjective individualism that typifies contemporary revivalism must always flirt with eroticism, since it is ultimately more powerful than tenderness and mutuality.[63] One could also acknowledge that the language of desire for God is naturally erotic.[64] Eros drives the search for God, and its present inculcation in charismatic Christianity is arguably a healthy sign: the rational balanced with the emotional. The revivalist worship we have so far discussed may just be *'agape* that is strained to intensity'.[65] In this respect, one could be seeing a movement that is journeying beyond dualisms.[66] This seems unlikely, however, when one considers that some fairly repressed and fundamentalistic attitudes to sexuality persist in such movements. In spite of the stress on Eros, the moral code in relation to sexuality is still configured through a literalistic reading of a selection of Scriptures.[67]

Whilst I admit that these interpretations all have possibilities, none of them seem fully adequate. However, the first one suggested – namely 'releasing' white, middle-class, middle-aged women – does show promise.[68] A number of the evangelical-charismatic churches known to me personally frequently feature groups of women who have acquired power in leadership and prominence in worship through owning their own distinctive somatic religious experience. In some cases, they will be worship, prayer or study group leaders; some may even lead healing groups. Yet in the same churches, they are often absent from the pulpit (preaching), or presiding at the Eucharist. Might it be that evangelical women, who are also charismatic, are finding a way of avoiding the constraints of doctrines of headship, or reservations about their presence in positions of official leadership? If the somatic religious experience of women in revivalism can be seen as at least quasi-mystical, then Grace Jantzen is right to suggest that an emphasis on embodied, erotic and consummatory spirituality may re-empower women, who are often excluded from avenues of power, including the debates that are dominated by rational discourse.[69]

In fact, one could go further here and suggest that the occurrence of romantic and erotic language and subsequent somatized experience rises and falls in relation to women's real access to clerical power. This ambiguity of power is actually quite familiar to the evangelical-charismatic and revivalist worlds. The history of this has been carefully noted by Margaret Bendroth in her sharp study of fundamentalism and its relation to women's needs and roles.[70] Similarly, Michael Mason has noted that 'sex press(es) forward so persistently in the history of these popular movements . . . (because) the whole spirit of such episodes was disinhibiting.'[71] In charismatic and revivalist contexts, ecstatic experiences were part of the 'unfocused creeds' that were being supplanted by evangelists. In many nonconformist churches and emerging Victorian sects, this actually liberated women, giving them some local ecclesial prominence. As John Maynard suggests, this 'fits' with the ambiguous sexual and religious roles women were given in the Victorian era: there was disgust at sex, but a fascination with it too. In religion, especially religious poetry and literature, fallen-female or ideal-virginal sexuality could be explored and redeemed through the safe lens of analogy, with the 'excesses' of ecstacy often becoming sacralized.[72] Yet men still dominated these discourses, even though some women may have been partly emancipated by their interest.

This may seem slightly far-fetched, until one begins to see that in the Toronto Airport Church, home of the Blessing, women are relatively prominent as speakers and preachers, although still mainly denied titles such as 'pastor' or 'prophet'. Furthermore, and unusual in the history of postmodern revivals, the Toronto Blessing was introduced to Britain by a lay-woman.[73] The worship, visions and real physicality of a phenomenon like the Toronto Blessing appear to allow women to publicly own an embodied form of spirituality that is beyond the immediate reach of male control. Thus, although the leadership remains male and the ascriptions to God largely male, it is the romantic and erotic rhetoric that delivers a degree of limited power to women participants. The type of woman set free here is an issue. Few of the women are single, with a successful career. The type of release and power on offer seems to resonate with the same market which is enabled and empowered by certain types of romantic fiction, magazines and the like:[74] married middle-aged women, for whom the recovery of romance as a means of reconstituting relationships may seem attractive. Generally, this material will be quite erotic in places; women are given space to take sexual initiatives and are not just passive.[75] Yet like much romantic fiction, although exciting and adventurous, it is ultimately rather undemanding of the reader.

It is, of course, highly ironic that women can be specifically empowered in a context that is still dominated and controlled by men: how is this so? The answer must lie in the suggested possibility of a romantic, erotic relationship with Jesus, and a relationship with God (as father) who is simply intimate and caring. Yet it also rests with the theological message: that God is available directly and personally to the believer, and does not need to be mediated through a priest, sacrament or subscription to a certain kind of rational discourse. Many in this movement believe that to be the case. The spirituality of contemporary revivalism unintentionally offers an apparent ideological by-pass around patriarchy.[76] Women are given sacred, personal space to communicate with God and embody certain somatic religious experiences that are particular to their needs. Thus, we are back with Turner's theory of liminality here. The dominating power of the Lord, along with the intimate love of God ('You'), can be focused on a significance of romance and eroticism which is highly orectic. Conflicting signals are effectively held together in the romantic genre, which women can often master far better than men.

In view of this, I would suggest that romance functions here as a participative, processual drama in which many can reconfigure themselves. Once one is caught up in the romantic genre, the path to eroticism or intimate patriarchy opens up for individual women and men alike. Carol Arnott says it is easier for women (of her age and sociality) to imagine being married to Jesus, than it is to sing 'Onward Christian Soldiers'. Likewise, the romantic genre for men offers new scope for being intimate with the Father, and then attempting to copy that model personally and socially. Thus, men are encouraged to remain as leaders, heads and father-figures, but also to be more in touch with their emotional side. For both men and women, there is always the possibility of being re-parented by God in a more intimate, therapeutic way.

It is clear from analysing the worship of contemporary revivalism, along-side the analogies present in the Toronto Airport Church, that the power of the movement is partially derived from the intensity of the language which does have sexual overtones. There is a fervour in the language that speaks of longing desire: to consume God, and be consumed. This is a spirituality with a sensuous appetite.[77] Thus, the bride is waiting: hot, wet, passionate, and longing for Jesus to come to her. The somatic experiences that accompany this revivalism are simply evidence of the anticipation and result of consummatory desire, which is projected onto a passionate Christ who, it is said, holds, embraces and caresses his holy ones. It is, in short, a form of romantic fiction. Increasingly in this religious world, it is being written and spoken by women and for women. Happiness, bliss, consummation and fulfilment await the believer.

## Notes

1 See H. Lefebvre, *The Production of Space* (Oxford: Blackwell, 1991). This is well discussed in N. Wang, 'Logos-modernity, Eros-modernity and Leisure', *Leisure Studies*, vol. 15, no. 2 (1996).

2 See D. McLellan, *Ideology* (Buckingham: Open University Press, 1995), pp. 2–4.

3 By postmodernism, I mean the fracturing of modernist metanarratives and their associated concepts of truth, which was largely achieved through assorted 'philosophies of suspicion'. The postmodern mind suspects modernist ideology and metanarratives of foolishness and oppression, but probably only replaces the former with smaller, more avowedly local ideologies. There is no sign yet that postmodernity can produce anything that is more liberating (or oppressive) than modernist ideology, especially since the liberating strategy seems to be mostly content with subjective, individualistic interpretation. In other words, there is no deep truth, only 'surface meaning'. In my 'Is there a Charismatic Theology?', *Farmington Papers* (Oxford: Manchester College, 1996/7), I argue that contempor-ary revivalism should be seen as a postmodern movement, partly because it lacks a theology. What it has, in place of this, is a subliminal axial micro-ideology (based on distorted but favourable concepts of divine love and power), grounded on the interpretation of experience, with an added theological gloss. For further discussion on the postmodern condition, see D. Lyon, *Postmodernity* (Buckingham: Open University Press, 1995); S. Connor, *Postmodern Culture* (Oxford: Blackwell,

1989); J. F. Lyotard, *The Postmodern Condition* (Manchester: Manchester UP, 1984); and A. Thiselton, *Interpreting God and the Postmodern Self* (Edinburgh: T. & T. Clark, 1995).

4 See J. Habermas, *Knowledge and Human Interests* (London: Heinemann, 1978), p. 314.

5 See C. Geertz, 'Ideology as a Cultural System' in *Ideology and Discontent*, ed. D. Apter (New York: Free Press, 1964), p. 64.

6 McLellan, *op. cit.*, p. 83.

7 See M. Rubin, *Corpus Christi* (Cambridge: CUP, 1991), p. 2, commenting on J. Bossy, *Christianity in the West, 1400–1700* (Oxford: OUP, 1985), pp. 57ff.

8 See M. Poloma, *By Their Fruits: A Sociological Analysis of the Toronto Blessing*, published by the Toronto Airport Christian Fellowship, no date. Poloma is a sociologist of religion and an Episcopalian. She is sympathetic to the Toronto church, and has conducted a quantitative survey of people attending her church. Her findings are that many people who attend the church feel more positively disposed to God as a result of their visit.

9 In a preliminary way, I have discussed how this takes place in my *Words, Wonders and Power: Understanding Contemporary Christian Fundamentalism and Revivalism* (London: SPCK, 1996).

10 For example, the older English universities can no longer class the study of Islam within 'Orientalism', thus distancing the subject from mainstream culture, and also endowing it with a false mystique.

11 See R. Goring, (ed.), *Chambers' Dictionary of Beliefs and Religions* (Edinburgh: Chambers, 1992), p. 142. Of course, there was never one type of Dionysian religion, any more than there is one type of revivalist church. They vary from time to time, place to place. In Greek legend specifically, Euripides' play *Bacchae*, Dionysius comes to Thebes to introduce his cult. He is rejected by Pentheus, the King of Thebes, but Dionysius succeeds in driving the Theban women wild: they flee in to the mountains, where they perform erotic, ecstatic rites. For resisting Dionysius, Pentheus is eventually hunted down by the new, ecstatically possessed Dionysians, and torn to pieces.

12 See W. F. Otto, *Dionysius: Myth and Cult* (Bloomington: Indiana University Press, 1965), especially chapters 5 and 10; E. R. Dodds, *The Greeks and the Irrational* (Berkeley, California: Sather Classical Lectures, no. 25, n.d.).

13 Catharsis describes a purging, healing process that is achieved through intense emotional expression, and is followed by release. In psychotherapy, the operation and definition is imprecise: it can involve methods and insights from Primal, *Gestalt* or Bioenergetic therapy. Freud connected catharsis with the expulsion of painful childhood memories. William James worried that the therapy of emotional release (such as screaming) could become habit-forming, thus obviating its original impact. More recently, others have seen sexual orgasm as the ultimate physiological catharsis. Abreaction more specifically describes the process of expressing repressed feelings, bringing them into conscious awareness. See M. P. Nicholls and M. Zax, *Catharsis in Psychotherapy* (New York: Gardner Press, 1977), and A. Janov, *The Primal Scream* (New York: Putnam, 1970).

14 A title that many revivalists would surely be happy to own. When I visited the host church for the Toronto Blessing in Canada, a number of believers wore T-shirts bearing the slogan 'I'm a Jerk for Jesus', a jocular reference to the somatic phenomena that is particular to this movement. Others wore sweatshirts bearing a picture of a cartoon character laid out on the floor, in an ecstatic spiritual state, 'Slain in the Spirit'. For further discussion, see A. Danielou, *Shiva and Dionysius*

(London: East-West, 1982). Interestingly, Robert Palmer's *Dancing in the Street: A History of Rock 'n' Roll* (London: BBC Books, 1996), points out that the success of contemporary popular music is in many ways, profoundly linked to these same religious roots. Palmer helpfully emphasizes the sexual libido and liberation that rock 'n' roll brought to a society dominated (or exhausted?) by the modernist mindset. The attempted suppression of 'pop' music by modernist society in the 1950s can be seen as a marker in the transition from modern to postmodern society, rather in the same way that the proliferation of nuclear bombs – literally capable of 'atomizing' society – maps the same cultural moment in a technological manner. Aesthetically and architecturally, these shifts occurred about twenty years earlier.

15 See the report on the Toronto Blessing carried in *The Daily Telegraph Magazine*, 'Unzipper Heaven, Lord', by Mick Brown (04/12/94).

16 See J. Hopewell, *Congregation: Stories and Structures* (London: SCM, 1987). Hopewell has used Northrop Frye's seminal *The Anatomy of Criticism* (Princeton: Princeton UP, 1957) to equate tragedy with canonic, comic with gnostic, ironic with empiric and romantic with charismatic genres.

17 *Ibid.*, p. 78.

18 *Ibid.*, p. 78. Hopewell is citing a charismatic's testimony here. Of course, the ekstatis is not lost altogether. It can become a means of obtaining the inner feelings required. Certain types of demonstrative charismatic worship are pseudo-sacramental: meeting God 'outside yourself' is in the service of nourishing the internal, individual self.

19 See H. Cox, *Fire from Heaven: Pentecostalism, Spirituality, and the Reshaping of Religion in the Twenty-first Century* (New York: Addison-Wesley, 1994), especially pp. 310ff.

20 Cox's thesis is incautiously optimistic and enthusiastic about the possibilities for experientially-based religion in a new millennium. For a critique from an unrepentant subscriber to the secularization thesis, see Steve Bruce's 'Religion in Britain at the Close of the Twentieth Century: A Challenge to the Silver-lining Perspective', *Journal of Contemporary Religion*, vol. 11, no. 3 (1996), pp. 3–21.

21 See R. Knox, *Enthusiasm* (Oxford: Clarendon, 1950); D. Martin, 'Evangelical and Charismatic Christianity in Latin America' in K. Poewe (ed.), *Charismatic Christianity as a Global Culture* (Columbia: University of South Carolina Press, 1994).

22 M. Noll, *The Scandal of the Evangelical Mind* (Grand Rapids, Michigan: Eerdmans, 1994), p. 120. Noll compares a George Croly song (1860) with a Helen Lemmel song (1922) that is widely used today, to great effect.

23 I could have used any number of these images. I was especially struck in researching this chapter by Joanna Southcott's vision of Jesus. He came to her in the night, glistening with dew, wet hair, and wearing a linen robe. He then proceded to sit on her bed and talk to her. Southcott was an eighteenth-century schismatic mystic: her writings are published by the Panacea Society, Bedford.

24 Hadewijch, vision 7; *Hadewijch: The Complete Works* (New York: Paulist Press, 1980), pp. 280–1.

25 C. W. Bynum, *Fragmentation and Redemption: Essays on Gender and the Body in Medieval Religion* (New York: Zone Books, 1992), pp. 120ff. Victor Turner's work on liminality and dominant symbols can be found in *The Forest of Symbols* (Ithaca: Cornell University Press, 1967) and *The Ritual Process* (Chicago: Aldine Press, 1969).

26 Bynum, *op. cit.*, p. 20.

27 See Turner, *The Forest of Symbols* (1967), Chapters 2 and 3. This theory of liminality is consonant with the definition of ideology advanced in the introduction: there is further discussion in the conclusion to this article.

28 *Op. cit.*, Bynum, pp. 88 and 191.

29 *Ibid.*, pp. 135, 139, 190. For a fuller discussion of this dynamic in mysticism, see Grace Jantzen's *Power, Gender and Christian Mysticism* (Cambridge: CUP, 1995).

30 Naturally, this could also be done through stressing the motherhood of Christ; Julian of Norwich was the most systematic exponent of this. See Bynum (1992), p. 222.

31 See A. Giddens, 'Uprooted Signposts at Century's End', *The Times Higher Education Supplement* (17/01/92), pp. 21–2; N. Chomsky, *Keeping the Rabble in Line* (Edinburgh: Academic Press, 1994), pp. 124ff., and S. Connor, *Postmodern Culture* (Oxford: Blackwell, 1989).

32 I was fortunate to be able to spend part of the Summer of 1996 observing the Toronto Airport Christian Fellowship, which 'hosts' the Toronto Blessing.

33 *Spread the Fire*, vol. 2, no. 1 (February 1996). This is the official magazine of the Toronto Airport Christian Fellowship.

34 At one Toronto intercession meeting I attended, the two women in front of me 'lapsed' into a state of ecstasy. They sat astride their chairs, and then 'rode' them rhythmically with deep and quick pelvic thrusts, their backs arched and their heads in the air, for about 20 minutes. All the while they were breathing deeply, at times hyperventilating, sighing, and crying (with pleasure). Nobody in the prayer meeting found this strange: one of these women later delivered a 'prophetic message' about Jesus coming to his bride soon, and the need to be ready.

35 See Rollo May, *The Cry for Myth* (New York: Norton, 1991), *Power and Innocence* (London: Fontana, 1976). For Weber's viewpoint, see *From Max Weber: Essays in Sociology* (London: Routledge and Kegan and Paul, 1948), pp. 107ff.

36 Source: TACF homepage on 'Partners in Harvest' and 'Prophecy': http://www.tacf.org/etc/html.

37 Quotes variously attributed to Roger Forster, leader of an independent House Church network in London, and Paul Cain, itinerant prophet formerly allied with John Wimber's Vineyard churches and now with the Toronto Airport Christian Fellowship.

38 For a fuller discussion, see my monograph *Catching the Fire: The Sociology of Exchange, Power and Charisma in the Toronto Blessing* (Latimer House: Oxford, 1996).

39 *Ibid.*, p. 19.

40 'Intimacy with Jesus', Carol Arnott, taped talk (05/07/96).

41 Of course, I am not suggesting young teenagers can't have mature loving relationships. With parents and siblings this is most likely: but with sexual partners it is unusual. A recovery of the sensation of being in love for the first time is therefore regressive. In my view, the real value to the Toronto Church of speaking in this way is that it places passion above love. Furthermore, as Hopewell notes, this type of romanticism is ultimately a celebration of the self, not of the object of love or passion. Passion and romance, and the feelings and experiences associated with them, become the dominant form of self-knowledge. Ironically, 'otherness' is eventually lost, and replaced by pseudo-pneumasomatic phenomena.

42 N. Luhmann, *Love as Passion: The Codification of Intimacy* (Cambridge: Polity Press, 1993), p. 3.

43 See 'Receiving as a Child', *Spread the Fire*, vol. 1, no. 6 (December 1995).

44 These statistics are the from the Toronto Airport Church. See M. Poloma, *By Their Fruits* (Toronto: TACF, n.d.)

45 Freudians would clearly enjoy analysing this rhetoric in more detail. As for Freud himself, the general concept of God being 'nothing more than an exalted father' is nothing new. See his *Totem and Taboo* (1912/13), his 1907 paper 'Obsessive Actions and Religious Practices', and his subsequent short book, *The Future of an Illusion* (1927), which is a more systematic critique of the relationship between neurosis and individual religiosity. These extracts are all reprinted in the accessible *The Freud Reader* ed. Peter Gay (London: Vintage Books, 1995), pp. 504ff.

46 See my *Catching the Fire* (Oxford: Latimer House, 1996), p. 16.

47 On two occasions when I was there, victims of incest were singled out for ministry, and asked to stand in the midst of the congregation. They were led in a prayer of forgiveness for the abuser, and then told to 'release' their anger. They were then invited to 'give their dad a gift he didn't deserve . . . let God give him a hug.' Then the 'victims' were asked to sit down. This ministry lasted about five minutes, and at no point was counselling offered, or were 'victims' allowed to express their abuse and anger in their own terms. It was, in effect, an exercise in abrogation.

48 Promise Keepers is an organization begun in the early 1990s by Californian Pastor Bill McCartney. It is a Christian movement for men, that depends on men making themselves accountable to one another concerning their family and their ethical, social and religious life. Men meet in small groups, with one leader designated as a 'point man'. There are regular, large celebrations held in stadiums. The movement is essentially a sacralized form of the type of philosophy laid out for men by Robert Bly in his *Iron John: A Book About Men* (New York: Addison-Wesley, 1990).

49 See my *Words, Wonders and Power* (1996), Chapter 4.

50 Dave Bryant (1978), Thankyou Music/*Songs and Hymns of Fellowship* (Eastbourne: Kingsway, no. 292, 1985).

51 Eric Hoffer, *The True Believer* (New York: Harper & Row, 1965), p. 28.

52 See W. G. McLoughlin, *Modern Revivalism* (New York: Ronald Press, 1959); B. A. Weisberger, *They Gathered at the River* (Chicago: Quandrangle Books, 1958); W. R. Cross, *The Burned Over District: The Social and Intellectual History of Enthusiastic Religion in Western New York, 1800–1850* (New York: Harper & Row, 1961). This last book, although now over thirty years old, remains an unsurpassed history.

53 S. Sizer, *Gospel Hymns and Social Religion* (Philadelphia: Temple University Press, 1978), p. 52. Although Sizer coins the term 'community of feelings', I mean something different in employing the term. For Sizer, the 'community of feelings' is located in the intense emotionalism of revivalism, which eventually becomes domesticated in late nineteenth-century rhetoric. My application of the term refers more explicitly to a transcendent community that identifies itself by organizing and directing its feelings in worship, without reference to social or historical situations.

54 *Songs of the Vineyard I* (Anaheim: Mercy Publishing, 1982).

55 Arguably, this is the logical outcome of an inductive theological strategy.

56 All the songs are sung to a slow, 'smoochy' tune that is 'modern-romantic'. This is now the dominant form of praise in worship for charismatic churches, and is *intended* to create a climate of intimacy. Songs are often sung 5–10 times each, over and over again. One hour of praise may only contain four or five short songs. Some questions arise when considering these forms of worship: (1) What is lost

and gained for the worshipper by eschewing credal/dogmatic formulae? (i.e. the Trinity, incarnation, Good Friday/Easter, Christian year, etc.) (2) How are human feelings expressed and harmonized, and to what end? (3) How convincing is the romantic idealism of the songs? (4) How is God addressed, and why? (5) What kind of somatic effects might this type of worship produce? (6) Historically and sociologically, why is postmodern revivalist worship so different from the forms that are particular to Wesley, Edwards, etc.? and (7) Can a 'grammar of assent' create and control religious experience?

57 From *Catch the Fire Again* (Toronto: Rejoice Publishing, 1996). The last of these songs is set to a 'punchy' beat rather than a 'smoochy' one; however, the triumphant and insistent sexual overtones make it a song that is performed with great passion.

58 For a fuller discussion of metaphors and models of God, see Sallie McFague's *Metaphorical Theology: Models of God in Religious Language* (London: SCM, 1983).

59 Jude Del Hierro, 'More Love, More Power' (1982), in *Eternity/Isn't He* (1996).

60 Both comments, from a male and a female colleague, were referring to meetings at Holy Trinity, Brompton, a host church for the Blessing.

61 By 'culture' I mean all forms of media: advertising, magazines, TV, film, etc.

62 See R. D. Kahoe, 'Ecstatic Religious Experience' in D. G. Benner (ed.), *Encyclopedia of Psychology* (Grand Rapids, Michigan: Baker House, 1985).

63 See Paul Ricoeur, 'Wonder, Eroticism and Enigma' in J. Nelson and S. Longfellow (eds), *Sexuality and the Sacred: Sources for Theological Reflection* (London: Cassell, 1994), pp. 80ff. In the same volume, Audre Lourde's essay 'Uses of the Erotic: The Erotic as Power' sees eroticism as a potential means of empowerment for women. Mary Pellauer's fine essay 'The Moral Significance of the Female Orgasm: Towards Sexual Ethics that Celebrate Women's Sexuality' shows how mutuality and the erotic can be combined.

64 See Paul Avis, *Eros and the Sacred* (London: SPCK, 1989), pp. 128ff.

65 A. Louth, quoting Gregory of Nyssa in *The Origins of the Christian Mystical Tradition* (Oxford: OUP, 1981).

66 Cf. Thomas Deidun, 'Beyond Dualisms', *The Way*, vol. 28, no. 3 (July 1988), pp. 26–38.

67 Interviewing pastors in Toronto, all agreed that practising homosexuals could not *really* be Christians, and were dammed to Hell unless they repented. Popular revivalist leaders such as Bill Surbritzky still insist that oral sex is a 'demonic' activity, not appropriate for Christians.

68 Sociologically speaking, Rosalind Coward suggests that the satisfaction of feminine desire is the lynch pin of a consumerist society. See her 'Female Desire and Sexual Identity' in M. Diaz-Diocaretz and I. Zavala (eds), *Women, Feminist Identity and Society in the 1980s* (Amsterdam and Philadelphia: J. Benjamins, 1991), pp. 25–9. Coward points out that the offer of pleasure, the new and the ideal, is part of a discourse that surrounds society and dominates it. She perceptively notes: 'Things may be bad, life difficult, relationships unsatisfying . . . but there's always the promise of improvements, everything could be transformed, you'll almost certainly feel better . . . dissatisfaction is displaced into desire for the ideal' (p. 29).

69 See Grace Jantzen, *Power, Gender and Christian Mysticism* (Cambridge: CUP, 1995). However, some of the strict revivalist churches (restorationist) tend to restrain women from Dionysian-type worship. Dancing, prophecy and public speaking may be forbidden, or strictly controlled.

70 See M. Bendroth, *Fundamentalism and Gender: 1875 to the Present* (New Haven: Yale University Press, 1993). Bendroth suggest that the emotional and 'domestic'

language about God in revivalism is a guarantee of some power for at least some women. For a different perspective on the same dynamic, see Elisabeth Ozorak, 'The Power but not the Glory: How Women Empower themselves through Religion', *Journal for the Scientific Study of Religion*, vol. 35 (1996), pp. 17–29.

71 M. Mason, *The Making of Victorian Sexual Attitudes* (Oxford: OUP, 1994), p. 137. Mason cites Edward Irwing as an example (pp. 29ff.). See also his *The Making of Victorian Sexuality* (Oxford: OUP, 1994). Both these volumes are well discussed in Simon Szreter's *Fertility, Class and Gender in Britain, 1860–1940* (Cambridge: CUP, 1996).

72 See John Maynard, *Victorian Discourses on Sexuality and Religion* (Cambridge: CUP, 1993).

73 Ellie Mumford, wife of Bob Mumford, pastor of a Vineyard church in London.

74 Although Meredith McGuire does not make the same connections, her study of Christian healing groups in suburban America does suggest that middle-class, middle-aged white women are a key 'market' for Hopewell's romantic/charismatic genre of spirituality. See M. McGuire, *Ritual Healing in Suburban America* (New Brunswick: Rutgers University Press, 1988).

75 I am not suggesting that Mills and Boon novels are the only ones to be read. The rise of more sexually explicit romantic fiction for women, such as Black Lace imprints, should be noted. In an odd way, this begins to take us into a related debate within feminism about whether there can ever be appropriate pornography for women. Some women claim it is sometimes liberating, others that it is always oppressive. In the case of contemporary revivalism, the truth about erotic language and somatized experience lies somewhere between these extremes.

76 Again, there are historical precedents. See Maynard, *op. cit.* (1993), pp. 22ff.

77 For a related perspective, see Joan Smith, *Hungry for You: From Cannibalism to Seduction* (London: Chatto & Windus, 1996). Smith, like Margaret Visser, is an anthropologist and food writer. She makes some excellent connections between sex and food, lust and desire, which have sacramental implications. One is immediately reminded of the Sheffield-based Nine O'Clock Service, with its erotically charged eucharists which invoked worshippers to 'Eat God'. Clearly, the infrequency of eucharists in revivalist churches makes the eroticism that much more sublimated.

# 9

# Things fall apart I:
# established religion and the presence
# of sexuality

In Chinua Achebe's *Things Fall Apart*,[1] the story of Africa's painful journey from tradition to modernity is narrated. The book is a portrayal of a primal but established society at the time of its first confrontation with Europeans. An Ibo legend and proverb provide the scenery against which bitterness and disillusion are projected, often conveyed with biting satire and irony. For any student of missiology, the book is an uncomfortable read. But beyond that, the early novels of Achebe hold up a mirror to Western tradition and establishment. Religious beliefs are threatened. The 'old ways' of doing things which bound people together through ritual, story and common purpose are slowly subverted by a creeping process of civilization. The enemy in *Things Fall Apart* is not so much Christianity as what the faith brings with it: modernity and secularization.

Proponents of the secularization thesis believe that numbers attending mainline denominational churches are steadily declining. Ironically, the discourse of theoreticians such as Steve Bruce and Bryan Wilson are endorsed by blueprints from surveys conducted by Christian groups that are more inclined to sectarianism. The best-selling *UK Christian Handbook* regularly cites the growth of 'new churches' as evidence of weakness in historic denominations.[2] Authors such as Ivan Clutterbuck celebrate the 'small is beautiful' thesis, and actually argue for the end of liberal, established religion.[3] It is certainly true to say that the historic denominations have lost power, influence and numbers in late modernity. However, the notion that this must simply be the responsibility of modernity (i.e. secularization) is crude and simplistic. It is probable that the fragmenting trends within religious belief simply mirror those within society. The Church corresponds with reality. There are altogether more complex reasons why established religion *appears* to be failing – and it may only be a momentary epiphany, as we shall note later.

What of fragmentation, though? There is nothing like a good argument to tenderize the Church and make any notion of unity look vulnerable and threatened. The Church of England in the 1990s has had to contend with a number of issues that have posed questions to its unity: the ordination of women, homosexuality and various clerical scandals have united and polarized parties in bizarre configurations. A service for the Lesbian and Gay Christian Movement at Southwark Cathedral brought howls of derision from the evangelical group Reform.[4] The argument was further fuelled by Anne Atkins, a prominent evangelical lay-woman, in a BBC Radio 4 broadcast in which she suggested that the declining number of laity and ordinands was directly linked to the lack of 'clarity' on moral issues within Anglicanism.[5]

It does seem as though indelible Anglican habits such as toleration, diversity and debate have been challenged in late modernity. Assertion and confrontation play a much bigger role in the Church of England's polity, and opposing views that used to coexist in flux and harmony now seem to harden positions and alienate the very concept of being in communion. Indeed, to live in a communion with people one disagrees with ought to be a sign of strength and maturity, not weakness. Yet issue after issue seems to invite the threat of schism and the cessation of complementarity. In turn, this becomes an issue for the study of power. It is therefore necessary to look at some of the deeper reasons for the apparent decline in established religion. In this chapter, the primary subject is Anglicanism, the second largest global Christian communion after Roman Catholicism. How does this commonwealth fare in relation to schism and the failure of ecclesial power to nurture and maintain unity?

## The Analogy of Family

J. Gordon Melton, in his *Encyclopaedia of Religion in the USA* (1st edition, 1978) categorizes expressions of American religious life according to 'families'. He identifies at least 17 different families, of which Anglicanism features as just one branch within the 'Liturgical Family (Western)'.[6] In choosing to adopt the word 'family' to describe expressions of religion, Melton is arguing for a structural understanding of religion that achieves two goals. First, it permits him to reject the simplistic European-centred distinctions of Troeltsch between church, sect and cult, which are potentially pejorative, besides being artificial and sometimes clumsy.[7] Second, it therefore allows religious expressions to be grouped together according to their ecclesial, social and doctrinal similarity, not according to size or social impact. Undoubtedly, there are some benefits in this approach, but it is not without its weaknesses. As fundamentalists have known for nearly a century, many of their family members often do not recognize each other, let alone talk to one another. The reason for the proliferation of family members in ecclesiastical history is not usually expansion, nor the indigenous enculturation of imported or exported religious tradition. It is much more likely to occur because of a breakdown in relationships, perhaps caused by disagreements over authority or interpretation, or by personality clashes, or perhaps because of simple rebellion or even open hostility.[8]

The history of the expansion of Anglican family members in the twentieth century is no different. The first edition of *The Encyclopaedia of American Religions* (1978) identified seven distinct Anglican groupings. The second edition of 1993, just fifteen years later, identified no less than twenty-six.[9] Granted, the discovery of nineteen new 'Anglican' groups does not mean they are all new: but many are, being a reaction to the perceived endemic 'liberalism' of American Episcopalianism. The situation in England is not dissimilar. Whereas there were once just a few Anglican splinter groups, the last few years have seen a remarkable growth in this area. The new traditionalism it seems, is deeply divisive in its drive towards the restoration of 'conservative values'. Instead of seeking revival for the whole body, new traditionalism seems to foster separatism, leading to eventual schism.

So, the burden of this chapter will be twofold. First, to record the recent schisms, to place them in their historical context, and to offer some kind of account for them. Second, to examine the viability of their ecclesiological future using broadly sociological insights, and to ask what Anglicanism can do to prevent accelerating theological and ecclesiological haemorrhaging in the postmodern era, in the light of the rationale of inclusivism, founded upon the quadrilateral of scripture, tradition, reason and experience.

## Schisms within the Anglo-American Anglican Communion

The main substance of the Anglican tradition in North America until the mid-1960s was provided by the principal episcopal church, the Anglican Church in Canada (part of the Church of England until 1955), the Reformed Episcopal Church (a nineteenth-century splinter group), and a few congregations of the Philippine Independent Church (PIC).[10] However, North American Anglicanism began to suffer splits when liturgical reform was introduced, shifting moral codes were apparently inculcated, and women were accepted into the priesthood in the Episcopal Church of the United States of America (ECUSA) in 1976, and into the episcopate in 1989. Some dissenting Anglicans initially looked to the PIC for the establishment of episcopal orders, in order to provide a form of 'continuing church'. Bishop Francisco Pagtakhan of the PIC duly consecrated a number of bishops in 1978. However, Pagtakhan's action alienated some of his own constituents, leading to a split within his own communion: by 1986 the Eglesia Filipina Independente was formally established in America. This historical pericope could easily serve as an atypical example for American Anglican schisms.[11]

North American Anglicans cannot be genuinely surprised at the proliferation of rival communions. Historically speaking, the very foundations of Anglican life in North America are bound up in schismatic tendencies.[12] The first Church of England church was established in Newfoundland in 1583, the Reverend Erasmus Stourton being the first Anglican cleric to reside in North America. Throughout the seventeenth century the Church of England spread in parallel with colonization, competing with Puritan and Catholic influences. The establishment of Anglicanism was especially successful in Canada following the Treaty of Paris (1763), by which the French government relinquished all territories to the British. However, the American Revolution almost destroyed Anglicanism, with the Church of England being identified as pro-monarchist and therefore anti-patriotic following the Declaration of Independence in 1776. It was not until 1784 that Americans were able to secure their own episcopal orders, and this was done through the disestablished Scottish bishops: Samuel Seabury, elected bishop by the remaining priests in Connecticut, was duly consecrated. However, by 1787, a working accord had been reached between ECUSA and the Church of England.

ECUSA consolidated its missiological and ecclesiological work throughout the nineteenth century with considerable energy and success. However, two minor schisms did occur. In 1873 the Reformed Episcopal Church was founded in New York City, a reaction to the growing influence of Anglo-Catholicism in ECUSA, which had arisen out of the Oxford Movement. During the 1860s doctrinal and liturgical-ceremonial divisions had occurred in the Church of England and in the USA, and Anglicans of evangelical persuasion had clearly felt threatened. Bishop George Cummins, a prominent evangelical prelate, resigned his office of assistant bishop to set up the new church.[13] In 1897, the Free Protestant Episcopal Church was formed out of a union between three small British Episcopates – the Ancient British Church (1876), the Nazarene Episcopal Ecclesia (1873) and the Free Protestant Church of England (1889) – the primary function of the union being to preserve a distinctive evangelical heritage.[14]

The situation in the USA had parallels with developments in England. The Free Church of England was officially formed in 1863, although its historical roots as a distinctive church can be said to have originated some twenty years earlier.[15] The Free Church of England, like its American counterpart the Reformed Episcopal Church, began as a response to the Oxford Movement; early leaders of the Free Church included James Shore and Thomas Thoresby, who worked partly in alliance with the Countess of Huntingdon's Connexion.[16] In 1922, the Protestant Episcopal Reformed Church was established to 'continue the distinctly Protestant theology and witness of the post-Reformation Anglican Church ... [taking] its stand with those who refuse to embrace the ecumenical movement, and the charismatic movement'.[17] The theological nemesis this time seems to be liberalism and modernism, rather than Anglo-Catholicism. In both the above cases, the function of ministers seems to be more akin to Presbyterian models of ministry than Anglican: deacons tend to be laity, and professional clerics presbyters. The exception is the office of bishop, which is retained in a somewhat functional manner for the role of someone acting as the president or superintendent of a group of churches.

In the first half of the twentieth century, ECUSA saw little in the way of further schism. The rifts caused by nineteenth-century Anglo-Catholicism had mostly subsided. The debates between 'liberals' and 'fundamentalists' were not yet affecting Anglicans ecclesiologically, and Pentecostalism and revivalism tended to impinge on other denominations. The formation of the PIC and its subsequent implications for ECUSA arose out of a one-off political situation, which did not suggest the proliferation of schism that was to occur from the 1960s onwards. Indeed, the only significant schism to occur in this period was the creation of the United Episcopal Church in 1945. Formed in Illinois by Bishops Julius Massey, Albert Sorenson and Hinton Pride, they envisaged a restoration of 'Celtic' heritage within a traditional Anglican framework.[18] The roots of the church are both Presbyterian and Old Catholic, with the 'fundamentals of the faith' (including the 39 Articles) not being open to 'alteration or debate'.[19] Yet there is a real sense in which this new schism marked the beginning of post-Second World War 'new traditionalism'.

The 1950s, 1960s and early 1970s saw further and increasingly dramatic partitions. The Southern Episcopal Church (1953) began with ten families from one church. Its constitution was formally ratified in 1965. The Anglican Church of North America (1955) traces its origins to the Independent Anglican Church of Canada, founded in the 1930s by William Daw. Its roots are Old Catholic, Liberal Catholic and Anglican: it accepts the St Louis Affirmations of 1977 (see below), which define and hallmark conservative Anglican-based schisms. The Anglican Orthodox Church (1963), founded by the Reverend James Parker Dees, separated from ECUSA over liturgical changes and liberalism. Dees was a low-churchman, and the emphasis of the church is very much on 'sound biblical doctrine'. The American Episcopal Diocese (South) is a splinter group from Dees' church, formed in 1988 following administrative disagreements. The American Episcopal Church (1968) was formed in Alabama partly out of racial motivation, following divisions in the Protestant Episcopal Church and the Anglican Orthodox Church. It is theologically conservative, and has around 5,000 members nationwide. The Anglican Catholic Church (1977) was also formed out of dissatisfaction with ECUSA over the ordination of women and a general 'theological and moral drift'.[20] The Anglican Catholic Church – mainly responsible for drawing up the St Louis Affirmations which set out such a clear conservative and anti-liberal agenda – is one of the larger schisms to have emerged from within Episcopalianism, although it has suffered its own divisions over authority and consecration subsequent to its foundation. The Anglican Province of Christ the King is one of those schisms. The Anglican Episcopal Church of North America was founded in 1972 by Walter Hollis Adams with the specific intention of bringing together traditional groups into a *via media*: Free Church, Orthodox and non-papal Catholic elements comprise the main influences. An attempt to unite with the Anglican Catholic Church in 1986 failed following a dispute over the validity and primacy of orders.

The late 1970s to the present is virtually a history of unmitigated fissure. The Continuing Episcopal Church (1984), the Holy Catholic Church, Anglican Rite (1981), the National Anglican Church (1988), the Provisional Diocese of St Augustine of Canterbury (1978, but now defunct), the United Anglican Church (1984), the Traditional Episcopal Church (1992), the Traditional Protestant Episcopal Church (1986), and the United Episcopal Church of North America (1980) all claim Anglican roots through episcopal lineage, yet are no longer part of ECUSA. Whether Protestant or Catholic in emphasis, anti-liberal or syncretic, what unifies these bodies as a *trend* is their desire to be conservative, traditional, separate and distinctive, whilst still claiming to be Anglican.[21]

The present situation in England, whilst nowhere near as prolific, is structurally somewhat similar. The decision in 1992 by the General Synod of the Church of England to ordain women to the priesthood has precipitated changes in some Anglican organizations, as well as triggering some new Anglican churches and movements. Organizations such as the Prayer Book Society have taken a stand against ordaining women, only to find that consultation with the whole membership revealed them to be deeply divided as a body.[22] The Additional Curates' Society, a traditional but open Catholic body, has also been polarized on the issue of women priests. An editorial in its magazine in 1993 explained:

> [we resolve to remain] true to our Tractarian origins . . . our attitude is
> not just about women priests, but about a general tendency in the

Church of England to take liberal attitudes in a whole arena of our common life ... note how the words 'equality' and 'justice' were bandied about. It is TRUTH we should be bothered about, for 'equality' and 'justice' are the key words in our modern pagan society ...'[23]

The editorial concludes with a call to 'draw back and follow the rest of our brethren'. Yet like the Prayer Book Society, the ACS turned out to be less than unanimous about women priests: some of their supporters were clearly relieved and glad that women had been ordained.

Some movements seem to have formed within the Church of England in direct response to the ordination of women. The Cost of Conscience movement has become Forward in Faith, devoted to maintaining a distinctive Catholic identity in the Church of England that does not recognize women priests. There was some attempt to create a 'Third Province' in the Church of England in addition to the Sees of York and Canterbury, that would cater for 'traditional clergy and parishes'. However, the appointment of three Episcopal Visitors ('Flying Bishops') by the Archbishop of Canterbury seems to have prevented this development. The ultra-conservative evangelical group, Reform, was forged out of an alliance between concerned evangelical clergymen, and bodies such as the Proclamation Trust (PT) and Action for a Biblical Witness to our Nation (ABWON).[24] Reform is a now pressure group that campaigns against apparently indiscriminate financial contributions to central diocesan funds, and argues against women priests on the grounds of biblical authority: 'I permit no woman to teach or have authority over a man' (1 Timothy 2:13). It also campaigns against what it sees as liberal trends in theological colleges and synods and in moral matters. There is some evidence to suggest that Reform may eventually consolidate its identity to the extent that it breaks away from the Church of England: some openly advocate a strategy that 'talks peace yet prepares for war', and of becoming a 'church within a church'.[25]

Yet all of the movements mentioned above still remain within the Church of England. So what of those that have departed? Perhaps the first thing to note is the number of people who have left the Church of England since the vote in 1992. Groups such as Cost of Conscience predicted that thousands of priests would leave and become Roman Catholics. In fact, only a few hundred who are presently in stipendary ministry have done so, although a slow haemorrhaging is likely to continue for a number of years. A number of these priests may be ordained into the Roman Catholic Church, following Cardinal Basil Hume's offer of hospitality in March 1994, and his subsequent clarification over the status of married Anglican priests in a Pastoral Letter.[26] The number of retired priests and non-stipendary ministers is more difficult to calculate, but the figures certainly run into hundreds, including the former Bishops of London[27] and Leicester. However, one must set against this those bishops who were opposed but who have since been 'converted' to the exercise of priestly ministry by women. In one or two isolated cases, whole congregations have asked to be received into the Roman Catholic Church. Prominent lay-people who have also converted to Roman Catholicism include John Gummer and Ann Widdecombe, two former Government ministers.[28]

Some Anglicans, however, have decided not to join the Roman Catholic Church, or to take advantage of the Provincial Episcopal Visitors scheme within the Church of England. The alliances formed and journeys undertaken at this point are still in a state of fluctuation. For example, one small 'daughter church' (St Barnabas and St Jude, Sandyford) of Jesmond parish church in Newcastle – a noted Reform stronghold – has left the Church of England, forming itself into the Newcastle Reformed Evangelical Church. It regards the Church of England as 'beyond reform', and does not even think that groups like Reform can save it.[29] The major divisions to have emerged in England in the last two years can be divided into five schismatic groupings, although more may emerge in future.

First, a branch of the Anglican Catholic Church (ACC) was formed in January 1992 by Leslie Hamlett, a priest from Stoke-on-Trent. He is now its presiding bishop, and the eccesiology of the church broadly attempts to offer 'a way forward to be an Anglican and a Catholic', yet without being compromised by existing moral and theological trends within the Church of England.[30] The membership of this group is unclear, but is probably numerically insignificant at present. The ACC has congregations in America (since its inception in 1977), New Zealand, Australia, Central America and India.

Second, there is the Traditional Church of England (TCE). Its presiding bishop is now Leslie Whiting, formerly a priest in London. The TCE is under the episcopal care of Archbishop Louis Falk, primate of the Traditional Anglican Communion and leader of the Anglican Church of America (ACA, founded in 1955). The TCE and the ACC in England, in spite of their doctrinal and liturgical similarities, regard themselves as being quite separate. They can even be quite hostile to one another, especially over episcopal lineage and the structure and autonomy of individual congregations.[31] Again, membership is still quite small.

Third, there is a Continuing Church of England (CCE), which seems to be catering for about five ultra-evangelical congregations. The presiding bishop is Dr David Samuel,[32] a former director of the Church Society and minister of the Proprietary Chapel in Reading. The CCE is still at the stage of developing its ecclesiology, but it is likely that it will be akin to similar nineteenth-century evangelical splinter groups. However, the CCE is in dialogue with the Traditional Church of England, since there is agreement about the need for doctrinal purity taking precedence over numerical growth.

The fourth and fifth groups can be treated together, since they are both movements that represent the interests of charismatic evangelicals. One of these, Pilgrimage to Orthodoxy, is headed by Michael Harper, a former director of Fountain Trust.[33] He claimed to have ten priests and nine congregations that were seeking reception into one of the many orthodox denominations.[34] However, a fifth option remains, namely joining a group of American (former) Episcopalians under the Charismatic episcopal Church, which is also active in the Philippines, and claims Apostolic Succession.[35] In both cases, the contemporary interest in pneumatology, a rejection of women priests, and the seeking of new structures in which to inculcate new experiences of the Holy Spirit seem to be the main motivation for leaving existing Anglican structures.

## Sociological and Ecclesiological Factors in the New Anglican Schisms

It is clear from our survey of the state of twentieth-century Anglo-American Anglicanism that liberalism is not the only reason for fissure. The factors that have prompted schism have included doctrinal issues, but also liturgical practice, ecumenism and difficulties over the recognition of 'valid orders'. Perhaps the first thing that needs acknowledging is the common thread of conservatism or traditionalism that unites these groups in their motivations and directionality. Each of the groups discussed is implying continuity with a real or imagined past that is somehow resisting the present and future. In this sense, the neo-conservative attitude is noetically similar to fundamentalism: clarity, certainty and security are delivered to the followers in return for an investment in believing that their faith is of long standing. In fact, much of the belief that is implied by rhetoric like 'the faith of our Fathers' or 'the faith once delivered' turns out to be a relatively recent 'invention', birthed in the nostalgic Tractarianism or Ultra-Protestantism that emerged in the nineteenth century.[36] So how are we to account for the proliferation of Anglican schisms? Is it entirely a reaction to the inculcation of liberal values as some claim,[37] or are there deeper forces at work?

Bryan Wilson's sociological approach to religion sees religious institutions as primarily 'the religious response to the world'.[38] This common-sensical statement invites us to assess the social, political and cultural situations that religions work within. The nineteenth century was one of post-Enlightenment turmoil: moral, religious and cultural values began to be relativized and slowly privatized in a broadly modernist world.

Against this, certain religious movements such as Pentecostalism, revivalism and fundamentalism seemed to resist modernist and rationalistic accounts. The response to secularization is nearly always sacralization: religious bodies re-selecting moral and behavioural phenomena which have lost their implicit religious dynamic, and making the religious explicit. Examples of this may include attitudes to family life, health and healing, or sexual practice.[39] Yet this response often requires a form of disjunction, breaking the link between Church and society to safeguard purity or belief: here Troeltsch is correct in noting that a schism may well be formed at this point. Schisms trust neither the society of their time nor their parent religion.

The social and cultural conditions of the twentieth century have seen the rapid development of postmodernity and pluralism. One of the characteristic hallmarks of the age is the struggle for identity and particularity. Given that pluralism is endemic, and relativity is implied by this, small religious groups and movements are more prone to separatism because of the lack of faith in universal principles or bodies. In other words, the recent proliferation and acceleration of Anglican schisms are a symptom of the postmodern and plural age, not necessarily a remedy against it. Thus, schismatic groups thrive by positing themselves against larger group interests such as the ecumenical movement, liberalism or the World Council of Churches, yet often fail to unite into successful federations to achieve deeper corporate goals. As I have remarked once before, neo-conservative groups imagine themselves to be strong because of their unity over a select range of fundamentals. Yet in interactive dialogue, even with one another, they often fail to agree on other issues, which can lead to dissipation of energy and eventual structural disintegration.[40] Ironically, it is liberalism that still tends to remain the stronger, because although little actually unites liberals in terms of structure or belief, almost nothing divides them either, since openness, toleration and mellowness lie so close to the heart of the liberal enterprise.[41]

But let us return to work of Bryan Wilson for the moment. Having noted the number of schisms in Anglicanism, we should now ask: What kind of schisms are they? Wilson's well-known typology of sects is underpinned by a generic definition of a sect. Wilson finds Troeltsch's definition to be socially and theologically inadequate, and proposes instead a circumscription that takes account of the phenomenological breadth of sectarian life:

> The sect must espouse some other principle of authority than that which inheres in the orthodox tradition, and claim superiority for it. The authority that a sect invokes may be the superior revelation of a charismatic leader, it may be a re-interpretation of sacred writings, or

it may be an idea that the revelation will be given to the truly faithful. Whatever it is, the sect rejects the authorities of the orthodox faith.[42]

So, sects do not necessarily reject the faith as such, rather they reject the present custodians of it. In terms of contemporary Anglican schisms, this is a critical observation. Innovative religion is not being advocated, but original belief is: in this sense, this form of neo-conservatism is closely allied to fundamentalism.

Wilson then goes on to suggest eight hallmarks that delineate sects: (i) voluntariness – although sects are voluntary bodies, family members tend to remain within them; (ii) exclusivity – clear boundaries demarcate them from others; (iii) merit – an act of subscription is required to join; (iv) self-identification – provision of a family or tribal group in which one can find oneself; (v) elite status – purity, salvation or chosenness guaranteed; (vi) expulsion – strict demarcation implies intolerance of deviant belief or anti-social behaviour; (vii) consciousness – distinct patterns of belief and behaviour develop out of elitism, possibly including antinomianism; and (viii) legitimation – ideological structures justify and underpin identity and praxis.[43] Most, if not all of the Anglican schisms discussed, largely fulfil Wilson's definition of a sect. Yet many within these groups would fiercely eschew being identified in this way: so, what sort of sects are we talking about?

At this point, Wilson's categories appear to be of little help. Of the seven types he offers, none exactly corresponds to contemporary Anglican schisms. They are not conversionist, revolutionist, manipulationist or thaumaturgical (i.e. magical-charismatic).[44] This leaves introversionist, reformist and utopian. But to describe Anglican schisms as introversionist places them in the same category as exclusive communities such as the Hutterites, which is hardly right or fair. Equally, although they are in some ways reformist, it does not do justice to the comprehensiveness of their beliefs. To describe them as utopian touches on their idealism, but again, it is not an apposite description. However, there is an eighth category which Wilson mentions but does not explicate: conformist. At first sight, this seems an oxymoronic typology for a sect. Yet if it is correct to identify contemporary Anglican schisms in terms of being 'neo-conservative' or 'neo-traditionalist', then 'neo-conformist' might be close to an accurate portrait, provided it is understood that it still indicates a sectarian response to the parent religion and, perhaps, to society in general.[45]

One of the main advantages of Wilson's work in tackling this subject is his appreciation of the relationship between mainstream religion and its offshoots. In a number of major works, he has carefully articulated the connection between society, religion and sectarianism.[46] The basic thrust of Wilson's more recent work is that secularization is the major force that is shaping sectarian responses to the world. As religion is placed on the periphery of Western society, becoming a privatized, almost alternative leisure activity, an increasingly sharp contrast develops between liberal and conservative religious values. The conservative religious values are more likely to become focused, but at the risk of becoming schismatic. The liberal religious values increasingly risk being absorbed into society and lost in a form of secularized osmosis.[47] The phenomenon of contemporary Anglican schisms highlights this dilemma precisely: the Anglican communion is struggling with how to be in the world yet not of it. The schisms present a challenge to Anglicanism: if it is pressed to identify itself too sharply, it risks alienating the body of society it serves by becoming exclusive. Equally, if it ignores the schisms, it risks being absorbed by society to the extent that it loses its identity, being outflanked by the sharpness of other beliefs.

Identity is therefore emerging as something of a key in this discussion. Anglican schisms, although difficult to place in any taxonomy of sects, nonetheless have clear self-perceptions. Indeed, the burden of the St Louis Affirmations of 1977 is essentially a chastening of North American Anglicanism for apparently changing and then losing its identity. Opinions vary as to whether or not there is a centre to Anglican theological methodology that issues identity, but many would concur with the notion that the 'quadrilateral' model defined in the last century is the most likely candidate.[48] Briefly, the Anglican Quadrilateral was defined in Chicago in 1886 and slightly modified at Lambeth in 1888. In response to the vigorous critiques of scripture in the nineteenth century, Anglicans moved from a faith that was too dependent on *sola scriptura* (even though it was implicitly a trilateral of scripture, reason and tradition) to one which fully acknowledged the equally important place of tradition (i.e. creeds, councils, synods, etc.), the sacraments and the episcopate. These last two are commonly understood to be codes for the inculcation of experience and reason respectively, so the quadrilateral is comprised of a dialectical relationship between scripture, tradition, reason and experience. Contemporary Anglican theologians argue that, with the exception of experience, this method has been explicitly central to Anglicanism since the time of Richard Hooker (1554–1600), and even implicitly predates him.[49] The reason for moving from an over-dependence on *sola scriptura* to articulating a quadrilateral model had much to do with the situation created by modernity: pluralism was increasing, scientific approaches to religion and humanity openly questioned fundamental beliefs, and the frontiers of religious life seemed to be shrinking. A comprehensive model for solving internal theological questions and engaging with the complex moral world beyond them was needed. Not only that, but the combination of pluralism and schism had made some realize that 'what Christianity entails [was and is] essentially contested':[50] there was neither unity of expression or belief – the signs of fracture were to be seen everywhere.

If the quadrilateral provided a fundamental template for Anglicans in which they could process theological and moral problems, it was clear even before it was formulated that conservative, fundamentalist and traditionalist groups would effectively take their leave of it as any kind of centre. The history of Anglican schisms and movements in the nineteenth and twentieth centuries shows that there is considerable dis-ease with the dialectical relationship between scripture, tradition, reason and experience. Ultra-Evangelical groups still insist on the primacy of scripture, ultra-Catholic groups of tradition, Charismatics of the experience of God, whilst liberals tend towards elevating reason. As a framework, it is one in which many can participate; in that sense, it is comprehensive. However, disputes about the superiority of one facet or another still bedevil inter-Anglican dialogue. And when that dialogue breaks down, usually on grounds of scripture or tradition, schisms are tending to occur with increasing regularity.[51]

It does seem that the very presence of problems in relation to sexuality poses a particular threat to Anglicans. If the ordination of women to the priesthood is a watershed for the Church of England, current debates over homosexuality threaten to engulf the Church altogether. Why should this be so? There are no easy answers, but it does seem reasonable to suggest that an agenda configured through sexuality challenges the rationalist assumptions of established religion. Concepts of revelation are ill-equipped to cope with what we know about sexual orientation: the language of sin needs so many qualifications that it effectively becomes neutered. Engagement with sexuality requires the culture and experience of individuals to be respected to the extent of precipitating reformation. Traditions about celibate priests are challenged, myths about women in pulpits or presiding over altars effectively destroyed. The presence of sexuality as an issue in established religion nearly always forces the church concerned to correspond far more honestly and closely with society than it would like. In a strange way, it does not actually threaten belief so much as idealism about belief. Serious theology in the presence of sexuality prevents the Church from being 'holier than thou', and from becoming too fond of its own imagined purity. From this position, its tenure on truth looks rather insecure. Ultimately, its sense of essentials and its own theological methods and moral reasoning are pressed to the absolute limit. This is a profound power issue: the very stability and unity of a social-transcendant body appears to be endangered by ordinary human affairs in the form of sexuality.

These remarks highlight the two fundamental weaknesses of the quadrilateral in the context of postmodernity. First, in explicating the quadrilateral as a central method, Anglicanism has explicitly formed itself into a pattern rather than a position. That is to say, the quadrilateral tells you how to arrive at resolutions on how to think and behave, but it does not necessarily prescribe what to believe or how to conduct oneself: in short, a method is provided, but not the conclusion.[52] This distinction has important implications for Anglican schismatics. Schisms tend to articulate belief through regularized dogma that is unambiguous in its moral and theological reasoning. The quadrilateral, by definition, invites a plurality of belief, interpretation and response. Thus, Anglicans can arrive at opposite conclusions over homosexuality or the ordination of women to the priesthood through processing their ideas via the quadrilateral. Yet agreement over appropriate praxis can still be reached even if there is disagreement, as the Church of England's appointment of Episcopal Visitors shows. However, this is not enough for some, and the subsequent strain can result in schism. Second, the quadrilateral can be so inclusive as to risk avoiding any serious praxis at all. Robert Carroll somewhat cheekily describes the quadrilateral as 'the Dodo's incorporative principle by which everyone wins'.[53] It is clear what is meant by this: a deeply liberal foundation underlies the quadrilateral, which ascribes meaning to scripture and tradition, but only authority where it is consonant with experience and reason. Neo-conservative Anglicans may not actually know this to be the case, but they certainly suspect it. The point is that schisms emerge when the liberal bias, inherent in the quadrilateral, appears to discriminate against scripture and tradition.

If the quadrilateral is some sort of centre within Anglican identity, however conscious or unconscious, then its failure in praxis to meet the needs of ultra-Evangelicals or ultra-Catholics is one of the deeper reasons for the proliferation of Anglican schisms, if not the deepest. Essentially, the quadrilateral fails these groups as a method because they are committed to a form of hegemony, not equality. Schisms have hierarchies of truth and method that deliver clear answers to complex moral and theological questions. In turn, this permits such groups to engage in a monological relationship with the world; the quadrilateral requires a series of dialogical relationships, and assumes a willingness to negotiate, which could ultimately lead to the transformation of fundamental principles. A physical way of expressing this would be to describe mainstream Anglicanism as an essentially fluid tradition, whilst its schisms, to varying degrees, are more solidified. Yet both are of essentially the same substance.

Of course, both before and after the formulation of the quadrilateral (1886), other theologians have sought to locate a unifying centre for Anglicans that might prevent schism in relation to modernity and postmodernity. Many could be mentioned, but two will suffice for our purposes. The romantic poet and theologian, Samuel Taylor Coleridge, was very much alive to the dangers of placing any doctrine or method as a centre for tradition:

> He who begins by loving Christianity better than truth, will proceed by loving his own sect or church better than Christianity, and end by loving himself better than all.[54]

Coleridge is engaging in a pre-emptive strike against fundamentalists and schismatics. The implications are clear: truth, by which Coleridge means God, is bigger than any doctrinal or ecclesial expression of it, so the focus of ecclesial life needs to attend to the directionality of love, which should be central. If love of truth or God is eclipsed by love of tradition, the 'spiral of schism' will begin.

If love feels too nebulous a centre, then a more practical suggestion comes from Paul Avis: baptism. In arguing for an 'authentic paradigm for Anglicanism', Avis suggests that unity is best understood through our common baptismal heritage. In effect, he suggests that it could become a 'supreme ecclesial fundament'.[55] However, there are problems with this view, since baptism is inextricably linked to views on communion and salvation. Not only that, but baptism presupposes a faith: is there real agreement over the creeds, councils and confessions that accompany baptism? Avis, although finding ground that is common to all Anglicans, whether schismatic or not, simply relocates the controversy over true ecclesial identity in baptism itself.

## Summary

The absence of a centre and the increase of sectarian churches and new religious movements appears to point to a massive failure of established ecclesial power. Many of the problems discussed here may seem particular both to Anglicanism and to any other historic denomination in late modernity. Actually, this is not the case. Secularization, as a thesis, has to negotiate the fact that church attendance has often risen and fallen in each generation. Medieval Christendom is an ambiguous concept to compare to today's post-Christian Europe. It is too naive to suggest that in the former, all subscribed to essentially the same religious and moral metanarratives. They did not. Christianity has always been a culturally related and relative religion. The number of believers and Christianity's power can never be reduced to a figure calculated from attendance. Its decline cannot be measured by the rise of new religions. Historically, the Hanoverian era was marked by religious apathy. George Eliot's *Middlemarch* portrays established and sectarian religion in an especially bad light. Alan

Wilkinson's *The Church of England During World War One*[56] portrays a revival in established religion (especially in church attendance) and general spirituality in the years following the Great War. And whilst it may be true that more people attended church in the past and believed in the religion of the state, it is no exaggeration to say that this was, at best, patchy. Belief in folklore, magic and esoteric religion has always competed against what the state has presented as normative. Religious syncretism and schizophrenia have always abounded. Suggesting that things are falling apart on the basis of church attendance figures is a slight argument, requiring much more depth, subtlety and empirical work.

Although the proliferation of Anglican schisms in recent times may seem alarming to Anglicans, the prognosis is not necessarily so bleak. There are several reasons for this, of which three deserve particular mention. First, the schisms, although relatively solidified, are nonetheless numerically rather small. The new schisms lack the financial and ecclesial resources to expand, and their appeal is limited to those who are not from within the movement. Any reading of sociology or history – especially in relation to charisma – suggests that although they may initially grow under the first generation of leaders, it is mainly a question of survival for their heirs.

Second, Anglicanism in the nineteenth and twentieth centuries is no different from the Old Catholic, Methodist or Baptist churches in terms of the number of schisms it has suffered. Indeed, if Melton's *Encyclopaedias* are anything to go by, Anglicans seem to be faring quite well by comparison. However, too much optimism would be mistaken. As has been suggested already, the lack or erosion of fundamentals within contemporary Anglicanism – such as the 39 Articles, or *The Prayer Book* – coupled with the inherent liberal bias in the quadrilateral, lays Anglicanism open to the possibility of suffering the same kind of split suffered by American Baptists in 1845, which led to the new denomination of Southern Baptists being formed. Anglicans are not immune to dividing into conservative and liberal groups, and the debates over the ordination of women to the priesthood or on homosexuality in the Church of England have sometimes produced an 'unholy alliance' of evangelicals and Catholics determined at preventative action. It is the modern equivalent of the friendship between Herod and Pilate (Luke 23: 12).

Third, the schisms themselves are part of a more general trend within global Christianity that even Roman Catholicism is not immune to, as Tridentine enthusiasts have shown. This trend encompasses conservative reactions to modernity and postmodernity, which seem to propel some individuals and groups into a separatist mentality that requires them to abandon their parent religion in the interests of protecting their identity and fundamentals. The presence of a cluster of issues around sexuality is merely one of many catalysts for such schisms: it is the excuse for late capitalist individualism to assert itself in corporate ecclesial polity. Coleridge would ultimately have seen this as a kind of 'falling out of love' with truth as a whole, and the beginnings of the process of falling in love with oneself. But given that ecclesial structures tend to mirror trends within contemporary society, and bearing in mind the present context of postmodernity (with its relativism, non-universalism, and its promotion of the self as the central assignee of meaning), the present proliferation of Anglican schisms is hardly surprising.

# Notes

1 Chinua Achebe, *Things Fall Apart* (London: Penguin, 1958).
2 See *The UK Christian Handbook*, ed. P. Brierley (London: Marc Europe, 1994–95). There are serious questions about the method and type of data collected, and then the gloss placed on them. Brierley seems to have a vested interest in *proving* the decline of established religion. For example, Anglicans in England find their membership calculated on the basis of returns for communicants and electoral rolls. Yet the Church of England tends to keep its rolls small for financial reasons, besides having no acknowledged concept of membership as such. Anglican influence and power is not dependent on numbers attending church, although this helps. It often comes through the established role it enjoys: through baptisms, weddings and funerals, it touches a huge percentage of the population annually. In contrast, a new independent church with a few hundred members that now has over 1000 may look like a spectacular success story. Yet the percentage increase indicated ignores the growth limits that small independent churches often place on themselves quite unconsciously. At the time of writing, some House Churches are experiencing numerical decline, in spite of Brierley's over-optimistic predictions from the mid-1980s.
3 See I. Clutterbuck, *A Church in Miniature* (Leominster: Gracewing, 1996). Clutterbuck, based on his experience of break-away Anglican churches in Canada, prescribes sects as normative for the future purity of belief. The book is fiercely anti-liberal in its stance.
4 16 November, 1996. The service celebrated 20 years of the LGCM organization.
5 *Thought for the Day*, Radio 4 (10/10/96).
6 J. Gordon Melton, *The Encyclopaedia of American Religions*, Vol. 1, (Charlotte, NC: McGrath Publishing, 1978), pp. vii–xii, and 49–56. Cf. F. E. Mayer, *The Religious Bodies of America* (St. Louis: Concordia Publishing House, 1961): Mayer identifies 11 families, and is more in debt to Troeltsch than is Melton.
7 *Ibid.*, p. ix. See also Ernst Troeltsch, *The Social Teachings of the Christian Churches* (New York: Macmillan, 1931). Troeltsch's work is well discussed in J. Gordon Melton's *Directory of Religious Bodies in the United States* (New York: Garland Publishing, 1977), pp. 25ff.
8 For an amusing but apposite discussion of this dynamic, see Garrison Keillor, *Lake Woebegon Days* (New York: Viking Penguin, 1985), p. 107.
9 (Detroit: Gale Publishing, 1993).
10 One of the best potted discussions of American Episcopalianism can be found in

William Sachs, *The Transformation of Anglicanism: From State Church to Global Communion* (Cambridge: CUP, 1993). But for further discussion see James Addison, *The Episcopal Church in the United States, 1789–1931* (New York: Charles Scribner, 1951); William Manross, *A History of the American Episcopal Church* (New York: Morehouse-Goreham, 1950); William Syndor, *Looking at the Episcopal Church* (Wilton, CT: Morehouse-Barlow, 1980); and Frederick Wolverton, *Colonial Anglicanism in North America* (Detroit: Wayne University Press, 1984).

11 The Philippine Independent Church (PIC) emerged out of the political struggles of the nineteenth century which led to full independence for Filipinos. After excommunication from Rome in 1899 following the overthrow of Spanish rule, the PIC was formally recognized by ECUSA in 1961, although Anglican lineage can be traced through consecration back to 1948, and communion had existed since 1931. Internal divisions within the PIC in the 1980s led to the formation of a splinter group now known as the Philippine Independent Catholic Church in the Americas. ECUSA recognizes both groupings.

12 Cf. Donald Armentrout, *Episcopal Splinter Groups* (Sewanee, TN: University of the South, 1985).

13 Present membership (approx.): 7000 members; 80 congregations; 150 ministers.

14 Present membership (approx.): 2000 members; 20 congregations; 30 ministers.

15 See *A History of the Free Church of England* (Morecambe, England: The Free Church of England Convocation, 1960).

16 Calvinistic-Methodist chapels and ministers dedicated to social work, established in the eighteenth century by Selina, Countess of Huntingdon, a Methodist peeress. Her ministers were not allowed to become Anglican chaplains, in spite of her attempts to get their ordinations validated.

17 This Church is also known as the Protestant Evangelical Church of England. Quotation from the *Canons and Constitution*, p. 1, adopted by Convocation in May 1992.

18 It is unclear how this body relates to the Celtic Evangelical Church (Anglican, 1981), the Old Episcopal Church (1977) and the Old Episcopal Church of Scotland (OECS), which has its origins in the attempt of William III to establish Bishops over the Scottish (Presbyterian) Church. The leaders of the OECS mostly migrated to Canada in the eighteenth century. There are fewer than 50 members.

19 Melton, *op. cit.*, p. 270. Membership is under 1000.

20 The St. Louis Affirmations, besides holding to the fundamentals of the faith, denounce women priests, alternative sexual patterns (e.g. homosexuality), ecumenism (specifically the World Council of Churches), whilst expressing a desire to remain in communion with the See of Canterbury. Melton, *op. cit.*, p. 258.

21 See *A Directory of Churches of the Continuing Anglican Tradition* (Eureka Springs, AK: St Martin's Press, 1983–4); Roderic Dibbert, *The Roots of Traditional Anglicanism* (Akron, Ohio: DeKoven Foundation, 1984); and *Opening Addresses of the Church Congress at St. Louis, Missouri, 14–17 September, 1977* (Amehurst, VA, 1977).

22 The recent AGM in London (23/06/95) failed to resolve these divisions.

23 *The ACS Magazine* (January 1993), p. 3.

24 The Proclamation Trust is dedicated to conservative evangelical values and the promotion of 'Biblical preaching'. Its most prominent leader is the Revd Dick Lucas. Action for a Biblical Witness to Our Nation is run by the Revd Tony Higton, and is more in touch with charismatic renewal.

25 See *Church Times* (24 March, 1995), p. 3, and *Church Times* (31 March, 1995), p. 5.

26 *Pastoral Letter* (2 July, 1995). However, some Roman Catholics are unhappy about

the acceptance of married former Anglican priests as Catholic priests, when their own celibacy is still enforced.

27 Graham Leonard has since been conditionally ordained as a Catholic priest, the actual validity of his orders being accepted on the basis that an Old Catholic bishop took part in his consecration.

28 For an excellent summary of the events surrounding November 1992, see Domitille Grosmaire, 'Women Priests in the Church of England' (unpublished dissertation, Anglia Polytechnic University, Cambridge, 1995). Three more systematic accounts of women's ministry in the Church of England are Sean Gill, *Women and the Church of England* (London: SPCK, 1994); Sue Walrond-Skinner, *Crossing the Boundary: What Will Women Priests Mean?* (London: Mowbray, 1994) and Margaret Webster, *A New Strength, A New Song* (London: Mowbray, 1994).

29 *The Independent* (14 April, 1995), p. 8.

30 A *Confession of Faith* is available from St Mary's House, Byatts Grove, Longton, Stoke on Trent, England.

31 The ACC claims the TCE has mixed parentage, insofar as its founders were not just Anglican, but Old Catholic and Liberal Catholic too. See *Church Times* (10 February, 1995), p. 5.

32 *Church Times* (30 June, 1995), p. 2.

33 For Harper's views on women priests, see *Equal but Different* (London: Hodder, 1994).

34 Personal letter: 01/03/95.

35 The Charismatic Episcopal Church is made up of some Reformed Episcopal groups that have experienced charismatic renewal, former Episcopalians, and others.

36 See *The Oxford Dictionary of Sociology* (Oxford: OUP, 1994), p. 537.

37 See Andrew Brown's report on contemporary ECUSA: 'Disorder of Service', *The Independent* (24 June, 1995), pp. 21–5.

38 Bryan Wilson, *Religious Sects* (New York: McGraw-Hill, 1970), pp. 36–47.

39 For a fuller discussion see my *Words, Wonders and Power: Understanding Contemporary Christian Fundamentalism and Revivalism* (London: SPCK, 1996).

40 *Ibid.*, Chapter 8.

41 See Daniel Hardy, 'The Strategy of Liberalism', in *The Weight of Glory: A Vision and Practice for Christian Faith*, ed. D. Hardy and P. Sedgwick (Edinburgh: T. & T. Clark, 1991), pp. 299ff., and Peter Berger, *The Heretical Imperative* (New York: Collins, 1984).

42 Wilson *op. cit.*, p. 28.

43 Wilson *op. cit.*, pp. 23–35.

44 Wilson *op. cit.*, pp. 38ff.

45 So, as a term, neo-conformist can therefore be set alongside nonconformist, as a slightly different response to conformity. Neither of these expressions necessarily implies sectarian or schismatic behaviour, but it obviously remains a possibility.

46 See Bryan Wilson, *Sects and Society: A Sociological Study of Three Religious Groups in Britain* (London: Heinemann, 1961); *Religion in Secular Society: A Sociological Comment* (London: Watts & Co, 1966), and *The Social Dimensions of Sectarianism: Sects and New Religious Movements in Contemporary Society* (Oxford: Clarendon Press, 1990).

47 *Ibid.*, 1990, p. 126.

48 However, for a typically postmodern account that eschews centralism, see Ellen Wondra, 'What Do We Mean by Center?' in *Anglican Theological Review*, vol. LXXVII, no. 1 (Winter 1995), pp. 26–41. For a more straightforward view, see Timothy Sedgwick, 'The New Shape of Anglican Identity', *Anglican Theological Review*, vol. LXXVII, no. 2 (Spring 1995).

49 See Richard Hooker, *Of The Laws of Ecclesiastical Polity* (Cambridge: CUP, 1989): originally published between 1593 and 1661, in eight books. Experience is deemed to be added through the legacy of Schleiermacher's influence (1768–1834). However, with slight justification, Methodists claim that the transition of the Trilateral into a Quadrilateral is a legacy of Wesley's, who also stressed the primacy of feeling. Undoubtedly, many Methodists do operate with a quadrilateral theological framework, which partly accounts for the relative ease of dialogue between Methodists and Anglicans over unity, as opposed to say, Baptists. Naturally, what constitutes tradition for Methodists and Anglicans is different, especially in respect of episcopal lineage and sacraments. Having said all of that, it should be noted there is nothing particularly original about either the Trilateral or Quadrilateral. The tenth century Jewish philosopher Saadia Ben Joseph (Saadya 882–942 AD) posited precisely the same trilateral and quadrilateral theological schemes for safeguarding Jewish tradition. For an introduction to Saadya, see David Neumark (ed.), *Essays in Jewish Philosophy* (Amsterdam: Philo Press, 1922). The point of this last observation is simply to state that Anglicans are above all reasonable, and happily inculcate good praxiomatic methods that maintain ecclesial structures and boundaries, from whatever source is to hand. One of the best introductions to Anglicanism remains Stephen Sykes, *The Integrity of Anglicanism* (London: SPCK, 1978).
50 Stephen Sykes, *The Identity of Christianity* (London: SPCK, 1984), p. 282.
51 This is in spite of the claim that Anglicanism is a mediating tradition or template, a *via media* between Catholic and reformed positions. See the *Anglican Theological Review*, vol. LXXVII, no. 2, p. 196.
52 Stephen Sykes, *Unashamed Anglicanism* (London: DLT, 1995), pp. 211ff.
53 Robert Carroll, *Wolf in the Sheepfold: The Bible as a Problem for Christianity* (London: SPCK, 1991), p. 62.
54 S. T. Coleridge, *Aids to Reflection* (London: Taylor & Hessey, 1825), p. 101.
55 Paul Avis, *Anglicanism and the Christian Church* (Edinburgh: T. & T. Clark, 1989), pp. 300ff. Cf. my review of this in *Anvil*, vol. 8, no. 1 (1991), pp. 76ff.
56 A. Wilkinson, *The Church of England During World War One* (London: SPCK, 1978): reissued by SCM, London, 1996.

# 10

# Things fall apart II: experiential religion and the absence of theology

> Look on my works, ye Mighty, and despair!
> Nothing beside remains. Round the decay
> Of that colossal wreck, boundless and bare
> The lone and level sands stretch far away.[1]

In the Gospel according to Matthew, Jesus tells two parables about size and structure that are relevant to a discussion of experientially-grounded ecclesiology. In the first pericope in Matthew 5:14, Jesus likens the Christian community to 'a city on a hill that cannot be hid': the suggestion is that in its growth, Christianity should be both progressive and visible. In a second parable (7:24–27), which has a Sunday School familiarity about it, Jesus suggests that the foundations for a stable religious life need to be built on rock, not on sand. Building on rock is thorough but slow, although it ultimately outweighs the short-term attractions of building on sand. When the rains and floods come, the house on the sand is washed away. The suggestion is that rapid expansion may not be the desideratum of Christianity: extensive growth should not be over-valued at the expense of intensive development.[2]

I want to suggest, at least for the moment, that we should think about revivalism and its ecclesial situation at the end of the twentieth century as being like 'a city on a beach'. I have deliberately conflated the metaphors Jesus uses to get to the heart of the present and potential future state of charismatic renewal, which is what we shall be discussing here. Another advantage of the metaphor is that it resonates with images that have already been deployed in describing the state of contemporary religion. One thinks immediately of the cry of despair in Shelley's 'Ozymandias', or Matthew Arnold's poem 'Dover Beach' (1867), which questioned where faith would go once it had left the stable rocks and shores of modernity. Building on this image, Anthony Thiselton sees the present postmodern religious situation as one in which 'everything is shifting, as every stable meaning is deferred and erased in an ever-moving, never-ending flux'. The image of experientially led religion as a city sited on these foundations has been suggested by commentators such as Harvey Cox in *The Secular City* (1965) and in *Religion in the Secular City* (1984).[3]

Let me expand on this. There is no question that revivalism or charismatic renewal is a major shareholder in the totality of Christian expression. But like a city, that expression is not monobehavioural: it is multi-faceted, diverse and expansive, capable even of being at odds with itself. It has its own distinctive districts of belief and behaviour (e.g. those who are pro-Toronto Blessing, those who are anti-, those who speak in tongues, those who do not, etc.) and also like a city, it increasingly sprawls and expands. Indeed, following Melton, we can say that although it is a loosely clustered group, the movement still belongs together.[4] Yet the location of this expanding city is far from secure. Ironically, charismatics frequently talk of being hit by waves (of the Holy Spirit), of revival falling like rain, and of being drenched, soaked, washed and refreshed by the Spirit. These metaphors cover a multitude of occurrences, but it is safe to say that in each instance, whilst bringing energy and revival to some, they bring schism, erosion and disaster to others. Waves of the Spirit tend to fragment the Neo-Pentecostal community, washing some away, whilst bringing others in. Part of the reason that charismatic renewal is so prey to the tides of revival lies in its foundations, namely, identity being heavily reliant on religious experience as the ground of actuality, even though there may be (often latent) fundamentalist or evangelical foundations. More will be said about this later but, for the moment, it is enough to reflect on and note how various waves – or fashions – in revival have expanded revivalism yet also destabilized it. Health and wealth movements, the Toronto Blessing, House Churches, Shepherding movements, dancing in the Spirit, healing ministries and flamboyant charismatic leaders have all played their part. The city on the beach, in spite of its size, has major structural problems that make its long-term future far from secure.[5] As many sociologists have noted, charisma fades over time, enthusiasm wanes, institutionalization sets in, and the individual communities that housed motifs of adventure and excitement tend to fall flat.[6]

Yet the influence of revivalism in this century has introduced progressive and radical change into nearly all existing Christian denominations, besides spawning its own groupings. In the nineteenth century, careful observation and questioning of an individual could have revealed much in a short space of time about their religious allegiance. Not so today: charismatics may be Anglican, Catholic, Methodist or any other denomination. Pentecostals and Neo-Pentecostals can be any colour or class. Historically, Black Pentecostals, who had once focused mostly on *glossolalia*, had had little time for the healing and prophecies of their middle-class white Assemblies of God counterparts, resulting in a chasm between them. Yet the present situation is much more conflated. The varieties and vagaries of contemporary religious expression are seemingly endless. Today, Charismatics, Pentecostals and Neo-Pentecostals signifi-cantly influence each other and the rest of the world's Christian population, as well as secular, social, political and moral arenas. From twenty thousand in South America in 1920, their projected numbers are twenty million by the year 2000. Globally, Charismatics, Pentecostals and Neo-Pentecostals may number as many as four hundred million, which is one-third of the world's Christian population. No part of the world is untouched by Pentecostalism and charismatic renewal.[7]

## Revivalism: Mapping a Disparate World

David Martin's *Tongues of Fire* (1990) assesses the explosive growth of Protes-tantism in Latin America in recent times. It is a predictably excellent survey, and it is his treatment of Pentecostalism that we are primarily concerned with here. Noting that Pentecostal churches are experiencing numerical growth at a time when 'liberal' or traditional denominations are declining, Martin presses the question as to how this shift has come about. Clearly, part of the answer lies in the successful enculturation of Pentecostalism into contemporary society, which itself is moving towards fragmentation, new autonomies, and a willingness to create and participate in a 'free spiritual market'.[8] Whilst it is true that there are only a handful of mainline Neo-Pentecostal denominations in South America, which accounts for most followers, there are nonetheless hundreds of offshoots and alternatives. Martin also notes that their expansion is linked to their acceptance by a wide range of social classes. For the poor, Pentecostalism can represent a popularized, accessible version of Protestantism (or more specifically, the value-system of the Protestant work ethic). Yet the movement also appeals to the middle classes because of its focus on conservative values mixed with adventurous and novel religious motifs. Testimony to the success of Pentecostalism in the middle classes of South America is chiefly visible in the types of buildings now emerging, but also in energetic evangelistic campaigns and forays into the media.[9]

The strength of Martin's work is his appreciation of how Pentecostalism both creates and is created by society, is a reaction against it yet adaptive of its trends. For example, he is mildly critical of accounts of Pentecostal-ism that indulge in what he would probably call 'crude parallelism'. That is to say, simply linking the growth of Pentecostalism to changes in social and economic situations, thereby implying that Pentecostalism is somehow 'a religion of the gaps'.[10] But Martin does not retreat into naive positivism in response to this; he is more subtle. He recognizes that Pentecostalism does offer a sacred canopy under which individuals and groups can shelter, and then make decisions about their response to modernity, secularization and the incessant ravages of pluralism. Thus, he notes that Pentecostalism 'offers participation, mutual support, emotional release, a sense of identity and dignity . . . [it] provides a substitute society'.[11] Clearly, this functions in different ways for different social classes. For the middle classes, this form of religion can be escapist, offering mythical legitimization for their affairs, without really pressing social questions. Yet for the poor, it can be essential: a means of social and psychological survival, with religious hope issuing a form of security and the promise of liberation. So it seems in South America at least that Pentecostalism has become a peculiarly adaptable expression of Christianity that benefits from the breaking up of old religious monopolies, and in turn mirrors a more general fragmentation in society. Traditional Protestants and Roman Catholics alike are losing their grip on the souls of the people, as the search for authentic, transformative and convincing religious experience gathers pace. In South America, this process is accelerating with some rapidity, so it is safe to suggest that the forms of Neo-Pentecostalism that will emerge in the near future will most likely be more novel and particular than before. Fissure will increase, and enculturation and conflation of beliefs in relation to society and culture will require continual redrawing of the revivalist map.

In Britain and Europe, the picture is slightly different. House Churches have led the way in charismatic renewal for many years. Andrew Walker's seminal *Restoring the Kingdom* (1985) charts the rise of restorationism, the principle vehicle for Neo-Pentecostalism in the last quarter of the century. Walker describes the House Church phenomenon in sociological terms that categorize churches according to whether they are 'R1' or 'R2'. The taxonomy employed allows for differentiation over styles of leadership, attitudes to authority, women, dialogue with other groups, ecumenism and orders. Sociologically speaking, R1 churches are tightly controlled, with an aggressive sectarian mentality. R2 churches, on the other hand, are more relaxed, though both types may well share similar fundamentals and core beliefs. However, since the 1980s, there is plenty of evidence to suggest that some House Church movements, at least in terms of their sociological identity, move between the R1 and R2 categories. This is no doubt caused by such variables as the particular charismatic leader or situation, what issues the church may be addressing, and how it continues to consolidate and expand in the plural and postmodern world.[12]

Interestingly, Roman Catholics have a similar structural variant on the House Churches as an agent of renewal, in the form of Neo-Catechumenate movements and communities such as the Mother of God, founded in Gaithersburg, Maryland in 1966. Whilst those involved in these movements would argue that they have not left the Church, and are therefore communitarian not sectarian, there is mounting evidence to suggest otherwise.[13]

Of course, revivalism has reached well beyond the House Church movement. Charismatic renewal is one of the most potent forces of change and development in existing denominations. Revivalists and healers such as John Wimber, Benny Hinn, Morris Cerullo, Bill Surbritzky and Reinhard Bonnke have re-introduced the principles of revival in recent times with some force. In Britain, Europe and the Commonwealth, they attract considerable audiences for their conferences, yet do not necessarily press for a change in denominational affiliation. Cynics would say that this ensures that their market is consequently much larger than those who remain with the House Church movement, such as Terry Virgo and Bryn Jones. In my view, there is no question that Wimber and others are sensitive to being over-identified with their own denominational expansion, lest they lose widespread ecumenical support in the process.[14] But it would be unfair to suggest that charismatic renewal has only been stimulated in traditional denominations by forces external to them. True, many agencies in the 1960s such as the Full Gospel Businessmen's Fellowship International (FGBFI) did engender a form of dispersed ecumenical revivalism, that tended to be rather personal. Yet there were more corporate examples of renewal emerging in the 1970s and 1980s. For example, the Church of England has seen bodies such as Anglicans for Renewal Ministries (ARM), SOMA (Sharing of Ministries Abroad), the Fountain Trust and assorted healing ministries become an established part of the established church.[15] Added to this, major Anglican centres for revivalism – Holy Trinity, Brompton, St Andrew's, Chorleywood and St Thomas Crooke's, Sheffield – attract people in their hundreds if not thousands, to experience the very latest and freshest experiences of renewal, usually winged in on a jet and a prayer from North America.

In North America, the picture is no less diverse. Catholic Revivalism has been explored in some depth in important works by Meredith McGuire and Mary Jo Neitz.[16] Their contributions to the study of contemporary charismatic renewal are vital because they shrewdly identify the 'suburbanization' of revivalism in North America. Quite simply, the religion of perennial revival is at home there. The focus of McGuire's work is on healing, a subject that persistently absorbs the American mind. In her view, there is no question that part of the reason for the appeal of revivalism in the USA lies in the notions of power that underpin healing ministries: groups and individuals that practice these therapies operate as brokers of power, enabling a sense of healing energy to flow into people. Participants are caught up in a dynamic matrix in which agents of power give rise to experiences that help individuals feel closer to one another and closer to God.[17] This occurrence forms the church: it is a framework in which one can simply *be*.[18] Neitz's work, although more general, is valuable for its portrayal of the diversity of Catholic charismatic renewal. We shall explore this in more detail later, but for the moment it is worth noting that revivalist groups have formed themselves into a significant *sub-culture* within American Roman Catholicism through informal home groups and cells. At the same time, high-profile individuals and influential publications have placed charismatic renewal firmly on the Church's agenda.[19]

The mapping of contemporary Protestant Pentecostalism in North America could begin almost anywhere and end just about everywhere: from Tele-evangelists such as Swaggart and Bakker, to Pat Robertson's and Oral Roberts' universities, to churches the size of small towns, right down to snake-handlers in the rural mid-west.[20] Phenomenologically, Protestant charismatic renewal is both behaviourally and doctrinally diverse, and is also dispersed through all denominations besides having many of its own. Are there any generic characteristics that bind the movement together? Harvey Cox suggests that revivalism has fallen prey to new theologies that are enhancing the numerical growth of the movement but at the same time betraying its original fundaments. Working with a fairly positivist notion of the origins of Pentecostalism, Cox notes its present preoccupation with Dominion Theology, excessive demonology, health and wealth movements, and spiritual phenomena more usually associated with the New Age.[21] The first of these, Dominion Theology, particularly concerns Cox as he sees it as a way of inculcating politically conservative values and fundamentalist social attitudes into Pentecostalism. The preoccupation with establishing God's reign on earth now – righteously dominating individuals and institutions in the name of God – has led to the dissolving of distinctions between pre- and post-millennialists. Dominion Theology syncretizes these positions, and invites revivalism to move forward to make a brave new world, in preparation for the return of Christ. Yet in spite of this new social dimension to revivalism, it would be a mistake to assume that concrete galvanization and authentic socio-political integration are taking place. In North America, it is still true that revivalism continues to incline towards being 'divisive, anti-intellectual, self-righteous and reluctant to assume responsibility for social and institutional reform'.[22]

The last area of revivalist expansion that needs mentioning is not so easily confined geographically. I am referring to the syncretic revivalist churches that have mushroomed in recent years. Sociologists are in general agreement that the principal locations for study in this field are Africa and the Pacific-Asian Rim, which include countries like South Korea. Indeed, David Martin uses both Korea and South Africa as 'instructive parallels' in his discussion of Neo-Pentecostalism in *Tongues of Fire* (1990). Martin notes, as others have, that the relationship between revivalist religion in these places and the existing structure of primal religion goes far beyond what many western Christians would find acceptable.[23] For example, it is no accident that churches that strongly emphasize demonology flourish in mainly animistic areas of Korea, whilst those that press the Protestant work ethic in conjunction with healing ministries do extremely well in the new urban areas and overcrowded inner cities of Africa and Asia. Harvey Cox goes so far as to describe the situation as one in which shamanism has met entrepreneurialism, and been largely adopted by revivalists. Looking at the work of pastors such as Paul Yonggi Cho, with his church membership numbered in hundreds of thousands, this is a difficult thesis to defeat.[24] Similarly, Africa, through primal religions that emphasize healing, God as *deus ex machina*, and the world of spirits and demons, is also prey to novel and heady concoctions of revivalism and local religious belief. However, it is important not to patronize Africa and Asia for their alleged syncretism; the idea that the First World somehow has a pure version of the Gospel which is being corrupted and diluted is deeply offensive. Are healing ministries, health and wealth movements, Dominion Theology and the Toronto Blessing not also examples of postmodern, middle-class syncretism? Nonetheless, it is estimated that indigenous African churches, many of which are strongly influenced by Pentecostalism, already number 100 million Christians, and are the biggest growth area in revivalism today.[25]

## A Deeper Problem for Experiential Religion?

Whilst studying as an ordinand, I undertook a two-week placement in a well-known Lake District village, hoping to learn something about rural ministry in a busy tourist setting. Once upon a time, the place had supported two Brethren churches – 'Open' and 'Closed', the buildings being at opposite ends of the town. Now, there were no Brethren left: one church was a carpet warehouse, and the other a Masonic Lodge.[26] The Anglican church was an unremarkable Victorian building. Yet with a population of only 1200, in 1989 there were three House Churches. One had been founded by a former youth worker attached to the Anglican church: he had fallen out with the vicar ten years before over guitars, spiritual gifts and the like. He left, taking the teenagers with him; they now rented the local library on Sundays. A few years later, having been joined by some adults, this church divided itself, this time on the issue of authority – a retired charismatic missionary was clearly better suited to run the church than the ex-youth worker, but no one could agree. Result: schism. Two years after that, a second schism developed, this time over the issue of health and wealth (Prosperity Gospel) hermeneutics, and again, authority and charisma. The combined numbers of these three House Churches was no more than forty people; the Anglican electoral roll was around 160.[27]

The problem lies with the absence of theology. In spite of the influence and scale of contemporary revivalism, there is very little that could be classed as charismatic theology. Like fundamentalism and Pentecostalism, revivalism has spawned its own seminaries, notable preachers and exponents, but a theologian of national or global significance has yet to emerge. Revivalists tend to appeal to the work of theologians who feed their theological outlook, without they themselves necessarily being paid-up revivalists.[28] There are some exceptions to this rule:[29] historians of revivalism, such as Hollenweger or Hocken, have written about charismatic thinking and praxis, but neither has constructed a charismatic theology. Gifted scholars such as Simon Tugwell and David Watson, who clearly can be identified as charismatic, have tended to produce popular 'testimony-teaching' books, not serious works of scholarship that outline a theology. Indeed, in the recently published *Dictionary of Pentecostal and Charismatic Movements*, there is no entry for theology at all.[30] Naturally, this does not mean there are no doctrines in revivalism: ideas about the person and work of the Holy Spirit are critical to revivalist identity. However, beyond this, there is unlikely to be a developed Christology, soteriology, doctrine of the Church and the like.[31]

This is a vital observation. Why is there so much schism in revivalism? Answer: there is no doctrine of the Church, and no theological template for tolerating plurality. (All that can be said to exist is a notion of gathered homogeneity, which emphasizes size.) Why is evangelism so poor, numerical growth usually coming from converting people who are already Christians? Answer: revivalism has no soteriology of its own. Why does revivalism apparently succeed so quickly where others have failed for so long before? Answer: there is no real Christology, creed, sacramental or Trinitarian theology and praxis to burden believers. Adherents are offered experience, not knowledge. Theology, if you can call it that, is done through the hormones and not in the head. Experience always precedes reflection. There is no charismatic exegesis of scripture, only eisegesis.

The observation that contemporary revivalism has no real systematic theology, as such, is not meant to be patronizing. There are actually good reasons why this is the case. But let me say something about how revivalism attempts to compensate for the void. First and foremost, revivalism has a strong background in biblical fundamentalism. Whilst not everyone who would identify themselves as charismatic is a fundamentalist, most will be fundamentalistic. That is to say, they will use the Bible in a literalistic, pre-critical fashion, hold their beliefs in a similar way to classic fundamentalists (i.e. intolerant of plurality and liberalism, prone to schism, monologue, etc.) and yet be looking for spiritual power that is linked to, but beyond, a tightly defined biblical authority. As one author puts it, revivalism offers 'an eschatologically justified, power-added experiential enhancement'.[32] As one convert puts it: 'Salvation is wonderful, but there was just something missing. I wanted very earnestly to do God's will. I wanted to glorify him. I realised that there was a deeper depth where I could get into the Lord. I hungered and thirsted for this.'[33]

Second, revivalism purports to be, at least in part, a movement that has distanced itself from theology. Harvey Cox sees revivalism as the major component in an experientialist movement, that is tired of the arid, over-rational religion of modernity that was split between liberals and conservatives. Revivalism is a self-conscious religion of experience and feeling that deliberately pitches itself against too much thinking about God.[34] Cox is at least partly right in his observation: whenever and wherever I have attended a revivalist gathering, believers are often encouraged to desist from rationalizing, to abandon critical faculties, and are instead to 'let God touch their heart'. Last, the absence of a theological, doctrinal or ecclesiological basis makes revivalists incredibly free in their reactions to and inculcation of contemporary culture. Indeed, social relevance is their trademark: they are not bogged down by centuries of tradition, nor do they have much of a past to justify or carry. Thus, they tend to use any theologian or any aspect of Christian history selectively, to resource their beliefs,[35] but at the same time eschew a depth of participation in theological, ecclesiological, historical or sociological processes, for fear it will weigh them down. Revivalist religion is essentially a matter of the heart, and works best when it travels lightly.

There are some problems that arise directly out of these observations that relate to the question of charismatic theology. First, although some people claim revivalism is an ecumenical, uniting movement, it tends to be anything but.[36] History shows that Charismatics tend to be highly divisive: each new revival within revivalism brings fresh division and more schism. Contemporary revivalism has no history of uniting denominations, although it sometimes brings together federations of like-minded people. But that is not ecumenical, any more than the nation tuning in to *Songs of Praise* is an inter-faith event; it is simply evidence of homogeneity. The reason that ecumenism and unity are difficult to achieve in revivalism is because of the subjective, individualistic nature of the religion.[37] Second, and linked to this point, the worship of contemporary revivalism compounds the problem of persistent ecclesial fracture. Classic revival worship, such as under Wesley, Moody or Edwards, had a tendency to use hymns as didactic material. In the case of Wesley, his theology was actually taught in his hymns and sung by converts. The creeds, sacraments and traditions of the Church were caught up in eighteenth- and nineteenth-century rhythm: people were partly bound together by shared doctrines. Contemporary revivalism, in contrast, attempts no such thing. It does not supplement sacraments, but replaces them: it is in worship that you meet God, not in bread, wine, word or creeds. Furthermore, the function of worship is not didactic but emotive: it is a vehicle to move people closer to God, to 'release' them, to stir the heart.

Consequently, most songs in contemporary revivalism are deliberately devoid of serious doctrinal content: they express feelings about or to God. This of course is no basis for theological or ecclesial unity – it just creates a 'community of feeling' which is always open to the ravages of subjective individualism.[38] Third, the fundamentalistic roots of revivalism also guarantee ecclesial problems. In such communities, it is never the Bible that rules, but always the interpreter.[39] Consequently, some revivalist churches can look quite totalitarian. Even here, there is a theological account for the lack of ecclesial breadth. Although revivalists have done much to promote the Holy Spirit in recent years, there has been no move towards developing a Trinitarian doctrine that could give an ecclesial basis for openness, mutuality and plural forms of sociality. Ironically, the stress on experience in revivalism means that there is no 'coping stone' to keep orthodox views together.[40] Schism occurs in revivalism precisely because one person of the Godhead is invariably promoted or ignored over another. There is never any agreement over the basis for ecclesial authority. It is nearly always driven by charisma, authority, power and emotion, and therefore always open to a charismatic counter-coup.

If the theology of revivalism is poor, what exactly is it that keeps revivalism together? Indeed, how has the movement come to be so popular in late modernity and postmodernity? Part of the answer must lie in its 'lightness of being'. Despite the colourful, and at times complex world Charismatics live in, there is not much to actually learn. But there is plenty to experience. To be charismatic is to belong to a charismatically led church, where the gifts (or charisms) of the Spirit are known and deployed. Revivalism offers healing and a sense of personal renewal to believers. Its theodicy can be dramatically dualist: Jesus versus the devil, Christians and angels versus demons. The worship alternates between being dynamic and punchy, to intimate and smoochy. It is above all a questing faith, that sees itself as restoring the values of the Kingdom of

God, prior to the return of Christ. Increasingly, it has a millennial edge to it.[41]

The future for an enthusiastic-experiential Christian movement without a real theology is potentially troublesome. It has no way of preventing schism, lacks depth in discernment, colludes in social abrogation, and may well be a spent force in a new millennium.[42] Then again, a movement that stresses personal empowerment, intimacy and love, yet is 'doctrine-lite' (but still with all the fizz of new wine), innovative and novel, may actually turn out to be a highly popular *credo* for a third millennium. Many mainstream denominations, for the moment at least, seem content to supplement their diets with the spice of enthusiastic, paranormal and esoteric religion. As one Anglican charismatic vicar explained to me recently, they have not 'sold out' to the consuming fire of total revivalism – they have just been 'warmed in a gentle way'[43], influenced but not possessed. Passion and enthusiasm may be the dish of the day, but it is not the only item on the menu. For a Western world that is increasingly privatized and individualistic, a postmodern, enthusiastically driven religion may be the one that proves to be the most popular in the next millennium: yet that is no guarantee of ultimate longevity. Experiential-revivalist religion is fashion-conscious, a populist, culturally relative and relevant phenomenon.

## More Issues for Revivalism

The previous sections suggested that the global breadth of revivalism, coupled with its lack of fundaments, poses serious problems for experiential religion. The key issues for the future are now beginning to emerge. For example, if communitarian groups like House Churches or the Roman Catholic Mother of God communities are to succeed, how will they avoid becoming increasingly sectarian? In Africa and Asia, how far can syncretism go before fundamental beliefs are changed, and core Pentecostal values lost? How will all these movements avoid routinization, as Weber would call it, and what are the implications of that for new denominations and movements? And are times of spiritual revival, renewal or refreshment really capable of being the ground for religious identity? Placing so much stress on religious experience is a perennial problem: how can anyone be sure that the ultimate sources of revival rest not in God, but in the restless human psyche, searching for certainty at the end of a millennium? Equally, how do Charismatics cope with the tension between word and Spirit when strange phenomena like the Toronto Blessing hit town? As before, the brevity of this discussion necessitates a somewhat sweeping portrayal.

Nigel Scotland, in his sympathetic portrayal of charismatic renewal, provisionally highlights some areas of concern that he hopes those within renewal movements will address. The most obvious concern, echoing Weber, is the 'routinization of charisma' over a period of time. Although charismatic renewal has had a substantial effect on traditional denominations, it has largely failed to transform the structures in which it finds itself operating.[44] Thus, instead of displacing the liberal hierarchy, it finds itself placed within it — just another 'also ran'. So radical agendas for growth are often ignored, sometimes justifiably, due to their theological and sociological paucity.[45] By the time the movement has come of age and is ready to engage in dialogue, it has lost its cutting edge. Allied to charisma being routinized and controlled, is the difficulty of charismatic divisiveness, which can occur over a range of issues. Nigel Scotland sees a number of problems arising already: disagreement over interpreting religious experience in relation to the authority of scripture, worship that 'focuses on the self', and (generally) poor theological methodology (although he is optimistic about this point).[46] Harvey Cox sees charismatic renewal becoming a 'battlefield', a kind of phenomenological war that is waged between fundamentalists and experientialists, and then again between separatists and ecumenists.[47] Jean Jacques Suurmond's treatment of charismatic renewal opens up yet more possibilities, arguing that the movement could become theologically and morally liberal as a direct result of its playful engagement with postmodernism.[48] The future, it seems, is still an open one for revivalism, although I am not inclined to be as positive as scholars such as Nigel Scotland, for the following reasons.

First, there is no escaping the sociological dimensions that accompany charismatic renewal, 'Latter-Rain' and Neo-Pentecostal movements. No matter what theological story is being articulated in these groups, there is a sociological script to follow as well. Following scholars of charisma such as Sohm and Weber, Thomas O'Dea has indentified 'five dilemmas of institutionalization' that affect charismatic movements.[49] Each dilemma reflects a fundamental antinomy between charisma and the pressure to routinize it for the sake of the institution so that religious experience is rendered continuously available for the masses in order to provide stability. The first dilemma concerns the status of the original message and the maintenance of its prescient power. Clearly, this places great emphasis on the original messenger, although postmodern revivalism apparently seems to be quite 'decentred' in this way. The second dilemma is over how the sacred or the experience of the numinous is to be objectified and reified. Typically, this is done in the context of worship, ritual clinics or preaching. But in spite of the organization, perceptions remain highly subjective. A third dilemma arises directly out of this, namely assessment of the appropriate structures for inculcating charismatic experience: there will always be disagreements over how it is routinized, and the consequent hegemonic ecclesiology. This leads to a fourth dilemma: delimitation. Definitions of charismatic phenomena tend to 'kill the spirit', but some limits have to be placed on acceptable phenomena, or the movement risks gross subjectivity and eventual relativity. Fifth, the exercise of power also poses a dilemma. 'Power language' is common to theology and sociology, and there is a great temptation in charismatic groups to conflate sacred and profane notions of power in order to protect 'the religion' itself.

O'Dea's observations begin to bear out the initial thesis of this chapter: that religious experience is insufficient in terms of the provision of a foundation for Neo-Pentecostalism. The very basis of the movement is riddled with antinomies that ensure fracture, fissure and instability. My second point, therefore, is that 'the routinization of charisma' always occurs in relation to contemporary social norms. At the end of this millennium, charismatic renewal finds itself reacting to an increasingly postmodern society. Naturally, following Niebuhr, its self-perception is that it leads the way in asserting 'Christ above culture', but the movement would be more adequately expressed as representing the 'Christ of culture'.[50] The movement taps into contemporary preoccupations with empowerment, fulfilment, healing and meeting individual needs. It treads lightly on complex social issues. It is playfully ambiguous in its treatment of absolute values, tending towards pneumatological situationalism in moral and theological questions. It is becoming a radically 'decontextualized' movement, that has more time for the symbolic and less for texts, yet is profoundly 'dislocated', capable of instantly operating at any time, in any place, and anywhere.[51] Ironically, this may be a subconscious missiological response to the cultural challenge of the new millennium – the provision of an adaptive, experiential religion that is accommodating of the new, emerging world, neither rejecting it too strongly nor affirming it too easily.[52]

Third, and linked to the above point, a theological observation that has sociological consequences needs to be made. If the foundations of the Neo-Pentecostal city are weak, what about the structures themselves: how do they cope with the 'rain' or dramatic religious experience? It is ironic that the theologian who first posited experience as being important for the Christian community should unintentionally offer a critique at this point. Friedrich Schleiermacher suggested that religion could be located in feeling and intuition, not just in dogma, and that the doctrine of the Trinity could therefore be seen as a 'coping stone' that sits atop the Christian faith. It provides no support for the walls. Its function is rather to prevent corrosive external elements from entering the walls and building and corrupting it from within. There is a sense then, in which a coping stone is an essential burden to any building: it is supported by the walls, but without the stone, the walls are very vulnerable.[53] Clearly, Schleiermacher saw the doctrine of the Trinity as a way of keeping out heresy and thus uniting the body of Christ. The question is, how does experiential-revivalism manage the same ends? In spite of Nigel Scotland's assertion that contemporary revivalism has 'renewed its interest' in this doctrine, it is fairly apparent that it may be too little too late. True enough, revivalism does know the persons of the Trinity individually, but that is not the same as knowing a doctrine of the Trinity that might serve as a coping stone. So, sociologically speaking, there is a theological account for the fracture and fissure so endemic to contemporary revivalism, namely the absence of a doctrine that promotes openness, mutuality, unity and coherence, and that is also anti-hegemonic.[54] In short, an economic doctrine of the Trinity. This means that revivalism is constantly open to the vagaries of 'charismatic weather': every time there is a 'latter rain' (e.g. the Toronto Blessing), the body divides against itself on grounds of authority, the interpretation of experience, or other factors. Renewal over erosion, sometimes severe, is a constant factor in this type of experiential religion.

It is perhaps worth commenting at this point that the house in Jesus' parable that is built on sand and falls flat does so for two reasons. First, it is built on sand; second, it rains. This suggests that the socio-theological observation concerning the absence of a dogmatic coping stone will have important implications for the future. Clearly, the fragmentation that is common to postmodernity will be in some way copied in revivalism. In turn, this will result in some abandoning an experiential-based religion and opting (again?) for the more 'solid' fundaments of conservative evangelicalism or fundamentalism. Either way, the future does not look likely to develop into one of consolidation and unity, in spite of the inevitable routinization of charisma.

## The Future of Revivalism: One City, or a Thousand Different Villages?

Given the remarks made in the previous sections of this chapter, we are now in a position to speculate about the next millennium. I have already suggested that revivalism increasingly mirrors postmodernist trends, so it seems appropriate to define more precisely what is meant by that. Modernism could be characterized as a movement that searched for inner truths behind surface appearances: the origins of sociology, phenomenology and psychology are birthed in this vision. Modernism was also expressed in cultural and aesthetic ways: it was or is progressive, secularized and consciously opposed to classicism. Fundamentalism and classic Pentecostalism represent the cognitive and intuitive reactions to modernity. In contrast, postmodernism supposedly represents the recovery of the romantic outlook. Yet it is not a reversion to tradition, because postmodernity sees the search for truth as a mirage; thus, it is decentred, with 'a profusion of style and orientation . . . any attempt to penetrate to a deeper reality is abandoned and mimesis loses all meaning'.[55] There is a sense in which revivalism reacts against this vision of truth, culture and life. Yet to be a reaction against it, it has to be a reaction to it, and the inculcation of postmodernist values is thus unavoidable, unless a strict communitarian line is imposed. Generally it is not, and revivalism therefore finds itself accommodating the new world, and in some ways affirming it. Thus, many in charismatic churches have quite unconsciously abandoned their modernist foundations of evangelicalism or fundamentalism, and traded them in for the experiential forms of personal certainty so beloved of postmodernity. Therefore, they can now share in Lyotard's description of postmodernism (including its sacred forms) as 'incredulity towards metanarratives'.[56] Three points can therefore be made in conclusion.

First, the general directionality of revivalism does seem to lie in a more 'playful' engagement with truth. This is partly because it is tending to abandon textually centred religion in favour of the visual, symbolic and intuitive.[57] One of the ideas implied in describing revivalism at the turn of this century as a city on a beach is that it connotes the notion of pleasure, leisure and play. But we are entitled to ask at this point, has the 'pleasure principle' in phenomena such as the Toronto Blessing become divorced from reality? It would certainly seem so: such phenomena seem escapist and self-indulgent to those outside the city, yet to those within, they are the very presence of God, in playful activity with his children. The playfulness with truth – guaranteed by the experiential nature of late revivalism – leads to a number of problems for the movement and its onlookers. Conservative evangelicals find it hard to accept phenomena that are not explicitly reflected in the canon of scripture. Neo-Pentecostals partly respond to this by searching for texts that connect with their experience, but the connections are usually very thin, if appropriate at all. In turn, the failure to locate biblical proof or scriptural legitimization for revivalist practice leads them to the very heart of the postmodern abyss. It contents itself with a movement from the pre-critical phase to the post-critical phase, without ever passing through a critical stage; in other words, it abandons the search for any ultimate truth, and engages in methodological pragmatism and playful experientialism.[58] The real problem with this position is that it reflects postmodern culture only too well. If it does transpire that postmodernity will permit liberalism or totalitarianism, but without an 'agreed ethical heart', revivalism might end up by offering a religion that has no real head for discernment.

Second, there is a finite limit to the number of times one can say, 'behold, I am doing a new thing'. Such proclamations are essential to the charismatic situation, and especially to the leadership. But there is a boredom threshold that has to be negotiated by the revivalist movement at the turn of the century. What happens when prophecy fails? How can the community of romantic and adventurous ideology be maintained? Will followers not become weary of quasi-immanence? There is already some evidence to suggest that revivalism is losing the present generation of 'twenty-somethings', who are turning their backs on a form of religious expression that is too narrow and particular, in favour of alternative modes that are sacramental, liturgical, ecological and more avowedly postmodern. Where this will leave revivalism remains to be seen, but Bryan Wilson notes that charismatic communities always ultimately disappoint: 'the specific prophecies ... fail, the essential miracles are heard about rather than seen ...'.[59] Because charisma and charismatic phenomena are such shaky commodities, it does seem justifiable to speak of Neo-Pentecostalism as founded on the shifting sands of religious experience and charisma. As such, the ground of being is subject to all the elements, including the wind: and who knows where it will blow in the future? And as for 'rain', is not the safety of that metaphor in conveying revelation and renewal doubtful? The source of rain appears to be heaven; but its actual source is the earth, created by hot air and complex climatic conditions.

Third, the core or centre of revivalism, if it exists at all, seems to be an interest in power. The exercise of power, both human and divine, characterizes the movement at the end of this millennium. The power of God is deemed to be a counter-power against the world, yet working within it. The task of the renewed ecclesial community is seen as identifying that power (especially new and novel sources, such as the Toronto Blessing), reifying and controlling it, and finally expanding its influence. What is confusing in the analysis of revivalism is that many studies focus on the agency of renewal (e.g. a guru, a text, phenomena, etc.) without seeing that the interest in the agency ultimately rests in its capacity to deliver power. Ironically, although revivalism can be said to be 'power-centred', this does not invalidate my earlier point, that the movement is becoming decentred, because it remains power-related. The subtlety of argument lies in the alliance between power and its agents.[60] At the end of this century, the reticulate nature of revivalism is expansive, with new agents for empowerment constantly being added: yesterday the Kansas City Prophets, today Toronto, tomorrow ... ? These agents are increasingly distanced from each other, assuming their own particularity, making the boundaries and communicative links in the city difficult to track. Yet 'power-centredness' still exists notionally as the desideratum of core experiences. The problem for revivalism is that the ways of accessing that power have now become so myriad that the movement as a whole is losing its corporate identity and is beginning to break up.[61] Postmodernity has, it would appear, finally come to revivalism. After the collapse of the 'grand symphony' of metanarratives in 'established religion', all we are left with is groups of enthusiastic music-makers.[62] There is no charismatic *City of God* to be found, because there never was a foundation of theology. Yet there are plenty of peripatetic tent-villages, each with their own local rituals. The poet W. B. Yeats expresses the situation like this:

> Things fall apart;
> the centre cannot hold . . .
> The ceremony of innocence is drowned.
> The best lack all conviction,
> the worst are full of passionate intensity.[63]

## Notes

1 From the poem 'Ozymandias', Percy Bysshe Shelley, 1792–1822.
2 See K. Barth, *Church Dogmatics* (Edinburgh: T. & T. Clark, 1958), Book IV, ii, Chap. xv, p. 648: 'we cannot strive for greater vertical renewal merely to produce greater horizontal extension and a wider audience.'
3 See A. Thiselton, *Interpreting God and the Postmodern Self: On Meaning, Manipulation and Promise* (Edinburgh: T. & T. Clark, 1995), pp. 81–5. Harvey Cox, *The Secular City: Urbanization and Secularization in Theological Perspective* (New York: Macmillan, 1965), argues that the waning of ecclesial power may not be disastrous; the Church instead should concentrate on the positive, affirming role it can play in the modern world. *Religion in the Secular City* (New York: Simon & Schuster, 1984), takes account of the postmodern situation, and argues for a more accommodating view of the role of religion in society. This culminates in the suggestion that the present religious situation can be likened to a 'carnival of faith' (p. 241), in which religion has become popularized and urbanized, yet has also moved from dogmatism or fundamentalism to experientialism: in other words, adapted for the postmodern era. Thus, Neo-Pentecostalism, in its urban comprehensiveness, can be likened to a city on a beach.
4 J. G. Melton, *The Encyclopaedia of American Religion* (Charlotte, NC: McGrath, 1978). Melton uses the notion of 'family' to describe the federation of charismatic movements, but the notion of city or *polis* is just as appropriate.
5 The question therefore begs, 'what would constitute secure foundations?' There are no easy sociological or theological accounts for this. Sociologically, one could speak of foundational identity being formed through 'tenuous opposition' (G. D. Suttles, *The Social Construction of Community* (Chicago: University of Chicago Press, 1972), pp. 247ff.), which resonates with Martin Marty's theological notion of fundamentalism and revivalism as only existing 'in opposition to' other foundations that are held not to be sacred, but secular (cf. M. Marty, 'Fundamentalism

Reborn' in *Religion and Republic* (Boston: Beacon Press, 1987), pp. 299–300). Or, one could opt for the foundations being based on locality, sociality and relationships, whereby 'religion', in the very etymology of the word, acts as a cultural-linguistic system, a 'binding force' that brings coherence and unity to a given group (cf. H. Newby, *Community* (Milton Keynes: Open University Press, 1980), p. 13; S. Greer, *The Emerging City* (New York: Collier Macmillan, 1962), p. 103 and G. Lindbeck, *The Nature of Doctrine* (Philadelphia: Westminster Press, 1984), pp. 33ff.). Theologically speaking, secure foundations have tended to be found in an evolving (and sedimenting?) system of agreed canons of Scripture, creeds, ecclesial offices and the like, over many centuries. As I argue later, the doctrine of the Trinity, which permits a degree of directional plurality, can be seen by some as the 'capping' of this constructive process. However, other forms of theological method can also issue security that largely prevents fissure. In a recent article, 'Falling Out of Love: The Ordination of Women and Recent Anglo-American Anglican Schisms Explored' (*Journal of Contemporary Religion*, vol. 11, no. 3 (1996), I argue that the Anglican foundations – a 'dynamic negotiating quadrilateral' of Scripture, tradition, reason/rationality and experience/culture has, until recently, ensured a healthy pluralism that has permitted mutuality and unity, even in the face of disagreement. Contemporary revivalism, with no such 'foundation', save perhaps a notional knowledge of evangelical or fundamentalist roots, is based too much on the subjectivity of religious experience and expression.

6 For a discussion of charisma in relation to institutions, see M. Weber, *Charisma and Institution Building* (Chicago: University of Chicago Press, 1968). For a discussion of adventure as a prominent theme in contemporary revivalism, see James Hopewell, *Congregation: Stories and Structures* (London: SCM, 1987).

7 The terminology 'Charismatic', 'Pentecostal' and 'Neo-Pentecostal' is used interchangeably in this chapter. Although there are slight differences in theology and ecclesiology between these movements, their overall similarity at the end of the twentieth century allows for my deliberate conflation. The origins of the groups differ – classic Pentecostalism emerged from holiness movements in response to modernity, and charismatic renewal from Brethren groups and House Churches in response to postmodernity, but all three groups are now behaviourally similar (cf. J. G. Melton, *Encyclopaedia of American Religion* (Charlotte, NC: McGrath, 1978). They are driven by a desire to see individuals filled and empowered by the Holy Spirit, with some kind of reifiable activity following, such as *glossolalia* or *charismata*. Although Charismatics and Neo-Pentecostals tend to be more ecumenical, there is growing evidence to suggest that traditional Pentecostal groups are also beginning to share this outlook. References to numbers of Charismatics needs to be handled with caution. D. Barrett, *The Encyclopaedia of World Christianity* (Oxford: OUP 1982), p. 838, suggests that there may be only 100 million Charismatics. Ian Cotton, *The Hallelujah Revolution* (London: Little & Brown, 1995) suggests 400 million.

8 D. Martin, *Tongues of Fire: The Explosion of Protestantism in Latin America* (Oxford: Blackwell, 1990), p. 52.

9 Martin cites the Jotabeche Cathedral in Santiago, which holds 18,000 people, as an example. Much of the work in radio and television is still in debt to North American efforts.

10 Martin, 1990, p. 82. Martin especially has in mind Cornelia Butler Flora's *Pentecostalism in Colombia: Baptism by Fire and Spirit* (Cranbury NJ: Fairleigh Dickinson University Press, 1976). The basic thesis is to treat Pentecostalism as the religious aspect of economic dependency.

11 Martin, 1990, p. 258.

12 A. Walker, *Restoring the Kingdom*, 2nd edition (London: Hodder & Stoughton, 1988).

13 See 'Charismatic Communities' in *A Dictionary of Pentecostal and Charismatic Movements* (Grand Rapids, Michigan: Zondervan Publishing, 1988), pp. 127ff., and Gordon Urquhart, *The Pope's Armada* (London: Bantam, 1995). Urquhart's book is especially good on the Neocatechumenate movement, and on the influence of Kiko Arguello's music as an ideological lynchpin for the communities, which seems to resonate with the influence of Wimber's style of music and its influence on his Vineyard churches and their followers. In Britain, the most obvious example of a charismatic communitarian group is the Jesus Army, headed by Noel Stanton.

14 John Wimber did have his own denomination at home in the USA (Vineyards), but was more reluctant to spoil his widespread following in the UK by setting up too many Vineyards abroad, that might compete with churches that presently support him. There are a few Vineyards in the UK and other Commonwealth countries, but plans for more serious expansion are not clear.

15 See M. Harper, 'Renewal in the Holy Spirit', in *Christianity: A World Faith*, ed. R. Keeley (Tring: Lion Publishing, 1985), p. 103. A full, if over-positive account of charismatic renewal in Britain can be found in Peter Hocken's *Streams of Renewal* (Exeter: Paternoster Press, 1986).

16 Meredith McGuire, *Pentecostal Catholics: Power, Charisma and Order in a Religious Movement* (Philadelphia: Temple University, 1982) and *Ritual Healing in Suburban America*, (New Brunswick: Rutgers University Press, 1988); Mary Jo Neitz, *Charisma and Community: A Study of Commitment within Charismatic Renewal* (Oxford: Transaction Books, 1987).

17 McGuire, 1988, pp. 38–78.

18 A likeable account of this phenomenon can be found in Harvey Cox's *Fire From Heaven: Pentecostalism, Spirituality, and the Shaping of Religion in the Twentieth Century* (Reading: MA, Addison-Wesley, 1994), pp. 263ff.

19 Individuals who are prominent include the Dominican Francis Macnutt, a popular healer and author, and Peter Hocken of the Mother of God Community, Gaithersburg, USA, publishers of *The Word Among Us*.

20 See entries in S. M. Burgess, G. B. McGee and P. H. Alexander, *A Dictionary of Pentecostal and Charismatic Movements* (Grand Rapids: Zondervan, 1988).

21 Cox, 1994, pp. 281ff.

22 J. Thomas Nichol, 'The Charismatic Movement', in *Christianity in America*, ed. M. Noll, N. Hatch, G. Marsden, D. Wells and J. Woodbridge (Grand Rapids: Eerdmanns, 1983), p. 484.

23 Martin, 1990, pp. 1135ff.

24 Cox, 1994, pp. 213ff. See also Ro Bong-Rin and Marlin Nelson (eds), *Korean Church Growth Explosion*, (Taichung, Taiwan: Asia Theological Assoc. and Word of Life Press, 1983). There is a short article in this volume by Paul Cho, but his 'prosperity Gospel' teaching is more clearly articulated in his *Salvation, Health and Prosperity* (Altamonte Springs, FL: Creation House, 1987).

25 Cf. D. Barrett, 1982.

26 The Brethren arrived in Coniston from the West Country in the last century to work in the slate mines. Both churches were of a good size, but had ceased to function as such since the 1960s.

27 I was able to meet with all three House Church leaders. All had separated from their parent church 'because God told us to'. When I pointed out there was no New Testament precedent for separatism, they were unmoved. None of the groups

had what could be called a doctrine of the church, or any foundational theology. The configuration of each group/church was: 'these are the people we agree and worship with' – at the moment.

28 The work of James Dunn is an obvious example here. See his *Baptism in the Spirit: A Study of the Religious and Charismatic Experience of Jesus and the First Christians* (London: SCM, 1979). The works of George Eldon Ladd, James Kallas and Walter Wink are also highly esteemed by revivalists.

29 A pleasing exception to the rule is Douglas Petersen's *Not by Might Nor by Power: A Pentecostal Theology of Social Concern* (Carlisle: Paternoster, 1996). Although I have reservations about the theological hermeneutics in this text, it does seem to be a decent attempt at a genuine Pentecostal theology. However, it remains the case that there is nothing of this type in the charismatic movement.

30 *A Dictionary of Pentecostal and Charismatic Movements*, ed. S. Burgess, G. McGee and P. Alexander (Grand Rapids, Michigan: Zondervan, 1988). This is a slightly misleading comment, since there are articles on the doctrine of the Holy Spirit, and leaders like Edward Irving (1792–1834), are exceptions to the rule.

31 Some branches of Pentecostalism abandoned the doctrine of Trinity, and became Oneness Pentecostals, believing that baptism in only the name of Jesus was necessary. Soteriological doctrines tend to be quite dualist (Jesus versus Satan), or 'borrowed' from 19th-century evangelical subsitutionary ideas.

32 For further discussion, see R. Spittler, 'Are Pentecostals and Charismatics Fundamentalists?', in K. Poewe ed. *Charismatic Christianity as a Global Culture* (Columbia: University of South Carolina Press, 1994), pp. 103ff. See also my 'Fundamentalism: A Problem for Phenomenology?' and 'Power and Fundamentalism' in the *Journal of Contemporary Religion*, vol. 10, nos 1 & 3 (1995), pp. 83–92; 273–82.

33 A testimony quoted in James Hopewell's *Congregation: Stories and Structures* (Philadelphia: Fortress Press, 1987), p. 76.

34 H. Cox, *Fire From Heaven: Pentecostalism, Spirituality and the Reshaping of Religion in the Twenty-first Century* (New York: Addison-Wesley, 1994).

35 See Percy, *Words, Wonders and Power* (1996), p. 172.

36 Harper makes this claim (1986), as do others. But if one examines the history of British Restorationism, or of John Wimber's Vineyard, all one sees is wave after wave of schism. Even when charismatic renewal occurs in historic denominations, it often involves division between those who regard themselves as 'real' Christians and those who are dubbed 'traditional' or unregenerate. If revivalism were ecumenical, it would presumably be in dialogue with partner churches on questions of unity, and be open to using the liturgies and practices of other churches. It seldom is.

37 Pentecostal–Roman Catholic dialogue has been going on for almost twenty years, but the level of contact is low.

38 See S. Sizer, *Gospel Hymns and Social Religion* (Philadelphia: Temple University Press, 1978) for a different conception of 'community of feeling'. See also my 'Sweet Rapture: Sublimated Eroticism in Contemporary Charismatic Worship' in J. Jobling (ed.), *Theology and the Body: Gender Text and Ideology* (Leominster: Gracewing/Fowler Wright, forthcoming), and *Words, Wonders and Power* (1996), Chapter 4.

39 See K. Boone, *The Bible Tells Them So: The Discourse of Protestant Fundamentalism* (London: SCM, 1989).

40 Ironically, it was Schleiermacher (1768–1834) who first suggested that the core of Christianity might not be doctrine, but 'the feeling of absolute dependence' (*The Christian Faith*, 1821). However, this prompted Schleiermacher to conclude that

doctrines like the Trinity were necessary as a frame for unity, even if they only looked ornamental, like a coping stone.

41 See for example the discussion of the Toronto Blessing in Damian Thompson's *The End of Time: Faith and Fear in the Shadow of the Millennium* (London: Sinclair-Stevenson, 1996), pp. 139ff. Thompson points out that the 'rapture' of this type of revival provides a 'shot in the arm' for revivalism, as it wanes slightly as it approaches the millennium.

42 For a fuller discussion, see my 'City on a Beach' in *Neo-Pentecostalism at the End of the Century*, ed. T. Walters and S. Hunt (London: Macmillan, 1997).

43 Private correspondence.

44 Nigel Scotland, *Charismatics and the Next Millennium* (London: Hodder & Stoughton, 1995), p. 251.

45 See for example B. Skinner and D. Pytches, *New Wineskins* (Guildford: Eagle Press, 1991), in which the authors effectively argue for the privatization of the Church of England, so that parishes can compete for success.

46 N. Scotland, 1995, pp. 249ff.

47 Cox, 1994, pp. 310ff.

48 Jean Jacques Suurmond, *Word and Spirit at Play* (London: SCM, 1994), pp. 74ff.

49 T. O'Dea, 'Sociological Dilemmas: Five Paradoxes of Institutionalization' in *Sociological Theory, Values and Sociocultural Change* (New York: Free Press of Glencoe, 1963), pp. 71–89, and *The Sociology of Religion* (Englewood Cliffs, NJ: Prentice Hall, 1983).

50 H. R. Niebuhr, *Christ and Culture* (New York: Harper & Row, 1951). Cf. Frank Brown, 'Christian Theology's Dialogue with Culture' in the *Companion Encyclopaedia of Theology* (London: Routledge, 1995), pp. 314ff.

51 Some of these insights are derived from David Lyon, *Postmodernity* (Buckingham: Open University Press, 1994), and Richard Roberts, 'Power and Empowerment' in *Religion Today*, vol. 9, no. 3 (1994), pp. 3–23.

52 See R. Wallis, *The Elementary Forms of the New Religious Life* (London: Routledge, 1984), for a discussion of accommodation, rejection and acceptance. For a discussion of Pentecostal mission in relation to the millennium, see David Bosch, *Transforming Mission: Paradigm Shifts in the Theology of Mission* (Marynknoll: New York, Orbis, 1994), pp. 313–27.

53 F. Schleiermacher, *The Christian Faith* (Edinburgh: T. & T. Clark, 1928), pp. 740ff. 54 My observation of charismatic communities such as the Jesus Army is that their Trinity is a theological hegemony that matches their ecclesial hegemony. A ruling Father, suffering Son and serving Spirit mirror the structure (Godly order) imposed on men, women and children. Michael Harper has expressed similar views in some of his more recent works.

55 See A. Giddens, 'Uprooted Signposts at Century's End', *The Times Higher Educational Supplement* (17/01/92), pp. 21–2. See also Grace Davie, *Religion in Britain, 1945 to the Present* (Oxford: Blackwell, 1994), p. 192, and D. Lyon, *Postmodernity* (Buckingham: Open University Press, 1994).

56 See Jean-Francois Lyotard, *The Postmodern Condition: A Report on Knowledge* (Manchester: Manchester University Press, 1984), p. xxiii.

57 Cf. R. Porter and P. Richter, *The Toronto Blessing – Or Is It?* (London: DLT, 1995).

58 Cf. my review of Suurmond's *Word and Spirit at Play*, in *Anvil*, vol. 12, no. 3 (1995), pp. 65–7.

59 B. Wilson, *The Noble Savages: An Essay on Charisma* (Berkeley: California University Press, 1975), p. 3. See also the work of James Hopewell on adventure and romantic notions in charismatic communities. Readers interested in psychological studies

of prophecy are referred to Leon Festinger's *When Prophecy Fails* (New York: Harper & Row, 1956), and *A Theory of Cognitive Dissonance* (Stanford: Stanford University Press, 1957).

60 Cf. M. Foucault, 'Space, Knowledge and Power' in Paul Rabinow (ed.), *The Foucault Reader* (New York: Pantheon-Random, 1984), p. 247: 'Nothing is fundamental ... there are only reciprocal relations, and the perpetual gaps between intentions in relation to one another.' This quote is not intended to signify that I doubt such a thing as divine power.

61 For a fuller discussion, see my *Words, Wonders and Power* (London: SPCK, 1996).

62 See S. Bruce, *Religion in Modern Britain: From Cathedrals to Cults* (Oxford: OUP, 1996), p. 234.

63 W. B. Yeats, 'The Second Coming', in *The Collected Poems* (Basingstoke: Macmillan, 1921), p. 110.

# Conclusion:
# the future of the power of God
# in a post-foundational world

The staircase spiralled upwards into the darkness, like a fire escape in hell, fixed there to delude the damned. He dragged himself up four flights, and limped along the narrow gangway between tall shelves of books. He was in Theology. Abelard, Alcuin, Aquinas, Augustine . . . he crept further along the shelving, past Bede and Bernard, Calvin and Chrysostom . . . his hand groped instinctively . . . [and] he seemed to make out a few paces away the shape of a door, etched in thin cracks of light. He lunged towards it.[1]

One of the themes running through this volume is the apparent absence or weakness of theological foundations within Christian communities that might illuminate some of the darkness and confusion of modernity. In inching their way towards light and clarity, churches seem to stumble and lack orientation, besides being remarkably unclear about their purpose. In considering divine, human and ecclesial power in these chapters, it is clear that the advent of modernity and postmodernity have posed questions to the churches and threats to the future of the power of God. At one level, churches do seem to be in decline and have less sense of a shared, or core, theological identity. At another level, however, the posturing of the secularization thesis from sociologists of religion looks quite tired as the millennium draws to a close. There are rumours of revival; church attendance is on the rise, and the interest in spirituality, New Religious Movements and the Church as resource for community suggest that modernity has not marginalized religion as might have once been supposed. Some recent surveys even suggest that established denominations may not be faring too badly.[2]

Yet gaining an accurate picture about how churches, religion and God might be coping at the turn of the millennium is quite tricky. For a start, it must be said that one cannot measure 'the power of God' through church attendance. The global religious economy is too complex to be measured by such a simple statistic. In some communities in Britain actual church attendance has never been very high, but the influence of and respect for religion nonetheless remains a vital part of community life. Equally, church attendance is no indicator of the strength of belief in society. Many have pointed out that the USA, with an apparently enviable culture of church attendance, remains a highly secularized and violent society.[3] Linking people's perceptions about the reality and power of God to their actual religious observance has always been extremely problematic. Some of the best-attended churches turn out to be the most socially abrogate and inward-looking. Some of the smallest Christian communities can be the most effective in outreach and social intercourse. Size is not everything.

These observations have important implications for placing any thesis of secularization in context. Scholars such as Steve Bruce and Bryan Wilson, who propagate the theory that religion is dwindling in direct proportion to the growth of modernist humanism, are guilty of imposing a metanarrative over a whole range of complex data that simply will not cope with one grand theory. A sizeable percentage of the population of many developed countries still affirms a belief in God, even if they do little about it from year to year. Religious festivals remain an influential part of the calendar; many people still seek a religious burial; and many still turn up for church on the strangest of days such as Harvest Festival, Remembrance Day, Mother's Day – not to mention Christmas and Easter. Reports of terminal decline are simplistic and greatly exaggerated.[4]

However, it is also the case that rumours of revival need treating with caution. In an established denomination in England such as Roman Catholicism, it has been assumed for some time that the 'fallout' from the Church of England over the ordination of women and attitudes to homosexuality would at least result in some growth through transference. Prominent converts (such as Ann Widdecombe, John Selwyn Gummer and the former Bishop of London) caused Cardinal Hume to remark gleefully that Catholics might look forward to the conversion of England once more. The *1997 Catholic Directory* tells another story. In 1995 the Catholic Church ordained just 52 priests – under ten per cent of the Anglican ordinations for the same year. Moreover, attendance at Mass is in steep decline: in terms of youth, some openly say that that there is a whole generation of people missing.[5] Outdated but enforced codes of sexuality, celibacy, and the like have taken the edge off any triumphalism. Possibly the last straw is to note that of the three hundred or so Anglican priests who turned to Rome, a not insignificant number have now turned back (43 by December 1997), preferring Anglican flexibility to papal infallibility. Within other mainline denominations, revivals and rumours of revivals also persist as the new millennium approaches. At present, *Alpha* courses and similar programmes appear to be re-invigorating many churches. Yet courses like these all too frequently fail to transform any new converts into actual church members. They tend to excite the existing church membership, but little more. The likely long-term influence of such courses has been greatly over-estimated. A focus on basic belief may be a helpful apologetic task for some, but it does not introduce people to the Church. This sort of evangelism is the Gospel un-earthed: slickly sold as a consumer item, but more often than not failing to relate the life of the body of Christ to any specific social or local context. Sound ecclesiology cannot be manufactured out of elementary missiology.[6]

In new and emerging churches, stories of revival also need handling with particular care. The burgeoning growth of the House Churches in the 1970s and 1980s seems to have come to a halt. Sociological and statistical reflection on the rise of House Churches shows that most growth was achieved through transference – possibly as much as 95 per cent.[7] In other words, House Churches have done little to enlarge the pool of Christians within the country: most converts already come from Christian backgrounds. It is arguably the case that most modern Christian revivals have been engaged in essentially the same exercise. Jon Butler suggests that revivals and their impact ought to be divided between those that preceded Finney's (*circa* 1830) and those that followed.[8] The revivals of Wesley, Edwards and Whitfield do seem to have produced a lasting, tangible and widespread form of social and religious change. But those revivals that have followed have been less universal, less effective in their sociality, and their results often 'talked-up' via reference to the enthusiasm of attendees and the pneumatosomatic phenomenon taking place. Butler takes the view that most late modern revivals are echoes of the past, and seldom achieve anything significant beyond their immediate locality. As we have noted with the Toronto Blessing, there is just no evidence of that event signifying a global revival. Revivals, in Butler's thesis, emerge as exaggerations of God's power for a people longing to see its magnification and globalization. Thus far, it is clear that it is not happening quite like that, just as secularization does not proceed smoothly as one 'movement' within modern culture.

Globally, the picture is complex. The power of God, where it might be registered and active in social bodies, waxes and wanes – it has always been so. Religion as a cultural and political force is ever-resurgent in response to perceived decline. At the turn of this millennium, Europe, North America, the Middle East and the Far East have not been able to escape fundamentalist movements that have lobbied for power and polity in the name of God.[9] The assumptions of democracy, even Christian democracy, are being challenged by those who would wish to create a theocracy. There is the hope of re-sacralizing the profane, and of bringing the power of God to bear on issues and principles that many would regard as secular. Yet as we have noted, the existence of fundamentalism, in all its various forms, is evidence of a deeply neurotic response to modernity. Power is only being appealed to because there is a perception that it has been eroded, and continues to be threatened. In a sense, all the issues that are studied under the theme of power in this book reflect that concern, namely an anxiety about keeping alive the possibility of the power of God in a world where it seems to be increasingly ignored and squeezed.[10] But each of the issues and situations discussed has also disclosed the difficulty of defending divine, human and ecclesial power. From social, ideological and theological perspectives, there seems to be a serious problem for the future of the power of God: what was universal is becoming local; what was once public and true is being turned into something subjective and personal. The options for the power of God seem to be precariously poised between weakness (but socially relevant or incarnate) or strength (but socially removed or abrogated). Three further (and brief) studies from within mainstream Western Christendom illustrate this only too well.

## Reformed Theology in the Pre-modern Kraal

Jim Packer is one of the foremost reformed and conservative evangelical thinkers in the Western world. A recent volume of essays – *Doing Theology for the People of God* – paid tribute to his work.[11] The occasion for the *Festschrift* was Packer's seventieth birthday, and the contributors are distinguished writers from the reformed world. Packer's influence amongst Evangelicals cannot be underestimated: John Stott sets the tone by stating that his contribution to the volume is 'like the shrimp paying homage to the whale'.[12] And so the honours continue – Packer is talked up as a giant of modern theology. Giant he may be, but surely only within the kraal of conservative evangelicalism? Packer is seldom found on any reading list within a mainstream university. The book confirms the suspicion: he represents a retreat to the pre-modern era. Although geographically dispersed to the four corners of the globe, the contributors fit into only two categories. The largest of these are testimonies from North American evangelical colleges or seminaries. The second category comprises some more obviously denominational contributions from Scotland, Australia (Diocese of Sydney, naturally) and England.[13] Only the Scottish contributions come from universities (Aberdeen and Edinburgh), where theology is but one subject within the scope of humanities: all the others come from places where evangelical foundations can be taken for granted. The book demonstrates at least three problems that relate to addressing the power of God in contemporary life.

First, as Mark Noll noted in his fine *The Scandal of the Evangelical Mind*,[14] evangelical scholarship is in its own ghetto. Rather than engaging in 'secular' faculties of theology and religious studies, evangelicals have tended to prefer the safety of their own seminaries and colleges where their fundaments can be propagated without dilution or interruption. The price to pay for this has been self-imposed marginalization. God's power – through reformed theology and concepts of inerrancy – is kept pure. In *Doing Theology for the People of God*, the failure of this agenda becomes all too clear. In Chapter 11 for example, Packer's contribution to the doctrine of the inerrancy of scripture receives rapt attention. But the author seems unaware that this 'debate' is something that is only really conducted within evangelical circles; in general theology, the subject of inerrancy is now more likely to occur in courses on recent Church history, or as a phenomenon in religious studies. (The same, incidentally, could be said of Packer's views on hell, where once again we find a quaint evangelical doctrine defended against 'liberal' evangelicals, but no one else.)

Second, there seems to be little consciousness that the general reformed agenda has ceased to be one of pilgrimage and challenge, and has slipped into a form of solidified tradition. Theology is no longer systematic, but dogmatic. It is largely assumed that the Bible and the original reformers were mostly right, and there is little else to say about anything. Thus, Packer has scant regard for the fastest-growing movement that competes with his own tradition, namely charismatic renewal ('laid-back Christianity', as he is wont to call it), and seems unable to grasp the present state of Anglicanism or Roman Catholicism, as is true of most of the authors. There is nothing to say about what he presumably regards as funny secular perversions like feminist or liberation theology. In his view, they will have their day, but the inerrant word of God abideth forever. This is the view from the kraal – it's a funny old world out there; best stay indoors and stick within the boundaries of the protectionist pre-modern evangelical village. Occasionally, a war party from the kraal will venture out into the open, usually on a matter to do with morality or sexuality. Apart from that, the tribe is kept out of the public domain by its own code of rules.

Third, it seems barely credible that theology can be done any more in the way that Packer and his supporters imagine. The sheer narrowness of the perspective, coupled with the self-serving dogmatism that guarantees the same old principles are exposited from the same old selection of biblical passages, is deeply alarming.[15] Here is a theology that produces nothing new, practically prides itself on its social abrogation, and is in dialogue with no one but itself. Packer may well have deepened many conservative evangelicals' self-understanding. And he may well have helped keep the Anglicans within this tradition as part of the established church by rebuffing Martyn Lloyd-Jones in 1966, with his invitation to Evangelicals to leave their denominations and form their own. But he has not led Evangelicals into the heart of mainstream theology, and at the end of the millennium, this looks like a monumental failure to some within the movement. The achievement of Packer is that he has contended with energy and vigour for 'true' evangelical theology – but only amongst Evangelicals themselves. He has established a deeply separatist form of theological discourse that is free and reformed, yet knows that it needs to remain within established denominations to be taken seriously by anyone. In short, the pre-modern kraal successfully protects the power of God, but only by turning its back on the world, and allowing its leaders to be turned into totems.

## Evangelicalism in the Postmodern Cradle

An altogether different response from Evangelicals is to embrace the challenge and opportunity of postmodernity. Dissatisfied, and perhaps bored with the apologetic approaches from the likes of Packer (anti-modernity, but in a modernistic way?)[16], some have clearly conceded much territory to modernity and are looking for a way forward in a postmodern world. Postmodern evangelicalism may also be a reaction against the rise of the 'new right' in evangelicalism, represented by groups such as Reform, the Proclamation Trust and ABWON (Action for a Biblical Witness to Our Nation). Groups like these have come to dominate a large percentage of the evangelical constituency through skilful lobbying and ecclesial politicization. Although still quite small numerically, they acquired an influential power base from which to articulate their beliefs. In turn, they have produced their own type of ordinand that has forced colleges that were once quite munificent to re-emphasize their evangelical roots, in order to accommodate the swelling ranks of a new breed of ultra-Protestant.

This has led to some uncomfortable re-definitions: some colleges now delimit themselves as 'open evangelical'. What this is intended to mean is this: although evangelical in core-matters of doctrine, morality and spirituality, they are nonetheless open to or aware of the insights of others. The model is one of accommodation, and is repeated by many evangelical individuals, and in groups, churches and colleges. But as we noted in Chapter 9, it does not always work. When divisive issues such as homosexuality or the ordination of women surface, Evangelicals have recently been faced with quite a stark choice: either lurching to the right and supporting tradition uncritically, or standing their ground (legitimate but ambiguous?) and risking being marginalized as 'liberal'. The question is this: is there an alternative?

David Tomlinson's *The Post Evangelical* suggests there is.[17] In a somewhat chatty book, Tomlinson outlines a vision for retaining some aspects of evangelical identity and culture, yet moving beyond it. As an *apologia pro vita sua*, it is a valuable piece of work. Tomlinson belongs to the more alternative culture of British evangelicalism that is tired of certain traditions. As such, he has become a leading light in experimental ecclesiology and worship. Correspondingly, the book embraces a number of aspects of postmodern Christianity. The author seems at home with the postmodern narrative theology of writers such as Bruggemann, challenges the concept of truth for Evangelicals in a postmodern culture, and critiques evangelical and fundamentalist approaches to the Bible.

It is not an especially scholarly book, although the author is clearly well-informed. There are better works on the challenges of religious pluralism in the 1990s.[18] Yet to compare Tomlinson in this way is to miss the point of his book: it is an event, a moment that marks a transition for some within the evangelical movement. Tomlinson is beginning to take his leave of the modernist God and faith-tradition that is so beloved of evangelicalism and so endemic to its culture, and is reaching out to the postmodern, with all its confusion, profusion and possibilities. Thus, throughout *The Post Evangelical*, Tomlinson is actually arguing for a more realistic engagement with postmodern society. For him, it is as though the world has tilted on its axis and things will never be the same again: adjustment and change are the only way to survive. Against the charge that the vision he advocates represents an *ex*-evangelical position, Tomlinson writes 'to be post-evangelical is to take as given many of the assumptions of evangelical faith, while at the same time moving beyond its perceived limitations'.[19] Sociologically speaking therefore, we have an argument for moving from modernity to postmodernity, although without serious rupture in continuity of tradition and culture. Tomlinson is not trying to 'throw the baby out with the bath water'; it is more a case of 'wake, O sleeper, and arise'. In this way, Tomlinson stands in a long tradition of reforming and liberal Evangelicals who take their inspiration from the more Catholic and revisionist *Lux Mundi* (1889).

That last point begins to say something about why *The Post Evangelical*, although a small book, is nonetheless very important as an event for a discussion of power and foundations within evangelicalism. It represents an attempt to engage with the fundamental shift in genre and context that evangelicalism now finds itself in. *Lux Mundi* aimed at placing the Christian faith 'into its right relation with modern intellectual and moral problems'. The essays were primarily concerned with doctrine, biblical criticism and the maintenance of moral standards in a modernist society. Tomlinson's book shows how fast and far things have changed in a hundred years. Pluralism and moral-religious diversity are widely accepted. A grammar of shared or universal assent can no longer be seen, let alone assumed. Secularization, as a modernist theory, has itself found its place in a society tempered by New Age religion and postmodern expressions of 'traditional' religions. There is a new consciousness of the sacred. The age of the ultra-humanist metanarrative is gone: long live *différance*, diversity, competing convictions and religious individualism. It is against this background that *The Post Evangelical* should be read and understood. It is really an argument for being Christian in a postmodern world, but in an evangelical (cultural) *style*.

The urgency of Tomlinson's book for some within evangelicalism cannot be underestimated. One of the conditions that postmodernity places on religious culture is the requirement to be increasingly sharp and definitive about its beliefs. Peter Berger likens this to a process of 'demonopolization': universal orders of truth give way to privatization and pluralism. Thus, a religious tradition that could once be imposed with authority now has to be marketed – sold to a clientele that is no longer compelled to buy.[20] The modernist response to this reality is most typically ecumenism: reducing the number of competing units by amalgamation and also by dividing up the market between the larger units that remain. By contrast, the postmodern response to this is to embrace the potential chaos of the spiritual free market and delight in its opportunities. These might include the freedom and ability to constantly relaunch and re-define one's religious product with subtle re-profiling, alongside appeals to vague concepts such as tradition, newness and novelty. There is plenty of evidence to suggest that some aspects of contemporary charismatic renewal have not been slow to realize religious capital from the postmodern culture. The harvest of health, wealth and prosperity movements further testifies to this: fulfilment is in, holiness and sacrifice are out.

Since Tomlinson clearly is an Evangelical and not an *ex*-Evangelical, he is faced with two choices at this point. One is to attempt a rehabilitation of modernist evangelicalism. This depends on the evangelical nemesis of liberalism still being a potent force of opposition in Church and society. There is every sign that it is not. Instead, the opponents turn out to be the more shifty pluralism, individualism and relativism, and although modernist evangelicalism can and does address these issues, it was not actually built to do so. The second choice, and his preferred option, is to be postmodern and evangelical – a 'post-Evangelical' in his terminology. Yet here is the irony. If postmodernism is, amongst other things 'incredulity towards metanarratives',[21] then what is to survive as evangelical in the post-Evangelical? How can the power of God or 'core' doctrines be rescued in a cultural scheme that contents itself with surface meanings? Anyway, who decides which are the core doctrines? How can a philosophy that denies absolute and universal truth be meaningfully reconciled with a religion that really begins by asserting the very opposite?

Clearly there cannot be any easy answers. Recent creative ways forward with other sorts of religious dogma place religious statements in phenomenological or analogical categories.[22] This certainly gives a postmodern lease of life to some modernist theologies, but it would be unlikely to satisfy the average card-carrying Evangelical. For most of them, language corresponds directly to reality, even unseen transcendent reality: there *are* absolutes, and they can be deduced and imposed on individuals, church and society. Thus, there are real questions about the viability of Tomlinson's thesis. The more numerous post-Evangelicals become, the less they will agree on their homogenous identity: celebration of *différance* will lead to polarization, specialization, and then to eventual schism. Equally, the semantics between *post-* and *past-* is not easily constrained, and I suspect a number of alternative Evangelicals will ultimately end up by not being evangelical at all. When one considers the short history of the Sheffield-based 'Nine O'Clock Service' (NOS), which was originally charismatic-evangelical, to its rapid inculcation of Matthew Fox's 'creation spirituality', the future paradigmatic and pragmatic die is already cast.

Packer and Tomlinson, although not equals in scholarship, offer two possibilities for holding on to the reality of the power of God within their traditions. Packer's version of God's story is contra-modernity, and its survival depends on tightly controlled frontiers of faith that deliberately limit the points of social and ideological engagement. Tomlinson, on the other hand, appears to have accepted much of modernity and is now situated in the cradle of postmodernity. Whether that spirituality and theology can survive in the ocean of relativity will depend on more than appeals to federations of fundaments. It will require the re-forging and re-casting of new theological methods, and will inevitably lead to a complete reconfiguration of the power of God and what constitutes a related or corresponding fundament of truth that gives the body its identity. At the time of writing, there is little to see here except a sense of progression and a desire for community: a place where recovering Evangelicals can find themselves again. It is an open question as to whether the movement is simply a religion of calculated psephology, rather than a correspondence with the spirit of truth.

## Process Theology and the Power of God

In Chapter 2 the issue of the purpose of divine power in healing miracles was discussed. In any consideration of a topic like this, questions about the actual reality of power also arise. Suspicion about the remoteness of transcendence led many theologians to invest the power of God in politicization or notions of social incarnation. The prospects for the power of God in this more liberal tradition enjoy a longer and deeper history in the twentieth century. To an extent, the work of Ritschl, Rauschenbusch and Harnack can all be seen as attempts to save the reality of the power of God for ecclesial communities by concentrating on immanence, and demoting transcendence.[23] The flowering of this tradition was to be seen in the work of Paul Tillich, who sought to reconstruct a theology of the power of God that worked apologetically in a modernist world.[24] Tillich's work – widespread, systematic and socially-related for its time – worked with a number of presuppositions.

First, theology should be apologetic – its task was to truly speak to the modern situation, in all its scientific, moral, political and cultural diversity. Second, theology had an obligation to discover or recover its common ground with contemporary culture, as well as drawing on divine revelation to re-infuse sociality with the power of God. Only this form of engagement would prevent theology from becoming pointlessly privatized and ultimately obsolete. Third, and in contrast to Barth, Tillich sought to resource his theological programme through a deep engagement with the philosophy of religion. At the midway point of this century that meant existentialism, which led Tillich to a fourth presupposition, namely that an appreciation of ontology was vital in considering the relation between divine and human power. In other words, the very ground of our being questioned divine providence as much as it interrogated human action.[25] These assumptions led Tillich to develop his method of correlation, which determined much of his systematic theology: explaining 'the contents of the Christian faith through existential questions and theological answers in mutual interdependence'.[26] Effectively, Tillich set up a dialogue between human and divine power, in which the power of God was deemed sufficient and able to invest itself in immanence rather than remove itself through transcendence.

In one sense, this is close to the theological strategy outlined in the preface of this book ('theology in a fourth way'), but is more mindful of the critiques that were levelled against Tillich. Tillich's method of correlation tended to be more idealistic than real, and it often erred on the side of reductionism in considering revelation. Moreover, reason itself came to be the definer of ontology, and it therefore followed that revelation was further constrained by the scope of human need and enquiry. Thus, existentialism itself, or the ground of being as a fundamental category, ceased to be something that needed redeeming and acquired for itself a form of divine-relational power. The natural remedy to this, which Tillich tried to stress, was to put theology and Christology into categories such as *Logos* or Wisdom, which effectively placed 'God above God'. Thus, the scheme of theology works something like this. Historical revelation is trumped by philosophical idealism; in turn, immanence supersedes transcendence; and finally, socio-incarnational Christianity, with a heavy dosage of reductionist theology, triumphs over dogmatic or confessional brands of conservative theology. Unsurprisingly, it was therefore possible to become a Christocentric atheist, since the actual reality of divinity is marginalized or maybe even dissolved in Tillich's thought. In spite of noting these reservations, it must be said that Tillich represents one of the most significant attempts from within liberal theology to hold on to the power of God whilst thoroughly engaging with the culture of modernity. Many liberal theologians remain in his debt, not least the British pairing of David Jenkins and John Robinson.

In North America, Tillich's theology became more developed (some would say remote) through process theology. Theologians such as Charles Hartshorne and John Cobb, along with a spiritualist tradition led by Pierre Teilhard de Chardin, envisaged a more fundamental reconciliation between theology and science. Process theologians set their face against what they regarded as 'antiquated concepts of God',[27] by which they meant a cosmic moralist, omnipotent, unchanging and Passionless being. Against God as absolute controlling power, they too sought a more immanent and temporal God through a new form of natural theology. In attempting to reconcile immanence and transcendence, process theology took seriously the idea of human growth and evolution coupled with the expansiveness of God. Naturally, in the case of Teilhard de Chardin this took phenomenology seriously.[28]

In the case of Cobb and Hartshorne, the world and God became interdependent. God was not aloof from the world, but involved and affected by it. God does not coerce but persuades, although retaining a divine prerogative in nature. And omnipotence is seen as a Hellenistic or classical attribution to God rather than a Christian one. The God of the Christian Bible may eventually be revealed to be all-powerful (in eschatology), but for the moment acts with restrained power in order to woo creation into relationality with itself and himself. It therefore follows that God is not omniscient either: our futures are open and unknown, even though God is committed to them. Futures are possibilities, but not known in actuality.[29]

Compared to Packer, this theology of the power of God and Christian foundations looks altogether more lucid, fluid and applied – at least to modernity. Cobb, for example, replaced the idea of controlling power at the centre of theology with the idea of God as creative-responsive-love. This God is calling humanity into the future: it is a 'teleological pull'.[30] In terms of Christology, the same kind of stress is placed on logos as would Tillich, with an emphasis on incarnation and embodiment. However, process theology seeks to go beyond the Enlightenment and its obsession with individualistic-centred reason, and instead to focus itself on persons in communion. The process of process theology is therefore about progress: gradual but significant revelation from God which is slowly drawing humanity into an anticipated consummation of history. Yet it is never coercive: the freedom of humanity is entirely respected.

Critics of process theology, understandably perhaps, believe that the power of God has been irredeemably weakened in this scheme. Moreover, the work of Teilhard de Chardin and others in the tradition, such as Whitehead, tends towards a metaphysics which results in the 'divinization of the world'.[31] It tends to place God in the cosmos as just one feature of it, rather than seeing God as its author and beyond it. This undoubtedly makes sense to many who think about God in late modernity, but as a theology, it always runs the risk of devaluing all transcendence and relativizing all immanence.[32] Expressed in an ecclesiological manner, one could say that this form of correspondence to the world – allowing culture to set the agenda for theology – has many risks. The Student Christian Movement declared itself open and removed its boundaries: but the life of the body flowed out, rather than the people coming in. As David Martin has pointed out, 'the unbounded is soon the empty'.[33] The cost of inculturation is the alienation of those who joined the body because it was different. Others have also pointed out that whilst God suffering with the world is an attractive concept in terms of solidarity with the powerless, there is no account of overcoming that, or of triumphing over evil. In summary, it creates a God who is strong on persuasion but weak on potency.[34]

Yet for all the weaknesses of process theology, it remains a hopeful form of theological discourse, one that attempts a combination of immanence and transcendence, of revelation and reductionism, and of reality and idealism. As a theological tradition, it combines the ambiguity and authority of the Gospel with appeals to the incarnation. To quote Launcelot Andrewes from a much earlier era, 'the Word that cannot speak' in the form of the infant Jesus is the paradigm of divine *potestas*. The true Word chooses the way of meekness and love, not power. Yet that is not the end of the story, for Jesus did not remain an infant: he grew up, and his power, stature and wisdom increased. The Word learned to speak words, with power and authority. As a movement, process theology has attempted to keep alive the possibility of an evolving and dynamic power of God without capitulating to dogmatic foundationalism or to scientific atheism. It is arguably the crown of liberal theological thinking in relation to divine power, and with its stress on love, sociality and persons in communion, remains constantly open to adaptation and rehabilitation.

On its own though, it is not enough – it always risks vacuity. As a type of theology, it runs the risk of identifying contemporary cultural concerns, science and philosophy, far too closely with divine reality. Moreover, the power of God loses its momentum in this cause. Mysticism becomes therapeutic reflection with a metaphysical turn; theology becomes weakly apologetic, conferring too much respect on modernity and not enough on transcendance. Just as Barth complained about liberalism as a product of modernity, so can others can complain that process theology does not adequately concede that the evils of modernity, such as the Holocaust, need prophetic judgement, not just armchair theodicies.[35] Ultimately, process theology remains open to the same types of cultural critiques that pre-modern and postmodern evangelicalism are subject to. A balance of divine and human power has not been achieved.

To achieve such a balance would require a special type of grace. If theology is indeed, as one theologian suggests, partly about being struck by the story of God and humanity, then there may be some ways forward that are mutually empowering for all the forms of ecclesiology described and discussed in this book. To be struck by something is simultaneously a single event and a process. Thus, in using this verb, we may infer that *episodic* accounts of the power of God, including interventionist and transcendant notions, are legitimate for descriptions of divine activity as it is experienced. Equally, however, 'struck' is a continuous *dispositional* form of power, with real space for the immanent theologies of power to emerge. Is it not the case that churches need room for both economies of divine power within their order and organization? Denial of episodic-transcendent divine power risks investing too much weight in beauracracy, tradition and the Church. Denial of dispositional-immanent power risks too much authority being invested in the magical and momentary, besides ignoring the subtleties of human powers.

In view of these remarks, I wish to suggest that, tempered with some of Nancey Murphy's vision for a syncretism between immanent and interventionist forms of power, there is the makings of a genuine ecclesial way of holding on to divine power in the third millennium.[36] Liberals, with their links with establishment, need to keep their nerve; experientialists to deepen their tradition; conservatives to be willing to engage in dialogue with the world and not retreat behind the barricades of faith. But such a venture would require risk and grace from both liberals and conservatives. Such a vision requires the fostering of those quintessential

Anglican habits: passionate coolness and reasonable, morally sensitive, non-dogmatic and non-sectarian ways of thinking. A refusal to let go of the idea of *truth* and be seduced by postmodern relativism, and yet an ability to *argue* rather than *assert*.[37] Cool reasoning, deep intelligence and a faith that is open to the God of surprises can be combined. Were it undertaken, the prospects for the power of God might have more potentiality.

## Summary

Theology is always more than just thinking about God. It is art, dance, liturgy, protest and practice. It is an *activity*. As Paul Van Buren reminds us, it is the movement of people 'struck by the biblical story, in which they undertake to revise continually the ways in which they say how things are with their present circumstances, in the light of how they read that story'.[38] Where the story strikes there is power, response and religious community: the body of God, the Church. In this book there has been some attempt to show how the combination of theology and sociology, judiciously applied, opens up the arena of ecclesiology. Indeed, following Pierre Bourdieu, it is possible to see sociology as fieldwork in theology.[39] Most of the chapters in this book have worked with the assumption that the power of God is somehow real. However, that same power may only be a form of projection that is real to the people it dominates and serves. Furthermore, the power at issue can be assessed, partly, in complementary disciplines such as sociology.[40] Because God does not come to us neat, but through agents and ambiguity, it is necessary to examine how power is diluted and distorted – and perhaps even expose how we are deceived. It is not only theology that can speak about the power of God. Sociology may test the agents of power, as much as political science may examine their moral use and abuse: the *monarche* of God is generally transferred to states, individuals and ecclesial structures.[41] It is in these places that we find the power of God translated. Moreover, it has been noted in this chapter, in connection with process theology, that the process can be reversed, and God invested with ideologies of human power. Because these chapters have been concerned with divine and human power, the power of the Church, agents of power and definitions of power, it is impossible to draw one set of conclusions. However, four points for further reflection seem an appropriate place to end.

First, orientation in the culture of late modernity remains a serious issue for many who are religious and wish to defend some conception of the power of God, whether it be absolute or qualified. In part, a better orientation may be achieved if modernity and postmodernity are better understood. A clue to how this might be achieved comes, ironically, from a sociologist. Anthony Giddens prefers the term post-traditional to postmodern, and suggests that society is now engaging in social reflexivity.[42] According to Giddens, people have to filter rapidly growing amounts of information for themselves, such that they are increasingly reflexive about how they are influenced by ideas, and in turn, how their actions influence society. Social reflexivity is an individual and communal process of reflection and action, that allows foundationalism or metanarratives to have a bearing on the world without necessarily dominating. In other words, ideology participates in the world without becoming totalitarian.[43] In Giddens' view, therefore, moral fundamentalism is a much greater danger to society than (controlled?) moral relativism.[44] Clearly, the key to this conception of social, moral and religious orientation in a postmodern world lies in the quality and breadth of resources and a belief in the value of openness and dialogue. In such a world, power, whether of politicians, rock stars or God, can flourish and even compete: this is the Genesis of a post-traditional society (although one is tempted to ask when the Fall might come).

Reflexivity is an important concept here. It is no accident that post-liberals and 'post-Evangelicals' are at the forefront of constructing meaningful dialogue between traditions that were once alienated from each other.[45] But there are dangers to be heeded as well. Theology and ecclesiology might be swayed by culture rather than discerning it and exercising discrimination.[46] It is not clear what would test reflexivity: the very concept itself risks engulfment.[47] As we noted in an earlier essay (Chapter 9), even a sophisticated theological model like the Anglican Quadrilateral struggles with the profusion and pluralism of culture. Reductionism, relativism and failure most likely lie ahead if the reflexivity does not correspond to some form of revelation. As Von Balthasar notes, there must be a sociality that relates to what is limitless, beautiful, radiant, revealed and transcendant: reflexivity without this is just choice and self-evaluation.[48] Again, the Christian traditions of immanentism and interventionism could combine to counter-balance reflexivity, and in some ways reinhabit the gap created by the discourses of modernity.

And yet second, and linked to the first point, it does not follow that reflexivity with foundations leads to their compromise and eventual erosion. The suggestion being made by Giddens is that a post-foundational culture presents new opportunities for relating to fundaments. In an even more positive vein, Kieran Flanagan has suggested that power 'may reach a perfection in a theological context' that sociology and 'culture' cannot match, and that theology can enable (sociological) reflexivity and, in effect, call it to account.[49] Using the Weberian musical analogy, one does not have to choose between the totalitarian symphony on the one hand, or the banal and enthusiastic music-makers that Steve Bruce offers on the other.[50]

There is another, better way. The striking work of Jan Garbarek and the Hilliard Ensemble, which mixes the ordered polyphony of ancient plainchant with the spontaneity of modern jazz saxophone suggests a sociological and theological solution to Bruce's antinomy.[51] The music here is a marriage of two fundamental ideas in Western music: improvisation and composition – jazz and plainchant together. Even though they are separated by centuries, the synthesis suggests, at least analogically, that order and freedom can co-exist in harmony; indeed, in a harmony that is not tense but inspiring and liberating. Garbarek's work is not the only example here. Orlando Gough's speculative 'Latin Jazz' achieves the same effect through a different musical genre.[52] Still with jazz, Bossa Nova and Samba rhythms convey an order and mellowness that simultaneously carries a message of orthodoxy and liberalism. One could say that the jazz tradition, in many ways, is liberalism set to music.[53] Were one to extend the analogy further, from passive listening to active participation, the idea of a ceilidh gets close to the sort of socio-theological reflexivity envisaged here. In a ceilidh, patterns and improvisation co-exist: each form of dance is recognizable, yet the atmosphere is one of freedom rather than slavish correspondence. The dances must be taught, true enough. But this does not constrain participants: it enables them, liberating all who join in the harmony that is created by music and movement.[54]

Third, and linked to the second point, what Middleton and Walsh call 'anti-totalizing' metanarratives become highly desirable commodities as vehicles for the power of God in this new post-foundational situation. The question, already put, is how can any metanarrative be anti-totalitarian? As was noted earlier, this is especially problematic for faith-expressions such as evangelicalism that depend heavily on foundationalism as a form of absolutism. In appealing for metanarratives to be restored to evangelical faith, some exponents sound like children asking for their ball back, promising to never again kick it into the gardens of their neighbours.[55] You have a hunch the promise can't be kept. Evangelicals want their authority back, and with it the absolute power of God invested in revelation. Ironically, the idea of a non-totalitarian metanarrative might be rescued from the word 'meta' itself. When used in conjunction with narrative, the word means 'above': dominant, or reigning over. But in other usages, it can mean 'with', 'by' or 'beyond', as in the case of metaphysics. Perhaps the task for narratives about the power of God in a postmodern world is not to be 'over' the world but, as in process theology, both *with* it and *beyond* it. In other words, stories of power and domination become re-written as stories of love and relationship. Furthermore, 'with' implies a journey, where truth is encountered in the future through teleology or eschatology. Christianity is transformed from a propositional religion into a pilgrimage, in which God goes with us yet is beyond us.

Finally, in considering divine and human power, it is important not to lose sight of the reality of the struggle that is in us all. 'Power' comes into so much of what we do. Most of what we name, like or dislike is also linked to it. And in thinking and practising our faith, there is conflict between reason and revelation, divine will and human desire, between reality and illusion or (two-way) projection. Somewhere, sometimes, in all of that, there is actually something quite authentic, imbued with the real power of God. Simone Weil, facing her own death and ultimate sense of powerlessness, put this dynamic into words better than any theoretician:

> For it seemed to me certain, and I still think so today, that one can never wrestle enough with God if one does so out of pure regard for the truth. Christ likes us to prefer truth to him because, before being Christ, he is truth. If one turns aside from him to go toward truth, one will not go far before falling into his arms.[56]

It is this embodied wrestling with divine and human and power, out of a pure regard for truth, that remains with all those who still believe in the rumour of a God who is alive in the world. They also hope, pray and work for change: 'Thy Kingdom come.'

## Notes

1 David Lodge, *The British Museum is Falling Down* (London: Penguin, 1965), pp. 100–1.
2 *The Independent* (10 December 1996), p. 3.
3 Actually, there is some doubt as to whether Americans go to church as much as they claim. For further evaluation, see the *Journal for the Scientific Study of Religion*, vol. 35, no. 3 (September 1996).
4 For an account of the secularization thesis in contemporary religious life in Britain, see Steve Bruce's *Religion in the Modern World: From Cathedrals to Cults* (Oxford: OUP, 1996).
5 *The Tablet* (14 December 1996), p. 1661.
6 Roman Catholics adapting Alpha courses know this. See *The Tablet* (4 January, 1997), p. 27.
7 Source: Andrew Walker, King's College, London.
8 See Jon Butler, *Awash in a Sea of Faith: Christianizing the American People* (Cambridge, MA: Harvard University Press, 1990).
9 See David Westerlund (ed.), *Questioning the Secular State: The Worldwide Resurgence of Religion in Politics* (London: Hurst and Company, 1996).
10 For a slightly different perspective on this, see Robert Rubenstein, 'Power and Collective Violence in Anthropological Perspective' in Tim Ingold (ed.), *Companion Encyclopaedia of Anthropology: Humanity, Culture and Social Life* (London: Routledge,

1994), pp. 990–2. Rubenstein offers some perceptive comments on the plight of the Cherokee Indians.

11 *Doing Theology for the People of God: Studies in Honour of Jim Packer*, ed. A. McGrath and D. Lewis (Leicester: IVP/Apollos, 1996).

12 *Ibid.*, p. 3.

13 I exclude Alister McGrath from these observations. His contribution to mainstream theology is not in dispute, and his work as a theologian is widely appreciated by many who are not evangelical, myself included.

14 Grand Rapids: Eerdmans, 1994.

15 At the time of writing, his *Knowing God* (1973) and *Fundamentalism and the Word of God* (1958) [both published by IVP, Leicester] have just been re-issued – without any alteration!

16 Or, anti-intellectual in an intellectual way. Some Evangelicals appear to think that this approximates to the New Testament or Pauline concept of Wisdom. Clearly, this is nonsense.

17 D. Tomlinson, *The Post Evangelical* (London: SPCK/Triangle, 1995).

18 Two quite recent books – Terrence Tilley's *Postmodern Theologies* (New York: Orbis, 1995) and Anthony Thiselton's *Interpreting God and the Postmodern Self* (Edinburgh: T. & T. Clark, 1995), would be better guides.

19 Tomlinson, *op. cit.*, p. 7.

20 Cf. P. Berger, *The Sacred Canopy* (Garden City: Doubleday, 1967), p. 138.

21 Jean-Francois Lyotard, *The Postmodern Condition* (Minneapolis: University of Minnesota Press, 1983), p. xxiii.

22 See Graham Ward's *Barth, Derrida and the Language of Theology* (Cambridge: CUP, 1995) and his 'Theological Materialism' in C. Crowder (ed.), *God and Reality* (London: Mowbray, 1997), in which he argues for foundations in a post-foundational world.

23 See for example Albrecht Ritschl, *The Christian Doctrine of Justification and Reconciliation* (Edinburgh: T. & T. Clark, 1900); Walter Rauschenbusch, *Christianity and Social Crisis* (New York: Macmillan, 1907); Adolf von Harnack, *What is Christianity* (New York: G.P. Putnam & Sons, 1901).

24 See for example *The Socialist Decision* (New York: Harper and Row, 1933).

25 For further discussion, see Robert Schrader, *The Nature of Theological Argument: A Study of Paul Tillich* (Missoula, Montana: Scholars Press, 1975), and S. Grenz and R. Olsen, *20th Century Theology* (Carlisle: Paternoster, 1992).

26 See Paul Tillich, *Systematic Theology Volume 1* (New York: Harper & Row, 1967), p. 60.

27 Grenz and Olsen, *op. cit.*, 1992, p. 131.

28 See *The Phenomenon of Man* (New York: Harper & Row, 1961).

29 See C. Hartshorne, *Man's Vision of God and the Logic of Theism* (Hamden, Conn.: Archon Books, 1964); J. Cobb, *A Christian Natural Theology* (Philadelphia: Westminster, 1965).

30 J. Cobb, *God and the World* (Philadelphia: Westminster Press, 1965), pp. 42–66.

31 Grenz and Olsen, *op. cit.*, p. 143.

32 In this sense, the 'narrative' of God is close to Hopewell's Gnostic-Comic conceptions of divinity. See J. Hopewell, *Congregation: Stories and Structures* (London: SCM, 1987).

33 David Martin, reviewing Kieran Flanagan's work, *Journal of Contemporary Religion*, vol. 12, no. 1 (January 1997), p. 106.

34 Grenz and Olsen, *op. cit.*, p. 144.

35 For further discussion, see William Placher, *The Domestication of Transcendance:*

*How Modern Thinking about God Went Wrong* (Philadelphia: Westminster Press, 1996).

36 Nancey Murphy, *Beyond Liberalism and Fundamentalism* (Valley Forge, PA.: Trinity Press International), p. 156.

37 See John Habgood, *Making Sense* (London: SPCK, 1993), p. 12.

38 Paul Van Buren, 'On Doing Theology' in *Talk of God* (London: Macmillan, 1969), p. 53.

39 Pierre Bourdieu, *In Other Words: Essays Towards a Reflexive Sociology* (Cambridge: Polity Press, 1990), p. 28.

40 Cf. Kieran Flanagan, *The Enchantment of Sociology: A Study of Culture and Theology* (London: Macmillan, 1996), chapter 3.

41 See Daniel Hardy, *God's Ways with the World* (Edinburgh: T. & T. Clark, 1996), p. 184.

42 A. Giddens, *The Consequences of Modernity* (Cambridge: Polity Press, 1991), pp. 21–43.

43 For a political perspective in relation to power, see 'A Reply to my Critics', in D. Held and J. Thompson (eds), *Social Theory in Modern Societies: Anthony Giddens and His Critics* (Cambridge: CUP, 1996), p. 265.

44 See also A. Giddens, *The Transformation of Intimacy* (Cambridge: Polity Press, 1992).

45 See for example *The Nature of Confession: Evangelicals and Post-liberals in Conversation*, eds. T. Phillips and D. Okholm (Downers Grove, Il.: IVP, 1996).

46 Cf. Rowan Williams, 'Postmodern Theology and the Judgement of the World' in Frederic Burnham (ed.) *Postmodern Theology: Christian Faith in a Pluralist World* (San Francisco: HarperCollins, 1989), p. 103.

47 K. Flanagan, *The Enchantment of Sociology: A Study of Theology and Culture* (London: Macmillan, 1996), p. 26.

48 Hans Urs von Balthasar, *The Glory of the Lord*, Vol. 1 (Edinburgh: T. & T. Clark, 1982), p. 28.

49 K. Flanagan, *The Enchantment of Sociology* (London: Macmillan, 1996), pp. 207 and 213.

50 S. Bruce, *Religion in the Modern World* (Oxford: OUP, 1996), p. 234.

51 See *Officium* (Munich: ECM Records, 1994).

52 *Message from the Border* (London: Atalyst Records, 1995).

53 Here I am especially thinking of 'I wish I knew (how it would feel to be free)', Billy Taylor and the Billy Taylor Trio (London: Capitol Records, 1964).

54 Something Sydney Carter understood in his hymn 'Lord of the Dance', which is set to an old Shaker dancing tune.

55 J. Middleton and B. Walsh, *Truth is Stranger than It Used to Be* (London: SPCK, 1995), p. 107.

56 Simone Weil, *Waiting for God* (New York: Harper, 1973), p. 69.

# Bibliography

Achebe, C. *Things Fall Apart*, London: Penguin, 1958

Addison, J. *The Episcopal Church in the United States, 1789–1931*, New York: Charles Scribner, 1951

Archer, A. *The Two Catholic Churches: A Study in Oppression*, London: SCM, 1986

Arendt, H. *On Violence*, London: Penguin, 1969

Armentrout, D. *Episcopal Splinter Groups*, Sewanee: University of the South, 1985

Atwood, M. *The Handmaid's Tale*, London: Jonathan Cape, 1986

Autton, N. *Pain: An Exploration*, London: DLT, 1986

Autton, N. *Touch: An Exploration*, London: DLT, 1989

Avis, P. *The Resurrection of Jesus Christ*, London: DLT, 1993

Avis, P. *Eros and the Sacred*, London: SPCK, 1989

Barker, E. *New Religious Movements: A Practical Introduction*, London: HMSO, 1995

Barr, J. *Fundamentalism*, London: SCM Press, 1978

Barrett, D. *Encyclopaedia of World Christianity*, Oxford: OUP, 1982

Beckford, J. *Church-State Relations*, New Brunswick: Transaction Books, 1987

Bellah, R. (ed.) *Habits of the Heart: Individualism and Commitment in American Life*, Berkeley: University of California Press, 1985

Bendroth, M. *Fundamentalism and Gender: 1875 to the Present*, New Haven: Yale University Press, 1993

Benner, D. *Encyclopaedia of Psychology*, Grand Rapids: Baker House, 1985

Berger, P. *The Heretical Imperative*, New York: Collins, 1984

Berger, P. *The Precarious Vision*, Garden City: Doubleday, 1951

Berger, P. *The Sacred Canopy*, Garden City: Doubleday, 1967

Berger, P. with Luckmann, T. *The Social Construction of Reality*, Garden City: Doubleday, 1966

Berkowitz, L. *A Survey of Social Psychology*, New York: Holt, Rinehart and Winston, 1980

Bettis, J. *The Phenomenology of Religion*, London: SCM, 1969

Blau, P. *Exchange and Power in Social Life*, New York: John Wiley & Sons, 1964

Blau, P. *Inequality and Heterogeneity: A Primitive Theory of Social Structure*, New York: The Free Press, 1977

Blau, P. and Merton, R. *Continuities in Structural Inquiry*, London: Sage, 1981

Blau, P. and Schwartz, J. *Crosscutting Social Circles: Testing a Macrostructural Theory of Intergroup Relations*, New York: Harcourt Brace Jovanovich, 1984

Bly, R. *Iron John: A Book About Men*, New York: Addison-Wesley, 1990

Boone, K. *The Bible Tells Them So: The Discourse of Protestant Fundamentalism*, London: SCM, 1990

Bosch, D. *Transforming Mission: Paradigm Shift in the Theology of Mission*, Marynknoll, New York: Orbis, 1994

Bossy, J. *Christianity in the West, 1400–1700*, Oxford: OUP, 1985

Bourguinon, E. *Possession*, San Francisco: Chandler & Sharp, 1978

Bowker, J. *Is God a Virus? Genes, Culture & Religion*, London: SPCK, 1995

Bowker, J. *Licensed Insanities: Religions and Belief in God in the Contemporary World*, London: Darton, Longman & Todd, 1987

Brink, J. and Mencher, J. (eds) *Mixed Blessings: Gender and Religious Fundamentalism Cross Culturally*, New York: Routledge, 1996

Brown, A. 'Disorder of Service' *The Independent*, 24.6.95

Brown, F. 'Christian Theology's Dialogue with Culture' in *Companion Encyclopaedia of Theology*, London: Routledge, 1995

Brown, M. 'Unzipper Heaven, Lord' in *The Daily Telegraph*, 4.12.94

Bruce, S. 'Religion in Britain at the Close of the Twentieth Century: A Challenge to the Silver-lining Perspective' *Journal of Contemporary Religion*, vol. 11, no. 3, 1996, pp. 3–21

Bruce, S. *Religion in Modern Britain: From Cathedrals to Cults*, Oxford: OUP, 1996

Bryant, C. *Possible Dreams: A Personal History of the British Christian Socialists*, London: Hodder & Stoughton, 1996

Burgess, S. M., McGee, G. B. and Alexander, P. H. *A Dictionary of Pentecostal and Charismatic Movements*, Grand Rapids: Zondervan, 1988

Butler, Flora C. *Pentecostalism in Columbia: Baptism by Fire and Spirit*, Cranbury, NJ: Fairleigh Dickinson University Press, 1976

Butler, J. *Awash in a Sea of Faith: Christianising in the American People*, Cambridge, MA: Harvard University Press, 1990

Bynum, C. W. *Fragmentation and Redemption: Essays on Gender and the Body in Medieval Religion*, New York: Zone Books, 1992

Cassidy, S. *Sharing the Darkness*, London: DLT, 1988

Chittister, J. *The Fire in these Ashes*, Leominster, Hereford: Gracewing, 1995

Chomsky, N. *Keeping the Rabble in Line: Interviews with David Bausamian*, Edinburgh: Academic Press, 1994

Clegg, S. *Frameworks of Power*, London: Sage, 1989

Cobb, J. *A Christian Natural Theology*, Philadelphia: Westminster Press, 1965

Connor, S. *Postmodern Culture*, Oxford: Blackwell, 1989

Cotton, I. *The Hallelujah Revolution*, London: Little, Brown, 1995

Cotton, I. *The Hallelujah Revolution: The Rise of the New Christians*, London: Little, Brown, 1995

Coward, R. 'Female Desire and Sexual Identity' in M. Diaz-Diocaratez and I. Zavala (eds.) *Women, Feminist Identity and Society in the 1980s*, Amsterdam & Philadelphia: J. Benjamins, 1991

Cox, H. *Fire From Heaven, Pentecostalism, Spirituality and the Reshaping of Religion in the Twenty-first Century*, New York: Addison-Wesley, 1994

Cox, H. *The Secular City: Urbanisation and Secularisation in Theological Perspective*, New York: Macmillan, 1965

Cross, R. *The Burned Over District: The Social and Intellectual History of Enthusiastic Religion in Western New York, 1800–1850*, New York: Harper & Row, 1961

Crozier, B. *A Theory of Conflict*, London: Hamish Hamilton, 1974

Dahl, R. 'The Concept of Power' *Behavioural Science* no. 2, 1957

Danielou, A. *Shiva and Dionysius*, London: East-West, 1982

Daniels, D. Gilula, M., Ochberg, F. (eds) *Violence and the Struggle for Existence*, Boston: Little, Brown & Co., 1970

Davie, G. *Religion in Britain Since 1945: Believing Without Belonging*, Oxford: Clarendon, 1995

Davis, C. *Religion and the Making of Society: Essays in Social Religion*, Cambridge: Cambridge University Press, 1994

de Jouvenal, B. *Power: The Natural History of Its Growth*, London: Heinemann, 1945

Deidun, T. 'Beyond Dualisms' *The Way*, vol. 28, July, 1988

Derrida, J. *Spectres of Marx*, London: Routledge, 1994

Dibbert, R. *The Roots of Traditional Anglicanism*, Akron, Ohio: DeKewen Foundation, 1984

Dodds, E. R. *The Greeks and the Irrational*, Berkeley, California: Sather Classical Lectures, 1973

Douglas, M. *Purity and Danger*, London: Penguin, 1966

Dulaika, J. and Bouglass, W. *Terror and Taboo: On the Fables and Follies of Terrorist Discourse*, New York: Routledge, 1966

Dumouchel, P. (ed.) *Violence and Truth: On the Work of Rene Girard (1985)*, London: Athlone Press, 1988

Dunn, J. *Baptism in the Spirit: A Study of the Religious and Charismatic Experience of Jesus and the First Christians*, London: SCM, 1979

Ekeh, P. *Social Exchange Theory: The Two Traditions*, London: Heinemann, 1974

Eliade, M. *Shamanism: Archaic Techniques of Ecstasy*, Princeton: Princeton University Press, 1964

Elizondo, V. and Freyne, S. *Pilgrimage: Concilium 1996:4*, London: SCM, 1996

Evans, G. and Wright, J. (eds) *The Anglican Tradition*, London: SPCK, 1991

Festinger, L. *A Theory of Cognitive Dissonance*, Stanford: Stanford University Press, 1957

Festinger, L. *When Prophecy Fails*, New York: Harper & Row, 1956

Finney, C. G. *Lectures on Revivals of Religions (1835), Principles of Revival (1936)* ed. L. G. Gifford, Minneapolis: Bethany House Publishers, 1987

Flanagan, K. *The Enchantment of Sociology: A Study of Theology and Culture*, London: Macmillan, 1996

Foucault, M. *The Foucault Reader* (ed. P. Rabinow), New York: Pantheon-Random, 1984

Foucault, M. *Madness and Civilization*, New York: Random House, 1961

Freud, D. *The Ego and the Mechanisms of Defence*, New York: International Universities Press, 1946

Fridrichse, A. *The Problem of Miracle in Early Christianity*, Minneapolis: Augsburg Publishing House, 1972

Fuller, R. H. *Interpreting the Miracles*, London: SCM, 1963

Gay, Peter (ed.) *The Freud Reader*, London: Vintage Books, 1995

Geertz, C. 'Ideology as A Cultural System' in *Ideology and Discontent* (ed. D. Apter), New York: Free Press, 1964

Geisler, N. L. *Miracles and Modern Thought*, Grand Rapids: Zondervan, 1982

Giddens, A. *The Consequences of Modernity*, Cambridge: Polity Press, 1991

Giddens, A. *The Transformation of Intimacy*, Cambridge: Polity Press, 1992

Gill, S. *Women and the Church of England*, London: SPCK, 1994

Girard, R. *Violence and the Sacred*, Baltimore: Johns Hopkins UP, 1977

Goring, R. (ed.) *Chambers Dictionary of Beliefs and Religions*, Edinburgh: Chambers, 1992

Gorringe, T. *God's Just Vengeance: Crime, Violence and Rhetoric of Salvation*, Cambridge: CUP, 1996

Greer, S. *The Emerging City*, New York: Collier Macmillan, 1962

Grenz, S. and Olsen, R. *20th Century Theology: God and the World in a Transitional Age*, London: SPCK, 1989

Grey, M. *Redeeming the Dream*, London: SPCK, 1989

Griffin, C. D. *God, Power and Evil: A Process Theodicy*, Philadelphia: The Westminster Press, 1976

Habermas, J. *Knowledge and Human Interests*, London: Heinemann, 1978

Hadewijch, *Hadewijch: The Complete Works*, New York: Paulist Press, 1980

Hadley, J. *Bread for the World*, London: DLT, 1989

Hardy, D. *God's Ways with the World: Thinking and Practising Christian Faith*, Edinburgh: T. & T. Clark, 1996

Hardy, D. 'The Strategy of Liberalism' in *The Weight of Glory: A Vision and Practice for Christian Faith* (ed. D. Hardy and P. Sedgwick), Edinburgh: T. & T. Clark, 1991

Hartshorne, C. *Omnipotence, and Other Theological Mistakes*, New York: New York State UP, 1984

Hartshorne, C. *Man's Vision of God and the Logic of Theism*, Hamden, Conn: Archon Books, 1964

Hartshorne, C. *The Divine Relativity*, New Haven: Yale UP, 1948

Harvey, V. A. *Feuerbach and the Interpretation of Religion*, Cambridge: CUP, 1995

Henry, C. *God, Revelation and Authority*, vol. 4, Waco, TX: World Books, 1979

Hocken, P. *Streams of Renewal*, Exeter: Paternoster Press, 1986

Hoffer, E. *The Passionate State of Mind*, London: Secker & Warburg, 1956

Hoffer, E. *The True Believer*, New York: Harper & Row, 1965

Hollenweger, W. *Pentecostal Movements as an Ecumenical Challenge*, London: Concilium/SCM, 1996

Homans, G. C. *Social Behaviour*, New York: Harcourt Brace Jovanovich, 1974

Hooker, R. *On the Laws of Ecclesiastical Polity* (ed. A. McGrade), Cambridge: CUP, 1989

Hopewell, J. *Congregation: Stories and Structures*, London: SCM, 1987

Houston, J. *Reported Miracles*, Cambridge: CUP, 1995

Hudgins, A. *The Never Ending*, London: Houghton Mifflin Publishing, 1991

Hughes, J., Martin, P. and Shorrock, W. *Understanding Classical Sociology: Marx, Weber, Durkheim*, London: Sage, 1995

Hutton, W. *The State We're In*, London: Vintage, 1995

Hyams, E. *Terrorists and Terrorism*, London: J. M. Dent & Sons, 1975

Irwing, E. *The Making of Victorian Sexuality*, Oxford: OUP, 1994

James, W. *The Varieties of Religious Experience* (1902), Garden City, New York: Image Books, 1978

Janov, A. *The Primal Scream*, New York: Putnam, 1970

Jantzen, G. *Power, Gender and Christian Mysticism*, Cambridge: CUP, 1995

Jenkins, D. *God, Miracle and the Church of England*, London: SCM, 1987

Kahoe, R. 'Ecstatic Religious Experience' in D. G. Benner (ed.) *Encyclopaedia of Psychology*, Grand Rapids, Michigan: Baker House, 1985

Kallas, J. *The Significance of the Synoptic Miracles*, London: SPCK, 1961

Kee, H. C. *Miracles in the Early Christian World*, New Haven: Yale University Press, 1983

Keillor, G. *Lake Woebegon Days*, New York: Viking Penguin, 1985

Kelber, W. *The Passion in Mark*, Philadelphia: Fortress Press, 1976

Keller, E. and M.–L. *Miracles in Dispute*, Philadelphia: Fortress, 1968

Kelly, H. and Thibaut, J. *Interpersonal Relations: A Theory of Interdependence*, New York: John Wiley, 1978

Kermode, F. *The Genesis of Secrecy: On the Interpretation of Narrative*, Cambridge, MA: Harvard University Press, 1979

Knox, R. *Enthusiasm: A Chapter in the History of Religion*, Oxford: Clarendon Press, 1950

Lampe, G. *God as Spirit*, Oxford: OUP, 1977

Lash, N. *The Beginning and End of Religion*, Cambridge: CUP, 1996

Lefebvre, H. *The Production of Space*, Oxford: Blackwell, 1991

Lewis, I. *Religion in Context: Cults and Charisma*, Cambridge: CUP, 1996

Lewy, G. *Religion and Revolution*, New York: Oxford University Press, 1974

Lindbeck, G. *The Nature of Doctrine*, Philadelphia: Westminster Press, 1984

Lodge, D. *The British Museum is Falling Down*, London: Penguin, 1965

Louth, A. *The Origins of the Christian Mystical Tradition* (quoting Gregory of Nyssa), Oxford: OUP, 1981

Luhmann, N. *Lover as a Passion: The Codification of Intimacy*, Cambridge: Polity Press, 1993

Lukes, S. *A History of Sociological Analysis*, New York: Basic Books, 1978

Lukes, S. *Emile Durkheim: His Life & Work*, Harmondsworth: Penguin, 1973

Lukes, S. *Power: A Radical View*, London: Macmillan/British Sociological Association, 1974

Lyon, D. *Postmodernity*, Buckingham: Open University Press, 1995

Lyotard, J.–F. *The Postmodern Condition: A Report on Knowledge*, Manchester: Manchester University Press, 1984

Maitland, S. *A Big Enough God? Artful Theology*, London: Mowbray, 1995

Manross, W. *A History of the American Episcopal Church*, New York: Morehouse-Goreham, 1950

Maris, R. W. 'Suicide' in *Encyclopaedia of Sociology*, ed. E. Borgotta and M. Borgotta, New York: Macmillan, 1992

Martin, D. 'Evangelical and Charismatic Christianity in Latin America' in K. Poewe (ed.) *Charismatic Christianity as a Global Culture*, Columbia: University of South Carolina Press, 1994

Martin, D. *Tongues of Fire: The Explosion of Protestantism in Latin America*, Oxford: Blackwell, 1990

Marty, M. 'Fundamentalism Reborn' in *Religion and Republic*, Boston: Beacon Press, 1987

Marty, M. and Appleby, R. S. *Fundamentalisms Observed*, Chicago: University of Chicago Press, 1992

Marx, K. and Engels, F. *On Religion* (1844), Moscow: Foreign Languages Publishing House, 1955

Mason, M. *The Making of Victorian Sexual Attitudes*, Oxford: OUP, 1994

Mauss, M. *The Gift: Forms and Functions of Exchange in Archaic Societies*, London: Cohen & West, 1996

May, R. *Power and Innocence: A Search for the Sources of Violence*, New York: Norton, 1974

May, R. *The Cry for Myth*, New York: Norton, 1991

Mayer, F. E. *The Religious Bodies of America*, St Louis: Concordia Publishing House, 1961

Maynard, J. *Victorian Discourses on Sexuality and Religion*, Cambridge: CUP, 1993

McGrath, A. (ed.) *Encyclopaedia of Modern Christian Thought*, Oxford: Blackwell, 1993

McFague, S. *Metaphorical Theology: Models of God in Religious Language*, London: SCM, 1983

McGrath, A. and Lewis, D. (eds) *Doing Theology for the People of God: Studies in Honour of Jim Packer*, Leicester: IVP/Apollos, 1996

McGuire, M. *Pentecostal Catholics: Power, Charisma and Order in a Religious Movement*, Philadelphia: Temple University, 1982

McGuire, M. *Ritual Healing in Suburban America*, New Brunswick: Rutgers University Press, 1988

McLellan, D. *Ideology*, Buckingham: Open University Press, 1995

McLoughlin, W. G. *Modern Revivalism*, New York: Ronald Press, 1959

Melton, J. G. 'Violence and the Cults' in *The Encyclopaedic Handbook of Cults in America*, New York: Garland, 1992

Melton, J. G. *Directory of Religious Bodies in the United States*, New York: Garland Publishing, 1977

Melton, J. G. *The Encyclopaedia of American Religions*, Vol. 1., Charlotte, NC: McGrath Publishing, 1978

Melton, J. G. (ed.) *The Encyclopaedia of American Religion*, Washington DC: Gale Publishing, 1994

Meyer, M. 'The Weberian Tradition in Organisational Research' in *Structures of Power and Constraint: Essays in Honour of Peter Blau* (ed. M. Meyer and W. Scott), Cambridge: CUP, 1990

Middleton, J. and Walsh, D. *Truth Is Stranger than It Used to Be: Biblical Faith in a Post-modern Age*, London: SPCK, 1995

Milbank, J. *Theology and Social Theory: Beyond Secular Reason*, Oxford: Blackwell, 1989

Molm, L. 'Linking Power Structure and Power Use' in Karon Cook (ed.) *Social Exchange Theory*, London: Sage, 1987

Montefiore, H. *The Probability of God*, London: SCM, 1985

Moriss, P. *Power: A Philosophical Investigation*, Manchester: Manchester UP, 1987

Morris, B. *Anthropological Studies of Religion*, Cambridge: CUP, 1987

Morrison, K. *Marx, Durkheim, Weber: Formations of Modern Social Thought*, London: Sage, 1995

Neitz, M. J. *Charisma and Community: A Study of Commitment within Charismatic Renewal*, Oxford: Transaction Books, 1987

Newby, H. *Community*, Milton Keynes: Open University Press, 1980

Nicholls, D. *Deity and Domination: Images of God and the State in the Nineteenth and Twentieth Centuries*, London: Routledge, 1989

Nichols, P. and Zax, M. *Catharsis in Psychotherapy*, New York: Gardner Press, 1977

Niebuhr, H. R. *Christ and Culture*, New York: Harper & Row, 1951

Noll, M. *The Scandal of The Evangelical Mind*, Grand Rapids, Michigan: Eerdmans, 1994

O'Dea, T. *The Sociology of Religion*, Englewood Cliffs, NJ: Prentice Hall, 1983

O'Dea, T. 'Sociological Dilemmas: Five Paradoxes of Institutionalisation' in *Sociological Theory, Values and Sociocultural Change*, New York: Free Press of Glencoe, 1963

O'Siadhail, M. *The Chosen Garden*, Dublin: Daedalus Press, 1990

Otto, W. F. *Dionysius: Myth and Cult*, Bloomington: Indiana University Press, 1965

Palmer, R. *Dancing in the Street: A History of Rock 'n' Roll*, London: BBC Books, 1996

Parson, T. *Theories of Society*, New York: The Free Press, 1961

Parsons, T. *Structure and Process in Modern Society*, New York: Free Press, 1968

Pattison, S. *Alive and Kicking*, London: SCM, 1989

Percy, M. *Words, Wonders and Power: Understanding Contemporary Christian Fundamentalism and Revivalism*, London: SPCK, 1996

Percy, M. 'City on a Beach' in T. Walters and S. Hunt (eds) *Charismatic Christianity: Sociological Perspectives*, London: Macmillan, 1997

Percy, M. *Catching the Fire: The Sociology of Exchange, Power and Charisma in the Toronto Blessing*, Oxford: Latimer House, 1996

Poewe, K. (ed.) *Charismatic Christianity as a Global Culture*, New York: Columbia UP, 1994

Poheir, J. *God in Fragments*, London: SCM, 1985

Porter, R. and Richter, P. *The Toronto Blessing – Or Is It?* London: DLT, 1995

Potter, H. *Hanging in Judgement: Religion and the Death Penalty in England*, London: SCM, 1993

Rauschenbusch, W. *Christianity and Social Crisis*, New York: Macmillan, 1907

Reeves, D. *Down to Earth: A New Vision for the Church*, London: Mowbray, 1996

Reeves, P. 'Living with the Bomb', *The Independent* (13 May 1995), p. 32

Richardson, A. *The Miracle Stories of the Gospels*, London: SCM, 1941

Ricoeur, P. *Freud and Philosophy*, New Haven: Yale University Press, 1970

Ricoeur, P. 'Wonder, Eroticism and Enigma' in J. Nelson and S. Longfellow (eds), *Sexuality and the Sacred: Sources for Theological Reflection*, London: Cassell, 1994

Ritschl, A. *The Christian Doctrine of Justification and Reconciliation*, Edinburgh: T. & T. Clark, 1900

Ritzer, G. *The McDonaldization of Society*, London: Sage, 1996

Robbins, T. *Cults, Converts and Charisma*, London: Sage with the International Sociological Association, 1988

Robbins, T. and Palmer, S. (eds) *Millennium, Messiahs and Mayhem: Contemporary Apocalyptic Ferment in the USA and Canada*, New York: Routledge, 1997

Robbins, T., Shepherd, W., and McBride, J. *Cults, Culture and the Law: Perspectives on New Religious Movements* (American Academy of Religion) Chico, California: Scholars Press, 1985

Roberts, R. 'Lord, Bondsman and Churchman: Power, Integrity and Identity' in *On Being the Church: Essays on the Christian Community*, D. Hardy and C. Gunton (eds), Edinburgh: T. & T. Clark, 1989

Rose, G. *Love's Work*, London: Chatto & Windus, 1995

Rubenstein, R. 'Power and Collective Violence in Anthropological Perspective' in Tim Ingold (ed.) *Companion Encyclopaedia of Anthropology: Humanity, Culture and Social Life*, London: Routledge, 1994

Rubin, M. *Corpus Christi*, Cambridge: CUP, 1991

Sachs, W. *The Transformation of Anglicanism: From State Church to Global Communion*, Cambridge: CUP, 1993

Saghal, G. and Yuval-Davis, N. *Refusing Holy Orders: Women and Fundamentalism in Britain*, London: Virago, 1992

Saliba, J. *Perspectives on New Religious Movements*, London: Mowbray, 1995

Schrader, R. *The Nature of Theological Argument: A Study of Paul Tillich*, Missoula, Montana: Scholars Press, 1975

Schussler Fiorensa, E. and Copeland, M. *Violence Against Women (Issue 5)* London: SCM, 1994

Scotland, N. *Charismatics and the Next Millennium*, London: Hodder & Stoughton, 1995

Shaw, G. *The Cost of Authority*, Philadelphia: Fortress Press, 1982

Sizer, S. *Gospel Hymns and Social Religion*, Philadelphia: Temple University Press, 1978

Sobrino, J. *Jesus the Liberator*, London: Burns & Oates, 1993

Spittler, R. 'Are Pentecostals and Charismatics Fundamentalists?' in K. Poewe (ed.) *Charismatic Christianity as a Global Culture*, Columbia: University of South Carolina Press, 1994

Stark, R. and Bainbridge, W. *A Theory of Religion*, New York: Peter Lang/ Toronto Studies in Religion, 1987

Shuttles, G. D. *The Social Construction of Community*, Chicago: University of Chicago Press, 1972

Suurmond, J. *Word and Spirit at Play*, London: SCM, 1993

Swain, J. *The Elementary Forms of Religious Life*, London: Allen & Unwin, 1915

Swinburne, R. *The Concept of Miracle*, London: Macmillan, 1970

Swinburne, R. *The Existence of God*, Oxford: OUP, 1979

Syndor, W. *Looking at the Episcopal Church*, Wilton: Morehouse-Barlow, 1980

Szreter, S. *Fertility, Class and Gender in Britain, 1860–1940*, Cambridge: CUP, 1996

Theissen, G. *Miracle Stories of the Early Christian Tradition*, Philadelphia: Fortress Press, 1983

Thiselton, A. *Interpreting God and the Postmodern Self: On Meaning, Manipulation and Promise*, Edinburgh: T. & T. Clark, 1995

Thompson, D. *The End of Time: Faith and Fear in the Shadow of the Millennium*, London: Sinclair-Stevenson, 1996

Tilley, T. *Postmodern Theologies*, New York: Orbis, 1995

Troeltsch, E. *The Social Teachings of the Christian Churches*, New York: Macmillan, 1931

Turner, R. H., Killian, L. *Collective Behaviour*, Englewood Cliffs: Prentice Hall, 1987

Turner, V. *The Forest of Symbols*, Ithaca: Cornell University Press, 1967

Turner, V. *The Ritual Process*, Chicago: Aldine Press, 1969

Urquhart, G. *The Pope's Armada*, London: Bantam, 1995

Van der Leeuw, G. *Religion in Essence and Manifestation*, London: Allen & Unwin, 1938

Wagner, C. P. *Territorial Spirits: Insights into Strategic Level Spirit Warfare from Nineteen Christian Leaders*, Chichester: Sovereign Publishing, 1991

Walker, A. *Restoring the Kingdom* (2nd edition), London: Hodder & Stoughton, 1988

Wallis, R. *The Elementary Forms of the New Religious Life*, London: Routledge, 1984

Wang, N. 'Logos-modernity, Eros-modernity and Leisure', *Leisure Studies*, vol. 15, no. 2, 1996, pp. 17–27

Wangerin, E. *Ragman and Other Cries of Faith*, London: Spire, 1993

Ward, G. 'Theological Materialism' in C. Crowder (ed.) *God and Reality*, London: Mowbray, 1997

Ward, G. *Barth, Derrida and the Language of Theology*, Cambridge: CUP, 1995

Weber, M. *From Max Weber: Essays in Sociology*, London: Routledge & Kegan Paul, 1948

Weber, M. *The Sociology of Religion*, London: Methuen, 1965

Weber, M. *Charisma and Institution Building*, Chicago: University of Chicago Press, 1968

Weber, M. *The Methodology of the Social Sciences*, ed. E. Shils and H. Finch New York: Free Press, 1948

Webster, M. *A New Strength, A New Song*, London: Mowbray, 1994

Weisberger, A. *They Gathered at the River*, Chicago: Quadrangle Books, 1958

Westerlund, D. (ed.) *Questioning the Secular State: The Worldwide Resurgence of Religion in Politics*, London: Hurst and Company, 1996

Whelan, R. *The Corrosion of Charity: From Moral Renewal to Contract Culture*, London: Institute of Economic Affairs, 1996

Wiles, M. *God's Action in the World*, London: SCM, 1986

Wilkinson, A. *The Church of England and the First World War*, London: SPCK, 1978

Wilkinson, P. *Political Terrorism*, London: Macmillan 1974

Wilson, B. *Religious Sects*, London: Weidenfeld & Nicolson, 1970

Wilson, B. *Religion in Secular Society: A Sociological Comment*, London: Watts & Co, 1966

Wilson, B. *Religious Sects*, New York: McGraw-Hill, 1970

Wilson, B. *Sects and Society: A Sociological Study of Three Religious Groups in Britain*, London: Heinemann, 1961

Wilson, B. *The Noble Savages: An Essay on Charisma*, Berkeley: University of California Press, 1975

Wilson, B. *The Social Dimensions of Sectarianism: Sects and New Religious Movements in Contemporary Society*, Oxford: Clarendon Press, 1990

Wink, W. *Naming the Powers: The Language of Power in the New Testament*, Philadelphia: Fortress Press, 1984

Wink, W. *Engaging the Powers: Discernment and Resistance in a World of Domination*, Augsburg: Fortress Press, 1992

Wink, W. *Unmasking the Powers: The Invisible Forces that Determine Human Existence*, Philadelphia: Fortress Press, 1986

Wollheim, R. *Hume on Religion*, London: Collins, 1963

Wolverton, F. *Colonial Anglicanism in North America*, Detroit: Wayne University Press, 1984

# Index

# Index